A Significant Contribution to the Golden Dawn Literature

Now, for the first time, the majority of the Kabbalistic teachings from the Golden Dawn are presented in one unified, fascinating book. Originally, Golden Dawn adepts had been spoon-fed this material over a number of years as they went through the various grade ceremonies.

For those of you already familiar with Regardie's two published works on the Golden Dawn, you will not be disappointed— much of the material presented here has never before been published.

A great deal of the Golden Dawn's Kabbalistic teachings came from the translation of portions of the *Zohar* by Knorr von Rosenroth. This book takes you through the structure and contents of the *Zohar,* then pro-ceeds to give the Golden Dawn knowledge lectures on the subject.

Pat Zalewski, 7=4 adept of the Golden Dawn, presents the previ-ously unpublished diagrams, sigils, and verses of the Schemhamphoresch. He discusses the full aspects of the Golden Dawn diagrams before, during and after the fall of Adam, as well as the Partsufim theory of Kabbalistic thought. There are numerous quotes of the *Zohar* made from translations by Golden Dawn members. Also presented are the Four Worlds of the Kabbalah, plus the various Sephiroth and Paths; a previously unpublished account of the Qlippoth, or demons of the Tree of Life; and a detailed comparison of the Kabbalistic Soul with the seven subtle bodies of West-ern esoteric thought.

One of the most interesting parts of the book is the chapter on alchemy and the Kabbalah as seen from the Golden Dawn perspective. This opens new doors to alchemical application and thought. The Seven Heavens and Seven Hells of the Kabbalists are also given.

About the Author

Pat Zalewski and his wife, Chris, live in Wellington, New Zealand, where they are co-chiefs of the Golden Dawn Temple, Thoth-Hermes. Both were initiated and instructed in the Golden Dawn teachings by ex-members of the New Zealand temple Whare Ra, which was founded in 1912 and closed in 1978. Both are keen astrologers and have a strong interest in Wiccan craft and the study of comparative religions. They have written a number of books together on the Golden Dawn theme.

To Write to the Author

If you wish to contact the author or would like more information about this book, please write to the author in care of Llewellyn Worldwide and we will forward your request. Both the author and publisher appreciate hearing from you and learning of your enjoyment of his book and how it has helped you. Llewellyn Worldwide cannot guarantee that every letter written to the author can be answered, but all will be forwarded. Please write to:

Pat Zalewski
c/o Llewellyn Worldwide
P.O. Box 64383-873, St. Paul, MN 55164-0383, U.S.A.
Please enclose a self-addressed, stamped envelope for reply, or $1.00 to cover costs.
If outside U.S.A., enclose international postal reply coupon.

Free Catalog From Llewellyn Worldwide

For more than 90 years Llewellyn has brought its readers knowledge in the fields of metaphysics and human potential. Learn about the newest books in spiritual guidance, natural healing, astrology, occult philosophy and more. Enjoy book reviews, new age articles, a calendar of events, plus current advertised products and services. To get your free copy of *The Llewellyn New Worlds*, send your name and address to:

The Llewellyn New Worlds
P.O. Box 64383-873, St. Paul, MN 55164-0383, U.S.A.

Llewellyn's Golden Dawn Series

The Kabbalah of the Golden Dawn

Pat Zalewski

1993
Llewellyn Publications
St. Paul, Minnesota 55164-0383, U.S.A.

First Edition
First Printing

Cover design by Christopher Wells

Library of Congress Cataloging-in-publication Data
Zalewski, Pat, 1948–
    The kabbalah of the golden dawn / Pat Zalewski.
       p.   cm. — (Llewellyn's Golden Dawn series)
    Includes bibliographical references.
    ISBN 0-87542-873-8
    1. Cabala 2. Hermetic Order of the Golden Dawn.   I. Title.
II. Series.
BF1623.C2Z35   1993
135'.4—dc20
                                         92-31535
                                           CIP

Llewellyn Publications
A Division of Llewellyn Worldwide, Ltd.
P.O. Box 64383, St. Paul, MN 55164-0383

ABOUT LLEWELLYN'S GOLDEN DAWN SERIES

Just as, 100 years ago, the original Order of the Golden Dawn initiated a powerful rebirth of interest in the Western Esoteric Tradition that has lasted through this day, so do we expect this series of books of add new impetus to the Great Work itself among an ever broadening base of sincere students.

> *I further promise and swear that with the Divine Permission, I will from this day forward, apply myself to the Great Work which is: to purify and exalt my Spiritual Nature so that with the Divine Aid I may at length attain to be more than human, and thus gradually raise and unite myself to my Higher and Divine Genius, and that in this event I will not abuse the great power entrusted to me.*

With this oath, the Adeptus Minor of the Inner Order committed his/herself to undertake, consciously and deliberately, that which was ordained as the birthright of all Humanity: TO BECOME MORE THAN HUMAN!

It is this that is the ultimate message of Esotericism: that evolution continues, and that the purpose of each life is to grow into the Image set for us by our Creator: to attain and reveal our own Divinity.

These books and tapes will themselves make more easily accessible the Spiritual Technology that is inherent in the Golden Dawn System. It is a system that allows for individual as well as group endeavor; a system that works within or without an organized lodge; a system that is based on universal principles that will be shown to be global in their impact today.

And practical. The works in this series will be practical in their applications and requirements for application. You need neither to travel to the mountaintop nor obtain any tool other than your own consciousness. No garment need you other than that of your own imagination. No authority need you other than that of your own True Will.

Set forth, then, into the New Dawn—a new start on the greatest adventure there is: to become One with the Divine Genius.

Other books by the author

The Secret Inner Order Rituals of the Golden Dawn
(Falcon Press, 1988)

Golden Dawn Enochian Magic (1990)

Z-5: Secret Teachings of the Golden Dawn
Book I: The Neophyte Ritual 0=0 (1991)

With Chris Zalewski

Book II: The Zelator Ritual 1=10 (1992)

Equinox and Solstice Rituals of the Golden Dawn (1992)

By Chris Zalewski

Herbs in Magic & Alchemy
(Prism Press, 1990)

Forthcoming from Llewellyn Publications

Enochian Chess (by Chris Zalewski)

TABLE OF CONTENTS

DIAGRAMS

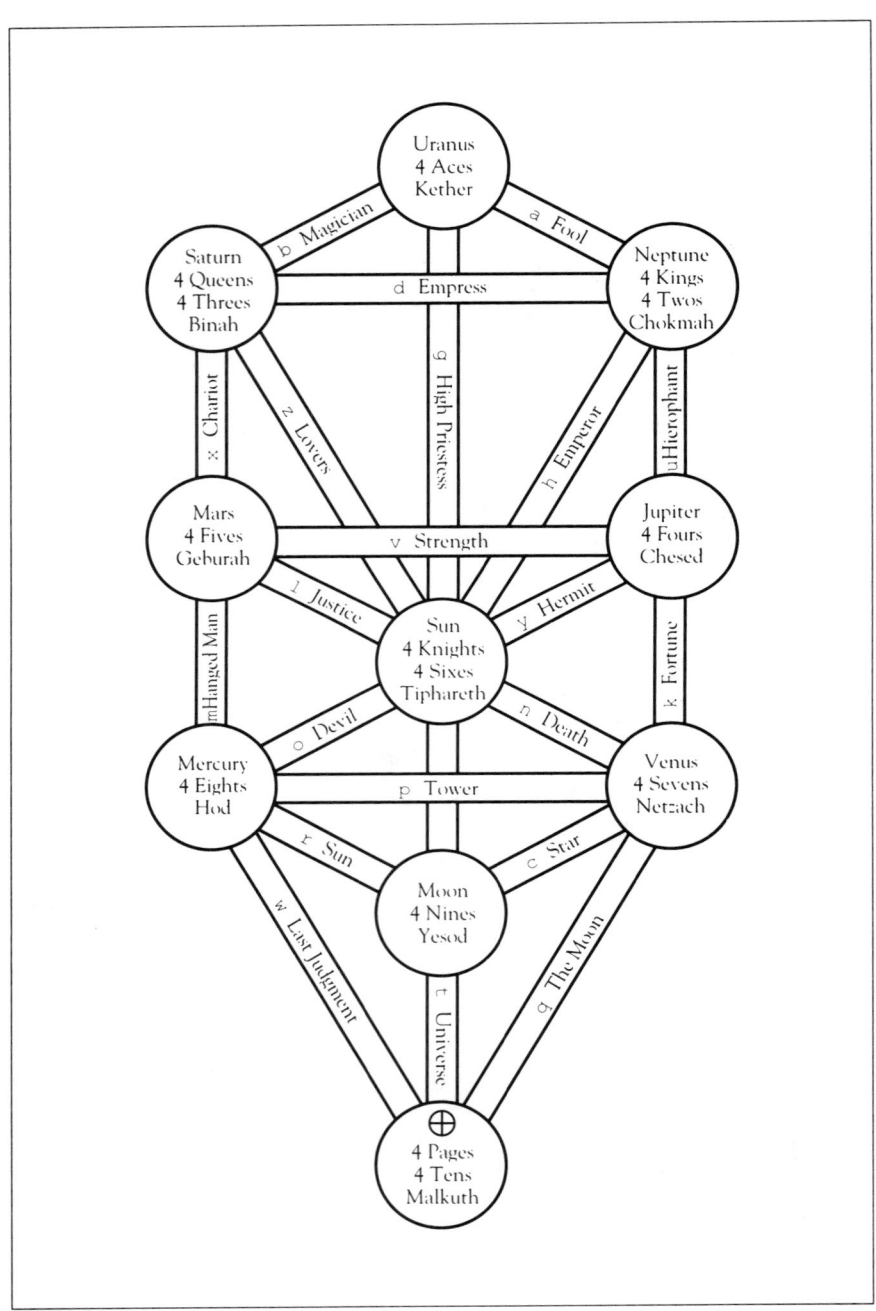

The Tree of Life

FOREWORD

All seekers on the path begin with questions such as "Who am I?" "Why am I here?" "What is the purpose of life?" Eventually, from a deeper level of consciousness, comes an answer, "perhaps it is to attain knowledge and wisdom" . . . direct knowledge about your own nature, the purpose of the world you live in and its relationship to God and Man.

If you have asked yourself these questions, perhaps the Kabalah will present you with answers and additional challenges as you travel the pathways to your ultimate goal. It is a tradition that is concerned with the transmission of the knowledge you seek. It is a most profound and effective system of esoteric training when applied in a practical approach.

This system of relationships among mystical symbols is used to open access to hidden parts of the mind, beyond reason; to learn the inner nature of man, the inner reality or essence of things. We determine this inner meaning based upon observance of the outer.

In a more practical way, we are using the techniques and principles of Kabbalah as calisthenics of consciousness; to develop the power of the mind, to realize conscious energy, to reduce the Earth plane to order and harmony, to live in this world, continually evolving toward the light. Heaven is a state of consciousness and our purpose is to be more than what we are today, to have an experience that transcends "our ordering self-awareness."

The Golden Dawn System of Magic is based on Kabalistic theory. The discipline and perseverance required in the pursuit of these studies in actuality rival those of the Eastern Yogic tradition.

Westerners, who in general require more active participation on their pathway of evolution, will find this approach more suited to their needs, and most often more easily assimilated into their daily lives. Instead of escaping from the material world, the task is to bring it wholly into a state of balance and harmony—thus releasing one from material worries and enabling him/her to move to the next level of development.

Alchemy is the transition from one state to another. This is an excellent way to describe what the student of magic or practical Kaballah is working to accomplish. Through these processes one is able to bring about changes on many different levels, which equate with the four worlds of Kabbalah:

> **Physical:** It is possible to retard aging, to heal, and to create evolutionary changes in the physical body.
>
> **Mental:** Through magic and the creation of changes on the astral plane one becomes the architect of his/her own environment.
>
> **Emotional:** If one begins with the proper foundqation, the result is the ability to accomplish psychological/analytical change.
>
> **Spiritual:** Evolvement of the soul, individuation, conversation with the Higher Self (our divine aspect)—all these are possible.

Soror M.A.A.E.M.
Ra Horakhty Temple
Federal Way, Washington

INTRODUCTION

The Hermetic Order of the Golden Dawn has attracted enormous interest in recent years, not merely from the many groups of practicing occultists who have based their activities on the Golden Dawn system, but also from a growing number of serious scholars and academics. Scholarly interest has concentrated on the pervasive influence of the Order on a number of celebrated writers, but particularly on the poet, W. B. Yeats. There have also been a considerable number of books over the past twenty years which have covered the history of the Order in some detail and have progressively revealed its ritualistic and magical secrets. Despite this publishing phenomenon, there is still much that is unknown about the Golden Dawn. As Golden Dawn historian and author R. A. Gilbert has noted, the Order "Yet remains as maligned, misunderstood and misappropriated as ever it was during its heyday."

One area that has not received the attention it deserves is that of the Kabbalah, which was the basis of all Golden Dawn rites. The idea of writing a book on the Kabbalah from the perspective of the Golden Dawn is something I had considered for many years. My first attempt at a similar venture was in the Golden Dawn Correspondence Course, in which a very detailed study of the Kabbalah was made in the form of a series of tabulations. It was based on the Golden Dawn manuscript "General Correspondences" which Aleister Crowley subsequently modified slightly and published as 777. While this course provided a great deal of original material, it did not cover many important areas of the subject. Originally I had intended to do a followup on the correspondence course, but due to an estrangement with the publishers, this did not eventuate.

The subject of the Kabbalah itself is well documented but there are too few publications written from the occultist's viewpoint, which differs somewhat from that of the Hebrew traditionalist. There are some useful books of this type available however, and one of the best texts is Dion Fortune's *Mystical Qabalah*, though she worked only on the Sephiroth. Another is A. E. Waite's book *The Holy Kabbalah*, which is really a monumental and impressive piece of work. Waite's commentary on the historical gleanings and folio references in the *Zohar* proved invaluable in the preparation of this work. My own personal favorite, though, is the *Kabbalah* by Charles Ponce, who does a brilliant job of condensing the vast and complex history of the Kabbalah into a very fine little volume. Ponce went further toward the occult viewpoint than Waite, while still retaining the integrity of the traditionalist.

My own work here, which is combined with the Golden Dawn viewpoint, takes things a step further toward the occultist's viewpoint. In many respects it is a Golden Dawn notebook on the Kabbalah, for it retains a number of previously unpublished Golden Dawn texts on the subject, as well as later ones which have been pruned and presented together. When Regardie published all the Golden Dawn rituals (Llewellyn Publications), only the bare bones of the Kabbalistic papers were included for reasons of space.

It is inevitable that there are some quotes from previously published Golden Dawn ritual papers, but these have been re-edited in such a fashion, with additional footnotes, that most of this material will be seen as it was intended by the Chiefs of the Golden Dawn. In context, therefore, it is very much a new type of work and direction.

Each Golden Dawn Temple had quite a number of lectures circulating on the Kabbalah that were never part of the five basic knowledge lectures, and even these differed from temple to temple. From 1900, when the Golden Dawn split into the Alpha et Omega Temples under Mathers and the remainder, who changed the name to Morgan Rothe,[1] the Order still continued to function on the practical level as it had before. Thus over the years from 1900[2] to the present day, quite a lot of Kabbalistic texts were added by various members of the Order as more translations of the *Zohar* became available.

---

[1]   This is German and roughly translated means Red Dawn.
[2]   A further split in the Order developed in 1903. One group was called the Holy Order of the Golden Dawn under Waite and the other was called the Stella Matutina under Dr. R. W. Felkin.

My own association with the Order came from ex-members of the New Zealand Temple Whare Ra. Under the tuition of my mentor Jack Taylor (a former Hierophant) I was given access to most of its documents. Some years ago, just before Taylor's death, I was given access to a large number of documents that had been the bases for lectures from Whare Ra on the Kabbalah since the temple's inception in 1912 to its demise in 1978. Most of these papers were undated (apart from the time that the lecture was given) and were partial translations of the *Zohar* from the French (apparently from the works of Pauly, Franck, Levi, and Papus) and from the Hebrew and Latin. In many instances the translations differ considerably from published texts, and where this is evident I have mentioned it. The Zoharic quotes I have used are from these translations, many of which have only been translated into English for the general public in the last decade or so. Taylor informed me that most of these translations were done by the two former Golden Dawn Chiefs, Mathers and Westcott. Mathers' wife Moina also claimed that full English translations of Levi's works were handed around the Order, some years before English translations became available.[3]

What the Golden Dawn did, in essence, was to take the eyes out of the Zoharic teaching and present these in rituals and knowledge lectures. Many of the associated diagrams and explanations which were provided in the Golden Dawn were omitted from Regardie's first publication of the Golden Dawn material. In Regardie's subsequent work, *Complete Golden Dawn System of Magic*, the missing explanations are given only in part and these are still barely skeletonic. These were of course taken from Rosenroth's works, that Mathers appended to the rituals. Many of the explanations given in this book are more complete than the rituals and are taken back to their original source, the *Zohar*. They are based on translations I uncovered here in New Zealand from various lectures on the subject given by Felkin and other Golden Dawn Adepts. What I have tried to do here is present, in one book, a synthesis of all major Kabbalistic teachings used by the Order, along with additional insight into the concepts they contain. I make no claim to be an expert on the traditional Kabbalah and its teachings, as my viewpoint is that of the Golden Dawn occultist and it is this viewpoint which is the basis for this book.

---

3 At Whare Ra I only found partial translation of Levi; the full ones were said to be left with Waite.

The part or volume number references to the *Zohar*, as given in the footnotes of this book, are modified from the traditional volumes to fall in line with the five-volume set of the Soncino edition, which is the more accessible of the English translations. I also noted that in the Soncino edition, the emphasis on the Holy Hebrew Names of God and their variations are surprisingly ignored, where the Nurho de Manhar single-volume edition has these included, as well as some folios left out by the Soncino edition. The English translations of the *Zohar* to date leave a lot to be desired.

Included in the section I have called "Sphere of Sensation," is a breakdown of the functions of the Kabbalistic Soul as applied to subtle body anatomy, or the aura, as it is commonly called today. This section of the book covers some of the teachings from the 6=5 and 7=4 Grades of the Thoth Hermes Temple, in New Zealand. In this section there is a discussion of the sexual teachings of the aura and its effect on the chakras and auric bodies. The theory was first outlined to me by Jack Taylor, in a rather general way, and I have taken the liberty of expanding it a great deal, with a more technical viewpoint.

On a final note, the reader may observe that one of the sections I have not covered in this work is that of the Tarot with regard to the Kabbalah. This is a work in itself and will be presented in a subsequent volume called *The Magical Tarot of the Golden Dawn*. The Kabbalistic teachings of Enochian Chess will also be presented in a separate volume by Chris Zalewski (soon to be published).

Pat Zalewski
Wellington, New Zealand.
Summer 1990

CHAPTER ONE

An Historical Outline

The Kabbalah is part of the ancient Jewish mystical tradition. There are many spelling variations of "Kabbalah," including Cabalah, Qabbalah, Gabbalah, and so forth. As "Kabbalah" is that favored by authoritative Judaic scholars such as Gershom Scholem, Aryeh Kaplan, and the first Chiefs of the Golden Dawn, it is this spelling which is used throughout this book.

The meaning of the term "Kabbalah" is usually related to the Hebrew root QBL meaning "to receive," which is itself commonly taken to refer to the traditional custom of handing down secret knowledge by word of mouth to ear. Other scholars have claimed that the Hebrew word is of Chaldeo-Egyptian origin, signifying occult science or doctrine.

Oral tradition has it that the Kabbalah was first taught to the archangels by God. These angels, said to be those mentioned in the Book of Enoch, then passed the secret teachings on to Adam (either directly or via Enoch, whom some identify with Adam).

The teachings were said to been originally handed to Adam from the Archangel Raziel (whose name means "secret of God"), a personification of Secret Wisdom. The Secret Doctrine then passed on from Adam through to Abraham, who taught it (in part) to the Egyptians. The Kabbalah at this point did not form the main body of Hebrew

1

teachings but was a type of mysticism that had been held strictly apart from the main body of Hebrew theology, and as such, it was communicated only to a select few. This was because the teaching of the "Hidden or Secret Knowledge" was considered so profound that few could be trusted with its essence, let alone fully understand its complexity. To express this in terms that could be readily understood, this mystical teaching was said to have been allied to the Old Testament, and was applied to interpreting some of the more abstract Biblical passages.

As to what this teaching was in its rudimentary form is almost anyone's guess save that it was mathematical in concept (based on a ten-stage system) and skeletonic in format. It is likely that it would also have required a system sufficiently flexible that could be applied equally both to the Macrocosm (the Universe) as well as the Microcosm (individual man or woman). At this stage one could safely say that general principles rather than detailed theories were the Kabalistic concepts of early years and these were deeply imbedded in the Hebrew religious thought and ideals of the period.

Little is known of Kabbalistic thought and development between the time of Abraham and that of Moses. Kabbalistic scholars, such as Ginsburg, have hinted that Moses reinjected some of the lost or modified Kabbalistic knowledge of the Egyptians back into the Hebrew teachings (since Moses was said to be learned in the Wisdom of Egypt) during the Exodus. The Ten Commandments have been said to have been part of lost Kabbalistic theosophy and were given directly to Moses from God, so that the purity of the teaching would be retained. Each commandment was said to represent a stage of Kabbalistic development.

TRADITIONAL HEBREW LITERATURE

The Talmud

This literature should not be confused with either the Old Testament or the Kabbalah. It is a composition of the laws and customs of the Jews in both civil and religious doctrine. Based on a doctrine of interpretations of the Hebrew Bible, it is divided into two parts, practical and oral, the latter being the secret tradition of Israel which gave birth to the Kabbalah. The Talmud can also be further divided into two literature sources. The first is the Palestinian Talmud which was compiled around the fourth century, and the second and largest is the Babylonian Talmud,[1] conceived about a century later. The latter is almost two-thirds larger than the former.

The substance of the Talmud is divided into two parts, the MISH-NAH and GHEMARAH.

The MISHNAH is a word relating to "repetitions,"[2-3] and signifying the methods of teaching. A large body of its teaching prior to the second century C.E. was compiled from earlier documents from the teachings of Rabbi's Hillel, Simeon, and Akiba with the final draft by Rabbi Judah Hamassi in 220 C.E.[4] It was divided into six sections:

1. Prayer in relation to produce and crops and their preparation and prohibition (11 chapters).

2. Observance of festivals and food preparations thereon. This also includes days of abstinence and annual sacrifice (12 chapters).

3. Marriage and prohibitions. Engagements, divorce, and adultery (7 chapters).

4. Damages, buying and selling. General punishments. Advice to judges. Matters of idolatry and moral proverbs (10 chapters).

5. Holy offerings. Taxation. The 36 sins of death (11 chapters).

6. Purifications (12 chapters).

---

[1] See *The Babylonian Talmud* by M. Rodkinson, 1896. Also a later edition by Epstein, 1935-52, of 35 volumes for an English translation. The original publications of both Talmuds were in Venice, 1520 and 1523 respectively.

[2] From the word "shanna,"–to learn.

[3] Before the creation of the MISHANAH, the vast quantity of Hebrew literature was called the MIDRASH, which was divided into two parts. The first is the HALKHA ("order of the march"— relating to the behavior of the Jews during the Exodus) which dealt in law, civil and religious. The second is the HAGGADA ("legend") which deals in the finer points of esoteric and mystical expression of Jewish ideals.

[4] He was also called the "The Prince" and went under the name of Mischino, according to Frank.

Once the MISHNAH was completed, commentaries (called MEDRASHIM[5]) and additions (called TOSEPHTOTH) were added by later followers of Rabb Judah.

The *Ghemarah* was formed from the MEDRASHIM and TOSEPH-TOTH, and simply refers to the bulk of the additional teachings added to the MISHNAH

The Kabbalah was said to have been hidden mainly within the first five books of the Pentateuch (written Torah or Law of the Old Testament), though it is also said to be found in some other later biblical books. At this point we have the written Torah for the masses and the oral Torah which, in part, was said to have been kept for the chosen ones. When the correct key was applied Kabbalistically, over 600,000 different meanings and applications applied to the written Torah (it is assumed that since this number coincides with the number of Jews who traveled with Moses that each person could interpret a different meaning to the Torah).

Tradition has it that Moses passed this Secret Wisdom of the oral Torah to 70 elders, which became the basis of Kabbalistic teachings for thousands of years to come.

---

[5] Some of these notable authors are Rabbi Eliezer (Jerusalem Talmud) and Rabbi Ashi and Rabbi Jose (Babylon Talmud).

[6] See *Cipher of Genesis* by Carlos Suares (Shamballah, 1985), for an example of how exactly the hidden ciphers within Genesis are utilized. Also see *Roots of the Bible* by Friedrich Weinreb (Merlin Books, 1986), for another variation of the same themes.

CHAPTER TWO

Letters of the Hebrew Alphabet

The origin of the Hebrew alphabet[7] should be discussed in some depth at this point because of its enormous effect on Kabbalistic thinking and thereby on the Golden Dawn.

From the time of the incorporation of the Kabbalah into the Christian magic of the Renaissance, the importance of correctly writing Hebrew letters, along with the necessity of producing perfect diagrams and symbols, was given major emphasis. The Golden Dawn was equally insistent on this requirement, and for this reason every Neophyte received a lecture on the Hebrew letters, their esoteric significance, and on the correct manner in which to draw the letters. The Neophyte was exhorted to become proficient in their execution and, of course, to learn them by heart. The Hebrew alphabet had seven main points of entry into Jewish lifestyle:

Northwest Semitic Script.
Cursive Script.
Square or Rectangular Script.

---

[7] See *The Hebrew Scripts* by S. A. Birnbaum; *Semitic Writing from Pictograph to Alphabet* by D. R. Driver; *The Bible in Ancient and Near East*; essays in honor of W. F. Albright; *A Study of Writing* by W. F. Albright; Facsimiles of manuscripts and inscriptions by C. D. Ginsburg; *The Samaritan Pentateuch and the Origin of the Samaritan Sect* by J. B. Peskham.

Numerical system applied to the letters
Braille
Manual
Shorthand

The first stemmed from the Pro-Canaanite and Cuneiform Canaan-ite script in the second millennium B.C.E., in which many of the names of the Hebrew letters used today have been identified. This developed into the Phoenician around 1100 B.C.E.,[8] and then into Aramaic in approxi-mately 900 B.C.E. The Hebrew script and alphabet from this point on developed independently of the Aramaic script. In the second century B.C.E., a further development of the Aramaic script was to square the let-ters, which the Jews adopted. It was around the second century C.E. that the letters started to appear with thick and thin bars in some type of polarization. It was not until at least the 6th or 7th century C.E. that the full Hebrew letters as we understand them today were finalized. The iso-lation of the Jews after the destruction of Jerusalem around 70 C.E. also had a great deal of effect on the different variations of script with each area, whether it be in Spain or China, having a distinct style of its own.[9]

The numerical system applied to the Hebrew letters was no doubt adapted from Greek origins. The first nine letters were for single units, while the next nine were for double digits, and the last for units of three digits. The five final letters were also used as triple digit numbers.

---

[8] B.C.E.—Before Christian Era.
[9] In texts such as the *Bahir* and the *Zohar* these differences are very noticeable when discussing the philosophical origins of the Hebrew letters through their geometrical shapes.

Hebrew Numerical System

Letter	Power	Value	Final	Name	Meaning
א	A	1		Aleph	Ox
ב	B	2		Beth	House
ג	G	3		Gimel	Camel
ד	D	4		Daleth	Door
ה	H	5		Heh	Window
ו	O,U,V	6		Vau	Hook
ז	Z	7		Zain	Sword
ח	Ch	8		Cheth	Enclosure
ט	T	9		Teth	Snake
י	I,Y	10		Yod	Hand
כ	K	20,500	ך	Kaph	Fist
ל	L	30		Lamed	Ox Goad
מ	M	40,600	ם	Mem	Water
נ	N	50,700	ן	Num	Fish
ס	S	60		Samekh	Prop
ע	Aa	70		Ayin	Eye
פ	P	80	ף	Peh	Mouth
צ	Tz	90,900	ץ	Tzaddi	Fishhook
ק	Q	100		Qoph	Back of head
ר	R	200		Resh	Head
ש	S	300		Shin	Tooth
ת	T	400		Tau	Cross

FORMATION OF THE 22 LETTERS

The following lecture, in abridged format, was written for the Hermetic Order of the Stella Matutina (called the Golden Dawn prior to 1900) by Mrs. Felkin, wife of the then Order head, R. W. Felkin. Though undated, I would place it about 1923. It is based on the work *Hebraic Tongue Restored* by Fabre d'Olivet, first published in English in 1921.

In studying the actual letters as we now possess them, we must of course admit that they have undergone a considerable modification since the days of Moses, the most important being their approximation to the Chaldean, owing to exile. From the Chaldean also was borrowed the vocalisation system by means of points placed above, below, or within a letter. Nevertheless, the hieroglyphic idea is retained in that each letter represents not merely a sound, but also an object, and the name of the letter is also the name of the object.

Aleph (Arabic *Alif*) not only means the letter A or E (or more accurately, the opening of the mouth to make a sound); it is also the name of an Ox. The word Beth is not only the letter B, but it is also the name of a house. There is another thing you have to bear in mind. In all ancient languages there was only one system of notation for both sound and number. Therefore, each letter is also a number, and each word has a numerical value equal to the sum of its numbers. Thus AL is not only a sound and a Divine Name. It is also 30 plus 1 = 31.

Moreover, a language like Hebrew had comparatively few words, but each word had numerous shades of meaning, indicated either by the context or the inflection, and also each individual letter had its own essential meaning. Therefore it follows that the word was the sum of or modification of those meanings, just as numerically it was the sum of those individual numbers. Thus AL, which signifies the number 31, is formed from Aleph, the sign of power, and from Lamed, the sign of extension. Its spiritual meaning is therefore "Extended Power," and hence *God*, the Power extended over all. Used in a restricted or materialised sense it may be translated as "towards, against, upon." The same letters reversed, LA, represent spiritually the prolongation of movement to infinity, which translated upon a lower plane becomes a negative and may be rendered as "no, not."

Now let us consider the abstract symbolism of each of the 22 Letters of the Hebrew Alphabet:

1. Aleph (Ox) is the sign of power, stability, Unity. It represents mankind as the ruler of earth.

2. Beth (House) is interior action. It represents virility, and an interior dwelling place. Unite these two letters and you have AB or ABA = Father.

3. Gimel (Camel) is the sign of organic development, hence the throat, or a canal which organises or controls inflection or sound, a glass of water.

4. Daleth (Door) is the sign of abundance from division, divisible nature, the source of physical existence: the breast, source of nourishment.

5. The letter Heh (Window) merits special attention. It is the symbol of Universal Life, the breath. It may be translated as either E or H and is closely akin to Cheth in meaning as well as form. It is frequently used as an article, and may be translated as "the, this, that, of." In this respect it is used as a prefix or an affix. It forms, when united with a vowel sound, the principle Deity names, and in this aspect it indicates an abstraction which no modern language can render adequately. Thus YH is Absolute Life, Eternal, Immutable. AHIH can be adumbrated as "That which Is—Was— Will be." It is the root of the verb "To Be, To Exist" and is used to denote the source of human life in the Name HIH which we translate as EVE, but which also may be given as HUA, the third person singular of the verb To Be, or simply HE. When the significant Yod is added it becomes TETRAGRAMMATON—YHVH, the Inviolable Name which must not be taken in vain and which was only intoned by the High Priest upon entering the Holy of Holies. Even today, no orthodox Jew attempts to utter it.

6. Vau (Pin or Hook) is a letter equivalent to O, U, or V. It is therefore convenient to use the point to indicate the sound since its symbolism differs widely according to its pronunciation. As a V, Vau is used as a conjunction and is placed at the beginning of a word; it may be translated as, "and, also, thus, then, afterwards," but it links words together more intimately than any of these. Used as a vowel (U or OU), it is a sign of action, and has the peculiarity of transforming a verb from the present to the past or from the past to the future. In these

aspects it no longer represents the junction of two things (as a hook, eye, knot, or link); rather it is the symbol of light, sound, air, wind. Hence RUCH "the wind, breath or soul," because Resh is movement:, Heh is life and Vau in the midst gives the peculiar human character to the word which indicates "expansion, inspiration."

7. Zain is a hissing sound of something passing through the air, hence a sword or arrow, javelin or spear. It also denotes the refraction of light, suggesting the dazzling appearance of a ray of light falling on polished metal. It may be transliterated as the letter Z.

8. Cheth (Fence, Enclosure) is a letter closely allied to Heh, both in form and in significance; but as it is more closed in form so it can be more guttural in sound and of a material connotation. It signifies life, but on a lower plane. It implies effort, labor, care. Thus in concrete example it indicates a field, an enclosure upon which labour must be expended.

9. Teth in its hieroglyphic form shows a coiled serpent protecting her eggs, hence the universal tradition of the serpent guarding treasure. From that we get the idea of a shield, shelter, a roof protecting man's family as the serpent protects her eggs. Finally a haven, refuge, or goal.

10. Yod is another letter of profound symbolism of deep significance. The hieroglyphic interpretation is that of a hand, but a hand held out in action, thus the symbol of creation. It is a symbol of the flame detached from any material base, free, the leaping creative impulse. By a natural transition we get the phallic symbol of creative power. On the abstract spiritual plane we have the Divine Creator. From this letter transmutes HUH, the feminine source of life, into YHVH—the Ineffable Supreme.

11. Kaph hieroglyphically represents the closed or half closed hand, a fist: hence the hollow, therefore a receptacle: the power of assimilation, reflection, meditation. It forms a link between Cheth, the sign of manifest life, and Gimel, the sign of organization, and carries in itself something of the symbolism of both of these. Used as an article of preposition it may be translated as "similar, according to." Vocalized by Yod it signifies KY, "because, for, then, when."

12. Lamed in a material form suggests any form of an extension, the outstretched arm of man, the unfolded wing of a bird, hence the

further symbolism of the whiplash or ox goad. But when these interpretations are raised to the spiritual plane we perceive at once how significant this letter becomes. It therefore represents an Extension of Power, omnipotence. Hence ALHIM (Alohim) is the extension of the Power of Life to the nth degree, the aspect of the Divine which is capable of creating without effort. Conversely LA signifies an indefinite, and therefore unknown and incalculable, quantity which brought down from the abstract to the concrete becomes negation, "no, not."

13. Mem is the sign of plastic or passive action; the genuine protective aspect of creative power. Hence vocalised as MEM it signifies water, always used in the plural since the Final Mem is collective as water is the condensation of moisture. With the letter Shin prefixed we get ShMIM (SHAMAIM), the Heavens, the ethereal water or atmosphere. Used as an article or prefix, Mem may be rendered as "from, out of, with, among." Hieroglyphically we may say that Mem indicates rough water, sea waves, while Mem Final suggests rather still, calm water, silence, or peace.

14. Nun shows an image of produced or reflected existence, offspring, fruit, or child; hence it represents hieroglyphically a fish, the inhabitant of water. Joined to Beth, the sign of interior action, it becomes BN (Ben—Son). This is more clearly defined when we realise that Nun Final is augmentative and emphasizes the individuality. Nun at the beginning of a word suggests passive action, contemplation folded in upon itself. Nun at the end of a word is the converse, unfolding. Thus NB represents inspiration, prophecy, ecstacy. From this is derived NBIA, a prophet.

15. Samekh represents the development of the hissing sound of Zain, so hieroglyphically it is a duplication. The duplicate link forms a prop, not merely joining but supporting. It is the image of all circular and spiral movement, possibly a deduction from the peculiar movement of the serpent.

16. Ayin, hieroglyphically, signifies an eye, and here we must find one of the most curious and erudite survivals of occult knowledge. Superficially, there seems to be little likeness between the letter and the symbol. When we come to consider it more carefully we find that it is indeed an extraordinary gift of the organs of vision. Externally we have two eyes (shown by the two Yods at the top of the letter), but inside our head lies a

small body, one (or rather two closely connected) of [the] so-called "ductless glands" of modern physiology—the pineal and the pituitary glands. These glands are connected with the external eyes by delicate nerves, as when the external eyes are exercised in certain methods they awake a definite response in the internal gland—the "third eye" of legend. The complete letter is an exact counterpart of the complete organism and signifies the whole visual apparatus. One of the secondary results is the reaction upon the general muscular system.

Phonetically, Ayin represents the opening of the glottis (in the throat to make a guttural sound), and therefore it is transliterated as AA – OO – WH or NG. Thus it symbolizes [an] interior hollow sound or noise and connotes materialism or emptiness, sometimes falsity or perversity. It is the physical aspect of Vau, and when used as a consonant almost always has an evil implication.

17. Peh as a hieroglyphic of an open mouth, naturally symbolizes speech. It is transliterated as either P, in which case it closely resembles Beth in meaning as well as form, or as PH, in which case it approximates rather to the meaning of Vau.

18. Tzaddi represents all ideas of severance, solution; concretely it represents the hook by which something may be caught or ended. In sound it falls into the same group as Zain and Samekh, though it is harder and more abrupt. Placed at the beginning or words it indicates the movement which carries us on towards an end. Placed at the end as Tzaddi Final, it indicates us on towards an end. On a much higher plane it represents a refuge for man.

19. Qoph is a letter that has a guttural sound like Ayin which suggests its materialistic tendency. Hieroglyphically it represents an ear. Symbolically it becomes an implement or instrument by which man may accomplish an act or defend himself. It marks at once, force and restraint. It is significant of repression and decision. In sound it is the harder and more guttural sound of Kaph. Abstractly we may trace a regular succession of descent and. development. Thus Heh—Universal Life, pure being; Cheth the Life of nature, Manifest Existence. Kaph assimilated Life holding natural form and Qoph, material existence giving the means of form.

20. Resh is the letter par excellence, the sign of movement. Hieroglyphically it is the head of man for Resh directs the move-

ment of his whole body. It can be described as being analogous to a captain, or by a slight alteration in focus, the initiative movement which predicates life and ultimate form, the culminating point of all things. Hence RASHITH HA GILGAL-IM—the vortex, the beginning of primeval movement, the Sphere of the Elements. It is the center unfolding to the circumference. The creative elemental fire, the renewal of all movement, the perpetual vibrations building up matter.[10] Hence the word AUR—fire, action, contrasted ASh with potential fire.

21. The letter Shin represents teeth, by which its sound is produced. It completes the symbolism of Zain and Samekh and is in a sense bound to them, for Zain is an arrow and Samekh the bow string, so Shin symbolizes the bow itself. Hence we are told that the Three Paths of the Tree of Life form QShT (Quesheth) the Bow,[11] the material sign of reciprocity between God and man. Shin is the symbol of movement and duration. Used as a prefix it indicates a double power of movement and of conjunction. It may be pronounced either SS or SH and it usually has a point above it to indicate which of the two sounds is to be used. Geometrically it represents the semi-arc of a circle whereas Resh is the straightforward movement of a radius and Samekh a spiral. By analysis we find that the Divine Name SHADDAI represents the oversearching heavens protecting the fecundity and abundance of nature—hence Providence.

22. Tau is the last letter of the Hebrew alphabet and represents a glyph of the cross, the name still retained to indicate the ancient form of the cross—the tau, sacred to THOTH. It is probable, indeed, that the letter was originally written in the form of a modern T and was gradually elaborated to distinguish itself from Daleth. It is the sign of reciprocity, of that which is mutual, interchanging, sympathetic. Joined to the first letter of the alphabet it indicates ATh—the essence, the innermost self of a thing or person, and in this form it is repeatedly used by Moses as a prefix in his account of creation to indicate that he is not describing a material or individual, but essential process which developed on a higher plane preliminary to any physical manifestation.

---

[10] See *Cosmic Doctrine* by Dion Fortune for detailed explanation of how this is accomplished.
[11] Refer to the 1-10 ritual of the Zelator of the Golden Dawn.

The Angels of the Schemhamphoresch.

CHAPTER THREE

Schem-Hamphoresch or the Divided Name

By the time an aspiring Golden Dawn member had reached the Grade of Philosophus, which corresponds to the Sephirah of Netzach on the Kabbalistic Tree of Life, he or she was permitted to study a manuscript called the *Schem-hamphoresch*.[12] It cannot be denied that this is a difficult paper, and one which concerns the deepest secrets of the Kabbalah in general, and of magic in particular. It is probable that, apart from the most gifted and dedicated members of the Order, few were able to utilize it correctly. Even the novice magician, however, is aware of the importance ascribed in Kabbalistic magic to the Holy Name of God in the Jewish tradition, the Tetragrammaton—YHVH. As the Jews were forbidden to utter this name, except in rare ritual circumstances, over the course of some 2,000 years the true pronunciation has been lost[13] and it was subsequently

---

[12] This text is not to be confused with that of the same name that was published by Andrew Luppis in 1686 in Wesel, Duisburg, and Frankfurt which is an inferior work to the one given here. I would refer the reader also to the work of Lenain in his eight-volume treatise *1a Science Cabalistique*, Amiens 1823, for a more indepth coverage of the Schemphamphoresch, which I feel is the basis for the Mathers paper given here. Also see "Schemamphoras," Mss 14- 785, 14-786, 14-187 at the Bibliotheque Nationale, and Harley 6482, British Museum Library.

[13] I have recently come across a reference to the true pronunciation of YHVH in the Edgar Cayce readings, which has it as YAHVAH.

necessary to vocalize the separate letters for invocation in the manner YOD HEH VAU HEH.

The ultimate aim of the Jewish mystic, or the Golden Dawn magician for that matter, was to attain to union with the source of all creation, the Lord of the Universe, or God. One of the ways to achieve this lay in the correct invocation of one of the God's names. Even in lesser magical or spiritual workings, the invocations of divine and angelic names was of crucial importance. For this reason the aspiring magician gave a great deal of study to the many arcane teachings involving the name of God.

One such teaching was the SchemHamphoresch document. "Schem-hamphoresch" is sometimes termed "The Complete Name," meaning that it includes all other names, each of which, by itself, is purported to express some one particular aspect or another of the Divine universal principle, namely, God.

The following paper is an abridged version written by Mathers for Golden Dawn members:

> This refers to the 72 Names derived from the Four Letters of the name of YHVH. Four is the number of letters of ADNI which is its representative and Key.[14] The latter name is bounded with the former and united thereto, thus IAHDVN-HY, forming a name of 8 letters. Eight multiplied by 3 (the number of the Supernal Triad) yields the 24 Thrones of Wisdom, the 24 Thrones of the Elders of the Apocalypse, each of whom wears on his head a Golden Crown of 3 rays, each ray of which is a name, each name an Absolute Idea and Ruling Power of the Great Name YHVH—TETRAGRAMMATON.
>
> And the number of the 24 of the Thrones multiplied by the 3 rays of the Crowns = 72, the Name of God of 72 letters, which is thus mystically shown in the name YHVH as under; or as the Book of Revelation says: "When the living creatures (the 4 Kerubi, the letters of the Name) give glory, etc., to Him, the four and twenty Elders fall down before him, and cast their Crowns before the Throne, etc. (that is, the Crowns which each bear 3 of the 72 names)."
>
> And these 72 names are written on the leaves of the Tree of Life, which were for the healing of the nations. These are also

---

[14] Mathers is referring to the fact that each of the 72 angelic names formed is related to a specific biblical verse which has the name YHVH in it, from Psalms. A Hebrew Bible is necessary for this process, but its verse numbers do differ from those given in the English Authorized Versions.

the 72 rounds on the Ladder of Jacob on which the Angels of God ascended and descended. It will presently be shown how the 72 angels' names are formed from the 72 Names of the Deity, and also how their signification is to be found.

The 72 names of the Deity are thus obtained: The 19th, 20th, and 21st verses of the XIVth Chapter of the Book of Exodus each consists of 72 letters. These are the verses.[15]

19th Verse

"And the Angel of Elohim which went before the camp of Israel, removed and went behind them; and the Pillar of the Cloud removed from before them and stood behind them."

20th Verse

"And it came between the camp of Egypt and the camp of Israel; and there was the cloud and the darkness, yet it gave light by night, and the one came not near the other all night."

21st Verse

"And Moses stretched his hand over the sea; and Tetragrammaton caused the sea to go back by a strong East Wind all the night, and made the sea dry land and the waters were divided."

These three verses are now to be written at length, one above the other, the first from right to left, the second from left to right; and the third from right to left; and as they each contain 72 letters, there will be 72 columns of three letters. Then each column will give a word of three letters and there will be 72 names of three letters each, which are the SCHEM-HAMPHORESCH, or the 72 names of the Deity expounding the Powers of the Name YHVH.

From these 72 names, 72 names of the Angels are formed by the addition in some cases of the name YH, which signifies Mercy and Beneficence, and in others of the name AL, which signifies Severity and Judgement. As it is said "And Thy Name is in Him." These 72 angels rule over the 72 Quinaries, or sets of 5 degrees of the Zodiac, and therefore each Decanate or set of 10 degrees of a sign has 2 Quinaries, and each sign has 3

---

[15] To obtain a clear picture of how this is done it is necessary to obtain a Hebrew translation of these verses.

Decanates, which are again allotted to the Planets in regular Order. And this is the formation as given above: Each Angel's name containing 5 letters, and each name of Deity 3.[16]

The 72 Angels of the SchemHamphoresch are further divided into Four Great Divisions of 18 each, each Division under the Presidency of one of the Four Letters of the Name YHVH. They are further classed as belonging to the Decanates of the Zodiac with 2 Quinaries to each decanate.

The first division of the 3 Signs is under the Presidency of YOD, the letter of Fire, headed by the Fiery Sign Leo. The second division of 3 Signs headed by the Watery Sign Scorpio is under the Presidency of Heh, the letter of Water. The third division of 3 Signs headed by the Airy Sign Aquarius is under the Presidency of Vau, the letter of Air. The fourth division of 3 Signs, headed by the Earthy Sign Taurus, is under the Presidency of Heh (Final) the letter of Earth.

NAMES AND MEANINGS OF THE 72 VERSES[17-18]

1st Angel

NAME: Vahuaih
SIGN: Leo
PLANET: Saturn
DEGREE: 0–5
MEANING: God the Exalter
PSALM 3:4: "And Thou, O Tetragrammaton, art a Shield about me, my Glory and He who lifteth up my head."

---

16 The Golden Dawn here has taken a modern approach to the Zodiac, using signs and planets, though in its inception, the formation of the Schem-Hamphoresch probably dealt with simply the degrees of the zodiac. It must be also pointed out that Mathers had the angelic names starting at a point 0 degrees Leo where other authorities have started the names from the inception of the zodiac measuring from 0 degrees Aries.

17 The verse arrangement is taken from the original Mathers paper which was omitted in *The Complete Golden Dawn System of Magic*. It is the most important section of the Schem-Hamphoresch, yet the publishers retained the section on the Magical Images of the Decans which is superfluous. I have included the Mathers translation of the Biblical verses (and resisted tampering with his translation), which, when repeated numerous times, along with the angelic name, for their desired effect, are considered part of the Practical Kabbalah. This document was given out in two parts. The second is given in the Appendix and has the Seals of the Angels and was given out at the 5=6 level.

18 See *Magical Evocation* by Franz Bardon for what can be considered a modern interpretation on the functions of the 72 angels.

2nd Angel

NAME: Yelauiel
SIGN: Leo
PLANET: Saturn
DEGREE: 5–10
MEANING: Strength
PSALM 22:20: "And Thou, O Tetragrammaton, be not far off, O my Strength, to help me make haste."

3rd Angel

NAME: Satiel
SIGN: Leo
PLANET: Jupiter
DEGREE: 10–15
MEANING: Refuge, Fortress, Confidence
PSALM 91:2: "I will say unto Tetragrammaton, My refuge and fortress, my God, I will be confident in him."

4th Angel[19]

NAME: Nghelamiah
SIGN: Leo
PLANET: Jupiter
DEGREE: 15–20
MEANING: Concealed, saving
PSALM 6:5: "Return O Tetragrammaton, deliver my soul, save me because of Thy mercy."

5th Angel

NAME: Mahasiah
SIGN: Leo
PLANET: Mars
DEGREE: 20–25
MEANING: Seeking safety from trouble.
PSALM 34:5: "I sought Tetragrammaton, and He answered me and out of all my fears He delivered me."

---

[19] Regardie gives this angel's name as Olmiah while Lenain gives it as Elemiah.

6th Angel

NAME: Lelahel
SIGN: Leo
PLANET: Mars
DEGREE: 25–30
MEANING: Praiseworthy, declaring.
PSALM 9:12: "Sing Psalms unto Tetragrammaton Who inhabiteth, shew forth among the nations His deeds."

7th Angel

NAME: Akaiah
SIGN: Virgo
PLANET: Sun
DEGREE: 0–5
MEANING: Long suffering
PSALM: 103:8: "Merciful and gracious is Tetragrammaton, long suffering and plentiful of Mercy."

8th Angel

NAME: Kehethel
SIGN: Virgo
PLANET: Sun
DEGREE: 5–10
MEANING: Adorable.
PSALM 95:6: "Come ye, we will bow down and bend before Tetragrammaton who hath made us."

9th Angel

NAME: Hazeyael
SIGN: Virgo
PLANET: Venus
DEGREE: 10–15
MEANING: Merciful
PSALM 25:6: "Remember Thy tender mercies, O Tetragrammaton, and Thy mercies, for from of old they were."

10th Angel

NAME: Eldiah
SIGN: Virgo
PLANET: Venus
DEGREE: 15–20
MEANING: Profitable
PSALM 33:22: "There shall be Thy mercy, O Tetragrammaton, upon us, as we have hoped in Thee."

11th Angel

NAME: Leviah
SIGN: Virgo
PLANET: Mercury
DEGREE: 20–25
MEANING: Meet to be exalted.
PSALM 18:47: "Liveth Tetragrammaton, and blessed by my Rock, and there shall arise the God of my salvation."

12th Angel

NAME: Hihaiah
SIGN: Virgo
PLANET: Mercury
DEGREE: 25–30
MEANING: Refuge
PSALM 10:1: "Why O Tetragrammaton, wilt Thou stand afar, why wilt Thou hide Thyself at times of trouble."

13th Angel

NAME: Iezalel
SIGN: Libra
PLANET: Moon
DEGREE: 0–5
MEANING: Rejoicing over all things.
PSALM 98:4 "Shout ye to Tetragrammaton, all the Earth, break ye forth, and shout for Joy, and sing Psalms."

14th Angel

NAME: Mebahael
SIGN: Libra
PLANET: Moon
DEGREE: 5–10
MAANING: Guardian and preserver.
PSALM 9:10: "And Tetragrammaton shall be a high place for the oppressed, a high place for seasons in distress."

15th Angel

NAME: Harayel
SIGN: Libra
PLANET: Saturn
DEGREE: 10–15
MEANING: Aid.
PSALM 94:22: "And Tetragrammaton is become unto me a refuge, and my God is the Aid of my Hope."

16th Angel

NAME: Hoqamiah
SIGN: Libra
PLANET: Saturn
DEGREE: 15–20
MEANING: Raise up, praying day and night.
PSALM 88:2: "O Tetragrammaton, God of my Salvation in the day I have cried, and in the night before Thee."

17th Angel

NAME: Laviah
SIGN: Libra
PLANET: Jupiter
DEGREE: 20–25
MEANING: Is Wonderful
PSALM 8:1: "O Tetragrammaton, our Lord, how excellent is Thy Name in all the Earth."

18th Angel

NAME: Keliel
SIGN: Libra
PLANET: Jupiter
DEGREE: 25–30
MEANING: Worthy to be invoked. Just to me.
PSALM 25:24: "Judge me accordingly to Thy righteousness, Tetragrammaton, my God, and let them rejoice over me."

19th Angel

NAME: Livoih
SIGN: Scorpio
PLANET: Mars
DEGREE: 0–5
MEANING: Hastening to hear.
PSALM 40:2: "Expecting, I expected Tetragrammaton, and He inclined unto me, and heard my cry."

20th Angel

NAME: Pheheliah
SIGN: Scorpio
PLANET: Mars
DEGREE: 5–10
MEANING: Redeemer, liberator.
PSALM 120:1, 2:[20] "In my distress I cried to Thee O Tetragrammaton, and He heard me." "Deliver my soul O Tetragrammaton, from lying lips, and from deceitful tongues."

21st Angel

NAME: Nelakhel
SIGN: Scorpio
PLANET: Sun
DEGREE: 10–15
MEANING: Thou alone.

---

[20] There are two verses associated here which when placed together, consecutively, give a fuller meaning than the single verse.

PSALM 31:15: "And in Thee I have confided, O Tetragrammaton, I have said Thou art my God."

22nd Angel

NAME: Yeiael
SIGN: Scorpio
PLANET: Sun
DEGREE: 15–20
MEANING: Thy right hand.
PSALM 121:5: "Tetragrammaton Keepeth Thee. Tetragrammaton is Thy shadow upon Thy right hand."

23rd Angel

NAME: Malahel
SIGN: Scorpio
PLANET: Venus
DEGREE: 20–25
MEANING: Turning away evil.
PSALM 121:8: "Tetragrammaton will keep thy going out and thy coming in from now until Ever."

24th Angel

NAME: Hahauiah
SIGN: Scorpio
PLANET: Venus
DEGREE: 25–30
MEANING: Goodness in Himself. Trust in Thy mercy.
PSALM 33:18: "From Tetragrammaton is a blessing upon those that fear Him, and those who trust in Him."

25th Angel

NAME: Nethhiah
SIGN: Sagittarius
PLANET: Mercury
DEGREE: 0–5
MEANING: Wide in extent, the enlarger, wonderful.
PSALM 9:1: "I will give thanks unto Tetragrammaton with all my heart, will tell of all Thy wondrous works."

26th Angel

NAME: Heeiah
SIGN: Sagittarius
PLANET: Mercury
DEGREE: 5–10
MEANING: Heaven in secret.
PSALM 119:145: "I have called with all my heart, answer me Tetragrammaton, I will preserve Thy statutes."

27th Angel

NAME: Irthel
SIGN: Sagittarius
PLANET: Moon
DEGREE: 10–15
MEANING: Deliver
PSALM 140:2: "Deliver me O Tetragrammaton, from the Evil Man, from the Man of violence preserve Thou me."

28th Angel

NAME: Sehaiah
SIGN: Sagittarius
PLANET: Moon
DEGREE: 15–20
MEANING: Taker away of Evils.
PSALM 71.12: "O Tetragrammaton be not far from me, O my Tetragrammaton make haste for my help."

29th Angel

NAME: Rayayel
SIGN: Sagittarius
PLANET: Saturn
DEGREE: 20–25
MEANING: Expectation.
PSALM 54:4: "Behold, Elohim helpeth me, and Tetragrammaton is with them who uphold my soul."

30th Angel

NAME: Evamel
SIGN: Sagittarius
PLANET: Saturn
DEGREE: 25–30
MEANING: Patience.
PSALM 71:5: "For Thou art my Hope, O Tetragrammaton: O Adonai, my confidence from my Youth."

31st Angel

NAME: Lekabel
SIGN: Capricorn
PLANET: Jupiter
DEGREE: 0–5
MEANING: Teacher.
PSALM 71:16: "I will go in strength O Tetragrammaton; O Adonai, I will make mention of Thy righteousness even of Thine only."

32nd Angel

NAME: Vesheriah
SIGN: Capricorn
PLANET: Jupiter
DEGREE: 5–10
MEANING Upright.
PSALM 33:4: "For Upright is Tetragrammaton of the Word, and all His works are in Truth."

33rd Angel

NAME: Yechuiah
SIGN: Capricorn
PLANET: Mars
DEGREE: 10–15
MEANING: Knower of all things.
PSALM 94:11: "Tetragrammaton knoweth the thoughts of man, that they are in vain."

34th Angel

NAME: Lehahaih
SIGN: Capricorn
PLANET: Mars
DEGREE: 15–20
MEANING: Clement, merciful.
PSALM 131:3: "Let Israel trust in Tetragrammaton, now and for ever."

35th Angel

NAME: Keveqaiah
SIGN: Capricorn
PLANET: Sun
DEGREE: 20–25
MEANING: To be rejoiced in.
PSALM 116:1: "I have rejoiced because Tetragrammaton hath heard the voice of my supplication."

36th Angel

NAME: Mendiel
SIGN: Capricorn
PLANET: Sun
DEGREE: 25–30
MEANING: Honourable.
PSALM 26:8: "O Tetragrammaton, I have loved the habitation of Thy house and the place of the abiding of Thine Honour."

37th Angel

NAME: Anaiel
SIGN: Aquarius
PLANET: Venus
DEGREE: 0–5
MEANING: Lord of Virtues.
PSALM 80:18: "O Tetragrammaton Elohim Tzaboath, turn us and cause Thy Face to shine upon us, and we shall be saved."

38th Angel

NAME: Chaamiah
SIGN: Aquarius
PLANET: Venus
DEGREE: 5–10
MEANING: Hope of all the ends of the Earth.
PSALM 91:9: "Because Thou, O Tetragrammaton, art my refuge, Thou hast Thy refuge in the Most High."

39th Angel

NAME: Reheael
SIGN: Aquarius
PLANET: Mercury
DEGREE: 10–15
MEANING: Swift to condone.
PSALM 30:2: "Hear, O Tetragrammaton, and be gracious unto me Tetragrammaton, be Thou my Helper."

40th Angel

NAME: Yeizael
SIGN: Aquarius
PLANET: Mercury
DEGREE: 15–20
MEANING: Making joyful.
PSALM 88:14: "Why O Tetragrammaton, repelled Thou my soul, and hidest Thy face from me."

41st Angel

NAME: Kehihel
SIGN: Aquarius
PLANET: Moon
DEGREE: 20–25
MEANING: Triune.
PSALM 12:2: "O Tetragrammaton deliver my soul from a lip of lying, from a tongue of guile."

42nd Angel

NAME: Mikhael
SIGN: Aquarius
PLANET: Moon
DEGREE: 25–30
MEANING: Who is like unto Him.
PSALM 121:7: "Tetragrammaton shall keep thee from all Evil,
He shall preserve thy soul."

43rd Angel

NAME: Vavaliah
SIGN: Pisces
PLANET: Saturn
DEGREE: 0–5
MEANING: King and Ruler.
PSALM 88:13: "And I, unto Thee, O Tetragrammaton, have
cried, and in the morning my prayer shall come before Thee."

44th Angel

NAME: Ilhaiah
SIGN: Pisces
PLANET: Saturn
DEGREE: 5–10
MEANING: Abiding for ever.
PSALM 119:108: "Let the freewill Offerings of my mouth,
please Thee, O Tetragrammaton, and teach me Thy Judgements."

45th Angel

NAME: Saelaih
SIGN: Pisces
PLANET: Jupiter
DEGREE: 10–15
MEANING: Mover of all things.
PSALM 94:18: "When I said, my foot hath been moved,
Thy mercy, O Tetragrammaton, will uphold me."

46th Angel

NAME: Ngharaiel
SIGN: Pisces
PLANET: Jupiter
DEGREE: 15–20
MEANING: Revealer
PSALM 145:9: "Tetragrammaton is good unto every man, and His Mercies are over all His works."

47th Angel

NAME: Aslaiah
SIGN: Pisces
PLANET: Mars
DEGREE: 20–25
MEANING: Just Judge.
PSALM 92:5: "How Great have been Thy Works O Tetragrammaton, very deep have been Thy devices."

48th Angel

NAME: Mihel
SIGN: Pisces
PLANET: Mars
DEGREE: 25–30
MEANING: Sending Forth as a father.
PSALM 98:2: "Tetragrammaton hath made known His salvation, in the sight of the Nations hath He revealed His justice."

49th Angel

NAME: Uhauel
SIGN: Aries
PLANET: Mars
DEGREE: 0–5
MEANING: Great and Lofty.
PSALM 145:3: "Great is Tetragrammaton and greatly to be praised, and unto His greatness there is not an end."

50th Angel

NAME: Deneyael
SIGN: Aries
PLANET: Mars
DEGREE: 5–10
MAANING: Merciful Judge
PSALM 145:8: "Merciful and gracious is Tetragrammaton, slow to anger and abounding in Mercy."

51st Angel

NAME: Kechasheiah
SIGN: Aries
PLANET: Sun
DEGREE: 10–15
MEANING: Secret and Impenetrable.
PSALM 104:31: "The Glory of Tetragrammaton shall endure for ever, Tetragrammaton shall rejoice in His works."

52nd Angel

NAME: Amamiah
SIGN: Aries
PLANET: Sun
DEGREE: 15–20
MEANING: Covered in darkness.
PSALM 7:17: "I will give thanks unto Tetragrammaton according to His righteousness, and I will sing Psalms unto the Name of Tetragrammaton Most High."

53rd Angel

NAME: Nangel
SIGN: Aries
PLANET: Venus
DEGREE: 20–25
MEANING: Caster down of the Proud.
PSALM 119:75: "I have known, O Tetragrammaton that righteous are Thy Judgements, and in faithfulness hast Thou humbled me."

54th Angel

NAME: Nithael
SIGN: Aries
PLANET: Venus
DEGREE: 25–30
MEANING: Celestial King.
PSALM 103:19: "Tetragrammaton hath established His Throne in Heaven, and His Kingdom ruleth over all."

55th Angel

NAME: Mibahaih
SIGN: Taurus
PLANET: Mercury
DEGREE: 0–5
MEANING: Eternal.
PSALM 102:12: "But Thou O Tetragrammaton, shall endure forever, and Thy memorial from generation to generation."

56th Angel

NAME: Puiael
SIGN: Taurus
PLANET: Mercury
DEGREE: 5–10
MEANING: Supporting all Things.
PSALM 145:14: "Tetragrammaton upholdeth all those who fall, and lifteth up all those who are down."

57th Angel

NAME: Nemamaiah
SIGN: Taurus
PLANET: Moon
DEGREE: 10–15
MEANING: Lovable.
PSALM 115:11: "Ye who fear Tetragrammaton, confide in Tetragrammaton, their Help and their Shield is He."

58th Angel

NAME: Yeileel
SIGN: Taurus
PLANET: Moon
DEGREE: 15–20
MEANING: Hearer of cries.
PSALM 6:3: "And my soul hath been greatly troubled, and Thou, Tetragrammaton, how long."

59th Angel

NAME: Herachael
SIGN: Taurus
PLANET: Saturn
DEGREE: 20–25
MEANING: Permeating all Things.
PSALM 113:3: "From the rising of the sun to the going down of the same, let the Name of Tetragrammaton be praised."

60th Angel

NAME: Metzrael
SIGN: Taurus
PLANET: Saturn
DEGREE: 25–30
MEANING: Raising up the oppressed.
PSALM 145:17: "Righteous is Tetragrammaton in all His Ways, and Holy in all His Works."

61st Angel

NAME: Vamibael
SIGN: Gemini
PLANET: Jupiter
DEGREE: 0–5
MEANING: The name which is over all.
PSALM 118:2: "Let the Name of Tetragrammaton be praised from this time forth and for evermore."

62nd Angel

NAME: Iahahel
SIGN: Gemini
PLANET: Jupiter
DEGREE: 5-10
MEANING: Supreme Ens or essence.
PSALM 119:159: "See how I have loved Thy Precepts, O Tetragrammaton, in Thy Mercy keep me alive."

63rd Angel

NAME: Nghaneauel
SIGN: Gemini
PLANET: Mars
DEGREE: 10-15
MEANING: Rejoicing
PSALM 100:2: "Serve Tetragrammaton with Joy, enter those who fear Him, unto those who hope in His mercy."

64th Angel

NAME: Mochaiel
SIGN: Gemini
PLANET: Mars
DEGREE: 15-20
MEANING: Vivifying
PSALM 33:18: "Behold, the eyes of Tetragrammaton is unto those who fear Him, unto those who hope in His mercy."

65th Angel

NAME: Damabaiah
SIGN: Gemini
PLANET: Sun
DEGREE: 20-25
MEANING: Fountain of Wisdom.
PSALM 90:13: "Return O Tetragrammaton how long! and repent Thee concerning Thy servants."

66th Angel

NAME: Menqel
SIGN: Gemini
PLANET: Sun
DEGREE: 25-30
MEANING: Nourishing All.
PSALM 38:21: "Forsake me not O Tetragrammaton, my God be not Thou far from me."

67th Angel

NAME: Aiael
SIGN: Cancer
PLANET: Venus
DEGREE: 0-5
MEANING: Delights of the Sons of men.
PSALM 37:4: "Delight in Tetragrammaton, and He shall give the desire of thy heart."

68th Angel

NAME: Chabeoiah
SIGN: Cancer
PLANET: Venus
DEGREE: 5-10
MEANING: Most Liberal Giver.
PSALM 106:1: "O give thanks unto Tetragrammaton, for He is good, for His mercy endureth forever."

69th Angel

NAME: Rohael
SIGN: Cancer
PLANET: Mercury
DEGREE: 10-15
MEANING: Beholding all.
PSALM 16:5: "Tetragrammaton is the portion of my inheritance and my cup, Thou maintainest my lot."

70th Angel

NAME: Yebamaiah
SIGN: Cancer
PLANET: Mercury
DEGREE: 15-20
MEANING: Producing by His Word.
PASSAGE: Genesis 1:1:[21] "In the Beginning Elohim created the substance of the heavens and the substance of the earth."

71st Angel

NAME: Heyaiel
SIGN: Cancer
PLANET : Moon
DEGREE: 20-25
MEANING: Lord of the Universe.
PSALM 108:30: "I will give thanks unto Tetragrammaton greatly with my mouth, and in the midst of many will I praise Him."

72nd Angel

NAME: Mevamiah
SIGN: Cancer
PLANET: Moon
DEGREE: 25-30
MEANING: End of the Universe.
PSALM 116:7: "Turn unto thy rest, O my Soul, for Tetragrammaton rewardeth thee."

---

[21] This is the only Biblical passage in the Schemhamphoresh that comes from Genesis and not Psalms.

CHAPTER FOUR

The Early Books

SEPHER BAHIR[22-23]

Most scholars of Hebraic literature are of the view that the Kabbalah was not committed to paper until the the end of the 12th century when the manuscript *Bahir*, or "Book of Brilliance" first appeared. It is also believed by the majority of Kabbalists that the book can originally be ascribed to Rabbi Nechunjah ben Hakana (around 75 B.C.). As such it is considered to be the very earliest Kabbalistic document. One of the founding Chiefs of the Golden Dawn, Wynn Westcott, made a deep study of the *Bahir*, and in 1896 he produced a translation under the title *Book of Brilliance*. There is little doubt that the concepts of the *Bahir*, like those of the *Zohar* or the Hekaloth texts, were applied by Westcott to the Sephirotic and Kabbalistic schemata of the Golden Dawn.

Because many concepts of the *Bahir* are expanded upon in the *Zohar* (as published in Rosenroth's translation), some have considered the *Bahir*

---

[22] For English translations see *Book of Brilliance,* translated by Wynn Westcott (privately printed, 1896), and *The Bahir,* translated by Rabbi Kaplan (Weiser, 1979).

[23] The name Bahir is given in Job 27:21 "And now men see not the bright light which is in the clouds."

to be an obscure part of those books, though on closer examination the distinction between the two is very obvious.

The *Bahir* consists of a series of discourses which have been compounded into roughly 30 brief pages, though the length of it seems to vary with the various editions. The various Hebrew teachers mentioned in the book include Rabbi's Akiba, Elizer, Rahaumai, and Berachai. The discussions in the *Bahir* are less sophisticated than those of the *Zohar* and give brief hints of things expounded more fully in the *Zohar*. In many instances reading the *Bahir* first and the various relevant texts in the *Zohar*, where more in depth information is given, one can trace a gradual development of the concepts. The *Bahir* really appears to be the basic essence on which the *Zohar* proper was built, and as such, is a text of prime importance.

The Bahir can be broken down into the following seven divisions:

1. Expounds the theory of Creation. The statement given here by Rabbi Nechunjah seems closely allied to the Chinese Taoist view of creation, as defined by Lao Tzu:

> There was something formlessly fashioned,
> That existed before heaven and earth;
> Without sound, without substance,
> Dependent on nothing unchanging,
> All pervading and unfailing,
> One may think that it is the Mother of all things under
>   heaven,
> Its true name we do not know.[24]

Following Nechunjah's statement, Rabbi Berachiah says that Chaos was always there, a belief that also echoes that of the Chinese Tao, or Dao as it is now called. It is a point that does not so much relate to creation as such, but more importantly refers to the transmutation of substance. At this point the importance of the Hebrew letters are brought into close scrutiny, such as the letter Beth being the first letter of the word *Bereshith*—Genesis.

---

[24] *Tao Te Ching.*

2. Gives explanations of the formation of the first eight letters of the Hebrew alphabet from Aleph to Cheth. When compared with the later *Zohar* there are vast number of differences regarding the esoteric significance of the formation of the letters. It is obvious that we are looking at two periods of development of the Hebrew letters when comparing their etymological origins. Rabbi Kaplan, in his translation of the *Bahir*, solves part of this problem by associating the descriptions to the Ashur type script, whereas the Westcott translation uses a later script.

3. Shemhamphoresch, name of 72 letters.

4. Discussion of the Seven Voices as heard by Moses on Mount Sinai. This relates to the manner in which the Torah was given to the Jews.

5. Descriptions of the Sephiroth, which are given for the first time.

> It is thus, the hands have ten fingers, relating to the ten
> Sephiroth with which both the heaven and the Earth
> were sealed.[25]

Though the Sephiroth are not named directly in the *Bahir*, notes made by both Westcott and Kaplan in their translations more than adequately explain some of the hidden references to them.

6. The functions of the Kabbalistic Soul. Although not as sophisticated as that found in the *Zohar*, the concept of the formation of the Soul is given, showing that both the male and female souls develop from each other.

7. Within the *Bahir* there is also a reference to what could possibly be described as the practical part of Kabbalism, insofar as it speaks of the making of a Golem[26] by Rabba.

---

[25] Westcott translation.

[26] The Golem was a man made of clay who was brought to life by Kabbalistic meditations and rituals. See *The Golem of Prague* by Yehuda Yudel Rosenberg (Warsaw, 1939), "The Kabbalah and its Symbolism" by Gershom Scholem, pages 158–204.

THE HEKHALOTH TEXTS

Ismael ben Elisha (in 130 C.E.), a disciple of Nechunjah ben Hakana, taught a particular form of Kabbalistic mysticism which later appeared in what is known as the Hekhaloth texts. These tell how his own teacher took him on a journey of the Heavenly Palaces, and of the visions he experienced there. The actual structure and formation of these palaces will be discussed in later chapters, but the framework from which they developed is very important. Generally the name "Merkabah" (Chariot) denotes the method, whereas the name "Hekhaloth" (Heavenly Palaces) refers to the place they visited, but over the years the two names have become confused with each other. The Lesser Hekhaloth text is such an example, as it is more concerned with the Merkabah itself.[27] One of the most interesting aspects of this manuscript from the occult viewpoint is the section on angelology. This gives definitions and functions not only of various angelic choirs, but of individual angels as well. Like the *Bahir*, the Lesser Hekhaloth text shows yet another stepping stone to Kabbalistic associations through the seven heavens.

The content of the Greater Hekhaloth is more in line with the title, providing details of additional Heavens or Palaces that the earlier Hekhaloth texts did not include.[28] A further Hekhaloth text is the Biblical Book of Enoch which most Christian churches have not deemed as "inspired." Considering the contents, it is not surprising, though most Biblical scholars firmly connect the book with pre-Christian times.[29]

Part of the Merkabah vision is the use of certain symbols to enter various spiritual or psychological levels[30] (which we will call "heavens" for the sake of argument). This is not unlike the "Book Of Pylons" from the *Egyptian Book of the Dead,* and one wonders whether or not this methodology was part of the teachings Moses brought with him from Egyptian learning. The application of putting any visionary experience to the test

---

[27] See Odeberg's "Enoch 3" in which the Lesser Hekhaloth text is given. Scholars such as Scholem have considered it 3rd century and a corrupt manuscript. It appears though that this manuscript in its original form was 1st century, since it concerns the teachings of Rabbi Ishmael ben Elisha, but was possibly added to by other authors over the centuries. Scholem's "Jewish Gnosticism, Merkabah Mysticism, and Talmudic Traditions."

[28] Instead of Seven Heavens, the Greater Hekhaloth relates to Seven Heavens in each Heaven.

[29] Also see "Secrets of Enoch" in *Forgotten Books of Eden* which some have considered as being 1st century. It tells of a journey through ten Heavens and not the usual seven.

[30] See "Hekhaloth Text" in Kaplan's *Meditation and the Kabbalah,* for various examples.

was singularly important. Apart from the experiences of Enoch, the next most important experience allotted to Merkabah is the Vision of Ezekiel.

A more modern viewpoint would term this an exploration of "Inner Space" in which the Kabbalist through special meditational techniques attempts to go through a series of projection workings where his visionary expressions accord with his teachings. These various archetypes, of course, varied from individual to individual, but since they were confined within certain belief structures many similarities between the visions would occur. This Inner Space concept was taken further by Golden Dawn Adepti who adopted the Merkabah concept to suit their own special needs, as shown in the following lecture:[31]

> The symbol, place, direction, or Plane being known whereon it is desired to act, a thought ray is sent to the corresponding part of the Sphere of Sensation of the Nephesch.[32] The thought ray is sent like an arrow from the bow, right through the circumference of the Sphere of Sensation direct unto the place desired. Arrived there, a sphere of Astral Light is formed by the agency of the Lower Will, illuminated by the Higher Will, and acting through spiritual consciousness by reflection along the thought ray. This sphere of Astral Light is partly drawn from the surrounding atmosphere.
>
> The Sphere being formed, a simulacrum[33] of the person of the Skryer is reflected into it along the thought ray, and this united consciousness is then projected therein. This Sphere is then a duplicate by reflection, of the Sphere of Sensation. As it is said, "Believe thyself to be in a place and thou art there." In this Astral projection, however, a certain part of the consciousness must remain in the body to protect the thought ray beyond the Sphere of sensation (as well as the sphere itself at that point of departure from the thought ray) from attack by any hostile force, so that the consciousness in this projection is not quite so strong as the consciousness when concentrated in the Natural Body in ordinary Life.

---

[31] This is from an unnamed and undated lecture from Whare Ra temple, copied by Taylor into his diary notes in the late 1920s. It appears to be in the style of Mathers, but this is speculation.

[32] Part of the Kabbalistic Soul which will be discussed in a later chapter.

[33] There are a number of definitions of this word but generally one takes it to mean the astral body.

The return taketh with a reversal of this process, and save to persons whose Nephesch and physical body are exceptionally strong and healthy, the whole operation of skrying and traveling in the Spirit Vision is of course fatiguing.

Also there is another mode of Astral projection which can be used by the more advanced Adept. This consisteth in forming a sphere from his own Sphere of Sensation, casting his reflection therein, and then projecting this whole sphere to the desired place, as in the previous method. But this is not easy to be done by any but the practiced Adept.

This method of Astral projection was practiced only after the postulant had reached the Inner Order of the Golden Dawn and was experienced enough both to use and understand the various symbols, and to use it as a system of checks and balances against negative influences during the Astral trip. The Merkabah relates to both ascent and descent, which can be explained Kabbalistically as traveling up and down the Tree of Life.

SEPHER YETZIRAH OR
BOOK OF FORMATION

The next Kabbalistic book of major proportion was the *Sepher Yetzirah,* or Book of Formation. The exact date of its origin is usually thought to be somewhere between the 3rd and 2nd century A.D. One legend asserts that the Prophet Abraham was the instigator of the theory of the book, which he received in a vision. Some Kabbalistic authorities have ascribed authorship of this volume to Rabbi Akiba ben Joseph, who was also said to have authored a text on the mysteries of the "Holy Alphabet." It is also interesting at this point to note that the *Sepher Yetzirah* was mentioned in the two Talmuds and may have formed a type of bridge between standard Rabbinical views and that of the Kabbalists. Phineas Mordell, in his 1914 edition of the *Sepher Yetzirah,* considers that it was written in two parts; the first being the original and the second being added around the 6th century. He disputes the claim of authorship to Rabbi Akiba and relates the true author as being Joseph ben Uziel, giving some very convincing arguments in favor of the latter. Adolphe

Franck, in his *The Kabbalah*,[34] divides the essence of the *Sepher Yetzirah* into the following: (1) In general, the composition of the world; (2) In the division of the year or in the distribution of time in which the year is the principal unit; (3) The structure of man, the main principal uniting all these factors being the application of the book to the Macrocosm as well as to the Microcosm.

It would be fair to say that up until the 9th century the main theme of Jewish doctrine was very much against Kabbalistic teaching, and in many instances was aimed at trying to prevent it from being taught. Gaon Saadiah (892-942 C.E.), head of the Persian Academy at Sura, and one of those who did an enormous amount of Hebrew Linguistic research into Kabbalistic teachings, was one of the first to give Kabbalism its full due as a metaphysical doctrine in its own right. He wrote a reputable commentary on the *Sepher Yetzirah* which still exists today and which brought a new understanding of Kabbalism to the Jewry of his own era. Gaon Hai (939-1038), a contemporary of Gaon Saadiah, also wrote a commentary on the *Sepher Yetzirah*, as well as other works that have strong Kabbalistic references, such as "The Voice of God in its Power."

The *Sepher Yetzirah* is a very different book in style from the *Bahir* and has none of the question and answer phrasing which is so characteristic of the Zoharic documents. Possibly one of the first published versions of the *Sepher Yetzirah* was in 1562, Mantua Edition.[35]

The actual title of the *Sepher Yetzirah* is a little ambiguous for instead of a being a study of the Sephiroth it in fact is concerned with the formation and structure of the Paths of the Kabbalah. The book itself is broken down into six chapters:

Chapter 1 gives the breakdown of the ten Sephiroth and the 22 paths. It also discusses the theory of the Lightning Flash and the hidden method of ascending "Jacobs Ladder" through meditation. The formation of the elements is then discussed; from Spirit came Air, and from Air came Water, and from Water came Fire. The Three angelic Choirs of the Auphanium, Seraphim and Kerubim are then named. The Name of YOD

---

[34] First French Edition 1843, Paris. First published English translation in 1967, by University Books. I found a number of English translations of various parts of the text at Whare Ra. For the most part they differ only slightly from the later English publication. When quoting from Franck, I will be using the old Whare Ra translations, which no doubt were done in the late 1880s by Golden Dawn members.

[35] Gulielmus Postellus did a Latin translation in 1552, but it was not for general publication.

HEH VAU is then given as the Name which sealed the six directions of the Universe.[36] The following are the permutations:[37]

(5) IHV — Height
(6) IVH — Dept
(7) HIV — East
(8) HVI — West
(9) VIH — South
(10) VHI — North[38]

An observant student of either the Golden Dawn or the Kabbalah will notice that of all the Kabbalistic texts it is that of the *Sepher Yetzirah* which directly influenced parts of the rituals, diagrams, and teaching of the Golden Dawn. This is particularly true of all the concepts involving geographical direction, when combined with permutations of the Divine name YHVH. For example, at one point during the ritual of the 4=7 Grade of Philosophus, the Candidate is shown a diagram (see following page) and is told by the Hegemon:

> The Sepher Yetzirah divides the ten numbers into a Tetrad, answering to the Spirit of the Living Elohim: Air, Water, and Fire; and a Hexad, consisting of Height, Depth, East, West, South, and North, the six sides of the cube sealed with the six permutations of the letters YOD HEH and VAU of the Sacred Name.

In Chapter 2, the Three Mother Letters of Aleph, Mem, and Shin are directly related to the concept of Air, Water, and Fire. The letters as a whole are then able to be broken down and related to everything created with particular emphasis being placed on the pronunciation. The 22 letters are then formed into 231 gates. These gates are formed by adding each Hebrew letter with another letter, following a certain pattern. For example the first letter Aleph is then placed with every other letter totalling 21 permutations. Beth is placed with every other letter (excluding the one before it, Aleph) which gives 20 permutations. Gimel is paired with every

---

[36] The first four directions are Spirit, Air, Water, and Fire, which are the throne on which the directions are based. The directions proper actually start in the text from the fifth.

[37] The actual formation of the letters here forms a cube, commonly called the "Cube of Space."

[38] The Altar as described in the Golden Dawn's Neophyte rituals is based on this chapter of the *Sepher Yetzirah*.

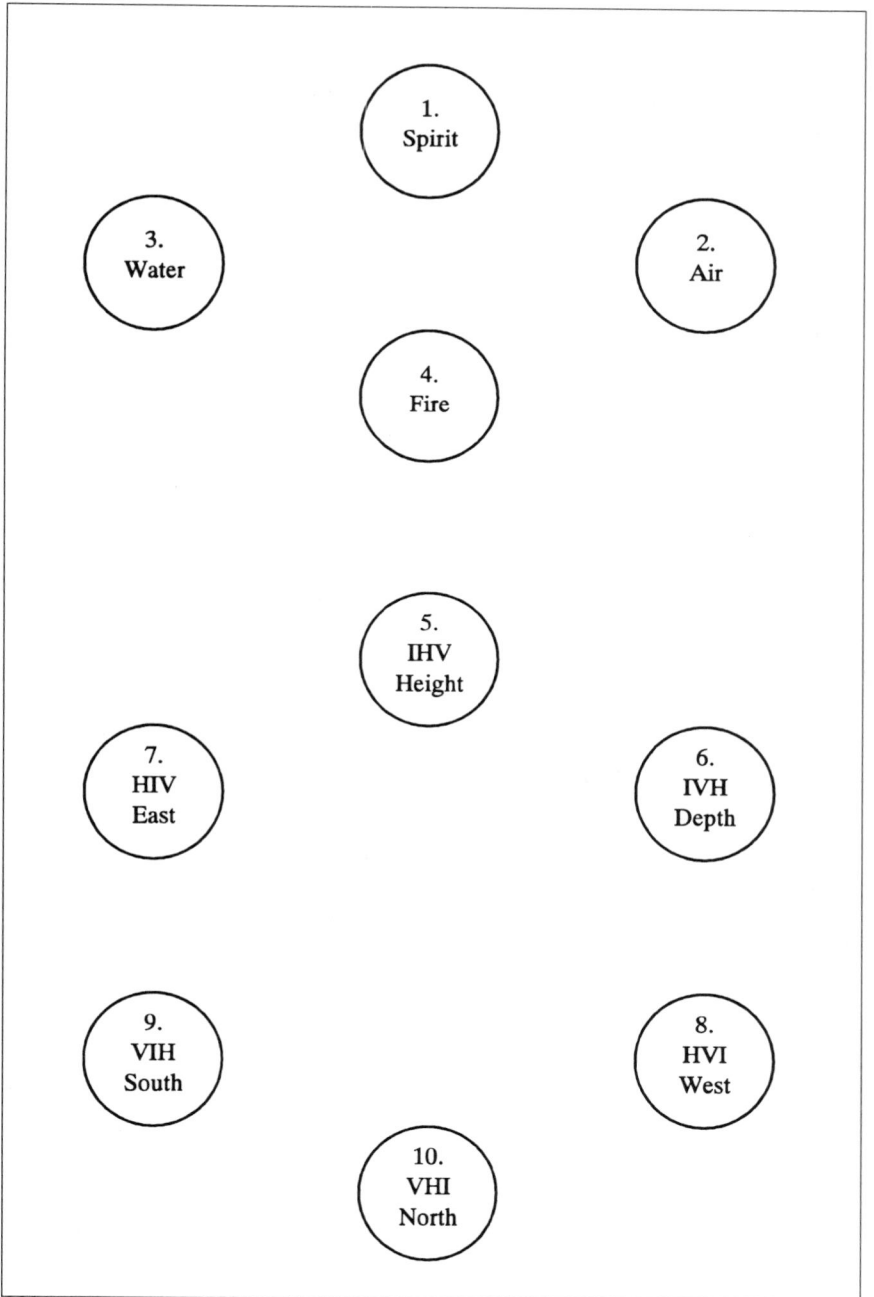

The Six Directions of Space

את אש אר אק אצ אפ אע אס אנ אמ אל אכ אי אט אח אז או אה אד אג אב
בת בש בר בק בצ בפ בע בס בנ במ בל בכ בי בט בח בז בו בה בד בג
גת גש גר גק גצ גפ גע גס גנ גמ גל גכ גי גט גח גז גו גה גד
דת דש דר דק דצ דפ דע דס דנ דמ דל דכ די דט דח דז דו דה
הת הש הר הק הצ הפ הע הס הנ המ הל הכ הי הט הח הז הו
ות וש ור וק וצ ופ וע וס ונ ומ ול וכ וי וט וח וז
זת זש זר זק זצ זפ זע זס זנ זמ זל זכ זי זט זח
חת חש חר חק חצ חפ חע חס חנ חמ חל חכ חי חט
טת טש טר טק טצ טפ טע טס טנ טמ טל טכ טי
ית יש יר יק יצ יפ יע יס ינ ימ יל יכ
כת כש כר כק כצ כפ כע כס כנ כמ כל
לת לש לר לק לצ לפ לע לס לנ למ
מת מש מר מק מצ מפ מע מס מנ
נת נש נר נק נצ נפ נע נס
סת סש סר סק סצ ספ סע
עת עש ער עק עצ עפ
פת פש פר פק פצ
צת צש צר צק
קת קש קר
רת רש
שת

01 + 02 + 03 + 04+ 05 + 06 + 07 + 08 + 09 + 10 + 11 + 12 + 13 + 14 + 15 + 16 + 17 + 18 + 19 + 20 + 21 = 231

Table of 231 Permutations

The 231 Permutations

other letter except the ones before it, giving a total of 19 permutations. Daleth is paired with every other letter except those before it, giving a total of 18 permutations, etc. The total number of pairings are 231[39] which were created from "nothing, the vast limitless space."

A major concept dealt with in Chapter 3 is that of balance, Aleph-Air, standing between Mem and Shin—Fire and Water. The text then goes on to say that the three Mothers are sealed with six rings—relating to the lower portion of the diagram.

The text then says:[40]

> The Three Mothers in the world are Aleph, Mem, and Shin: the heavens were produced from Fire[41]; the Earth from Water; and Air from the Spirit is as a reconciler between the Fire and the Water.

The translation by Papus is a little fuller:[42]

> Three Principles are Shin, Aleph, Mem; fire, air and water. The origin of the sky is fire, the origin of the earth is water. Fire rises, water descends, and air is the regulatory medium between them. Aleph—Mem—Shin is sealed with six seals and enveloped in the male and female. Know, think and imagine that fire supports water.

The Three Mothers are then associated with the year and the seasons, with Aleph (air, chest, lungs) representing the temperate climate, Mem (water, belly) for the winter, and Shin (fire, head) for summer. The same idea can be found almost identically expressed in the Mishna 3, Chapter 3, where it says:

> God created in the World—Fire, Water, and Air. In Man, the Head, Body, and Breast. In the Year, heat, cold and wet.

---

[39] Westcott states in his translation of the *Sepher Yetzirah* that this permutation adds up to 242 and cites the Postellus Edition as giving the reason why 11 are omitted to get a total of 231. Generating the permutations as I have given them adds up to 231, not 242.

[40] Westcott translation.

[41] The full aspect of this explanation is given in the section "Alchemy and the Kabbalah."

[42] This translation from the French was done by a former member of the Stella Matutina in New Zealand.

In Chapter 4, certain sensory associations are further given to the seven Hebrew "double" letters, which are called double because of the pairs of opposite meanings that can be associated with each letter (Beth, Gimel, Daleth, Kaph, Peh, Resh, and Tau) such as Life and Death, Peace \ War, Wisdom \ Folly, Riches \ Poverty, Grace \ Indignation, Fertility \ Solitude, Power \ Servitude. Also associated with these letters are the seven directions of space, the seven days of the week, seven heavens and earths, the seven Sabbaths, and the seven planets.[43]

Chapter 5 equates the 12 simple letters with the 12 zodiac signs, 12 properties, 12 directions, and the 12 months of the year.[44]

Overall this difficult chapter, chapter 6, shows the relationship of the elemental divisions of the zodiac in both partnership and opposites.[45] To simplify the associations of the Hebrew letters by way of analogy the astrological association is by far the easiest and most documented.

THE ZOHAR OR BOOK OF SPLENDOR

The formation of the *Zohar* in manuscript form is said to have come from Simon ben Jochai, who lived in or around 150 to 170 C.E. Condemned to death by the Roman Lucius Aurelius Verus (co-regent with Emperor Marcus Aurelius Verus), Rabbi Simon ben Jochai escaped to some secluded caves where, during his enforced 12-year captivity, he is said to have written down the oral tradition of the Kabbalah that he had received. It was here also that he communicated with the Prophet Elias, who further revealed to him the Kabbalistic mysteries. On his death (accompanied by many strange manifestations of light and sounds) his son (Rabbi Eliezer) and assistant (Rabbi Abba) were said to have gathered his teachings together, which formed the frame of the *Zohar*.

---

[43] The Zelator rituals of the Golden Dawn covers this in part in explaining the diagram of the seven-branched candlestick.

[44] This chapter relates to the 1=10 grade of Zelator when explaining the diagram of the Table of Shrewbread. This diagram, like that of the table of Shrewbread, were of great esoteric significance to the Golden Dawn. Although first introduced in the First Order, they were later studied in great depth in the Second Order.

[45] This entire chapter formed the basis for the complex Golden Dawn paper, "Convoluted Forces." For a simplified viewpoint of it see the forthcoming *The Magical Tarot of the Golden Dawn*, by Pat and Chris Zalewski.

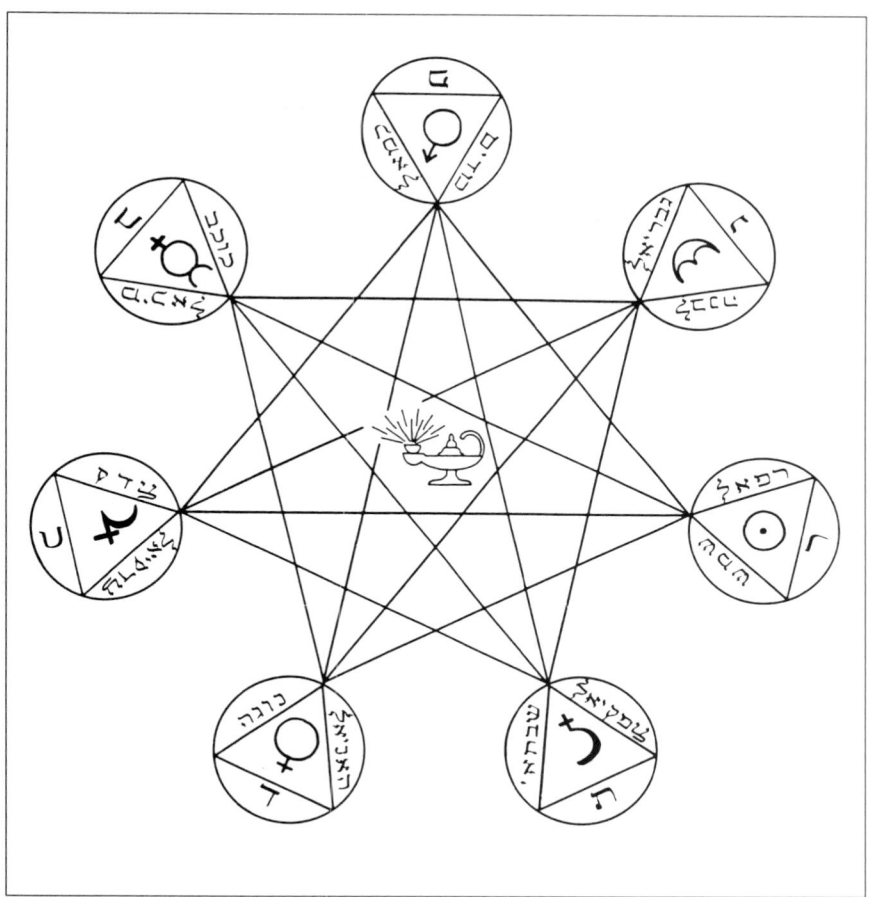

The Seven-Branched Candlestick

The *Zohar* first appeared in Spain in 1290 when Moses de Leon passed out various manuscripts (written in Aramaic) which were purported to be the *Zohar* as received by Simon ben Jochai.[46] When the *Zohar* was first received by Jewry, one Isaac of Acco came to visit de Leon and found that he had died. On asking de Leon's widow to see the original papers that de Leon had copied from, Isaac was informed that no original manuscript existed. Isaac offered her money but still she could not

---

[46] There is no doubt that a certain amount of later material was appended to the original manuscripts.

produce the original manuscript and told him that it had never existed and that de Leon had created the *Zohar* from his own teachings. Virtually in the same breath as these claims Isaac actually cites the *Zohar*[47] and quotes passages from it as belonging to Simon ben Jochai, long after he had visited de Leon's widow. His first criticism of de Leon, which outlines the events he encountered with his widow, is given in the *Divrey Ya Hamin*. Although something made him change his mind at a later date, Isaac's initial charge regarding the authorship of the *Zohar* seems to have stuck, and this has created a controversy that continues even today among Kabbalistic students.

The *Zohar* apparently had more than one name through the centuries and this has added to the confusion. It was also called Midrashi Yerushalmi, and is mentioned in the Geonim and also by St. Agobard (around 800 C.E.)

The first edition was published in 1558, Cremona (*Zohar ha Gadol*), 400 pages; the second in 1558, Mantua, (*Zohar ha Keton*), 700 pages.

The *Zohar* proper is based on the commentaries on the first five books of the Bible, with additions.

1. GENESIS
   (a) Commentaries
   (b) Tosseftoth (Additions)
   (c) Midrash ha Neelam (Secret Midrash)
   (d) Sithre Torah (Secrets of the Law)
   (e) Hashmaloth (Omissions)

2. EXODUS
   (a) Commentaries
   (b) Midrash ha Neelam (continued)
   (c) Raaiah Mehemnah (Faithful Shepherd)
   (d) Sithre Torah (continued)
   (e) Idra de Maschcana (Assembly of the Sanctuary)
   (f) Siphra Pi Zeniouthra (Book of Concealment)
   (g) Hecaloth (Palaces)
   (h) Additions

---

[47] Otzar Cahim.

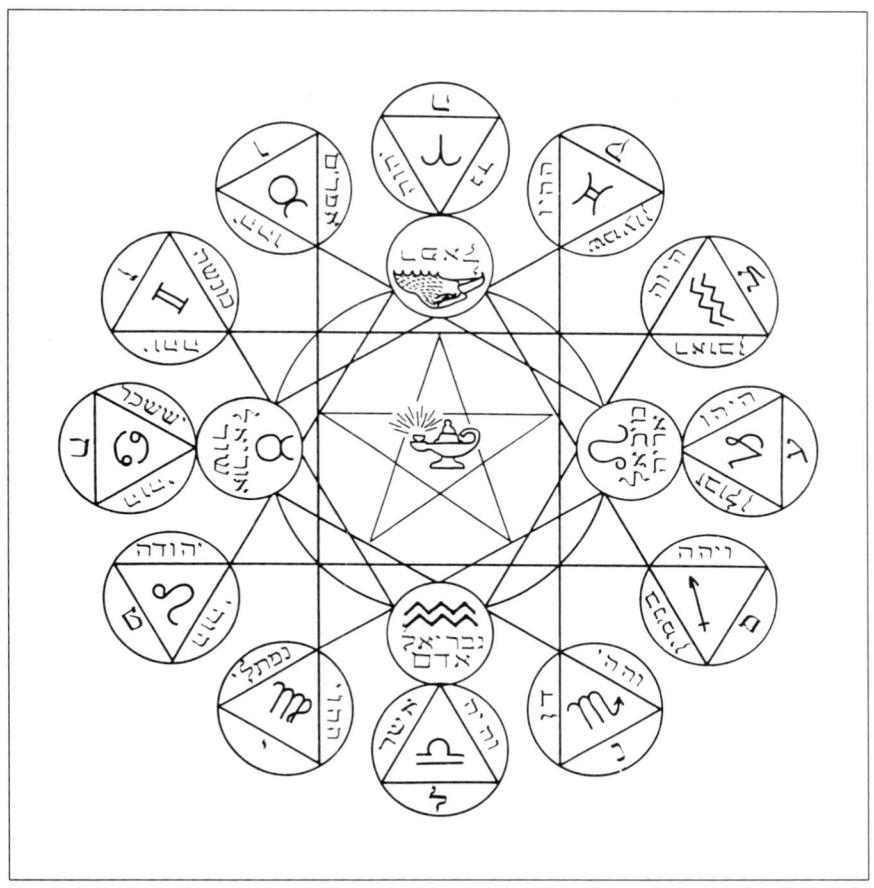

The Table of Shewbread.

(i) Sabah Di Mishpatim (Discourse of the Ancient One
    in Mishpatim)

3. LEVITICUS
    (a) Commentaries
    (b) Raaiah Mehemnah (continued)

4. NUMBERS
    (a) Commentaries
    (b) Raaiah Mehemnah (continued)

(c) Idra Rabba Kadisha (Great Holy Assembly)
(d) Additions

5. DEUTERONOMY
   (a) Raaih Mehemnah
   (b) Idra Zouta Kadisha (Lesser Holy Assembly)

There are additional pieces of the *Zohar* that in reality do not fall into any of the above five parts.
   (a) Midrash Ruth (Commentary on Ruth)
   (b) Raze Derazin (Secret of Secrets)
   (c) Midrash Hazeeth (Commentary on the Song of Solomon)
   (d) Pekoodah (Explanation of the Torah)
   (e) Yenookah (Discourse of Youth)
   (f) Maamar to Hazee (The beginning, come and see)
   (g) Hibboorath Kadmaa (Main Assembly)

The tabulations of these books, though, seems to vary slightly with each different edition of the *Zohar*.[48]

---

[48] For example, Gershom Scholem cites 19 divisions, while Knorr Von Rosenroth has eight and C. D. Ginsburg eleven.

CHAPTER FIVE

The Structure of the Tree

THE FOUR WORLDS

In Kabbalistic doctrine there are Four Worlds, or levels of existence, each becoming more definitive than the one before it. The worlds are said to represent the Four Letters of the Divine Name. Generally, they can be applied to four separate versions of the Tree of Life, or also divide the one Tree into four separate divisions.

The First World is that of **Atziluth** and is linked to the Yod Force of the Divine Name and, by the Golden Dawn, to the Tarot Suit of Wands. This is often called the Archetypal or World of the Spirit for here we have the very first impetus of an abstract idea that works on the broad outline of a concept of a plan.

The Second World is that of **Briah** and relates to the Heh force and to the Suit of Cups of the Tarot. This is the Creative World and shows that the idea or concept as formulated in Atziluth has now taken root in some sort of large framework and is being developed into some sort of workable structure.

The Third World is that of **Yetzirah** and is the Vau force as well as being linked to the Sword Suit of the Tarot. This is the World of Formation showing the actual development of the ideas through the framework

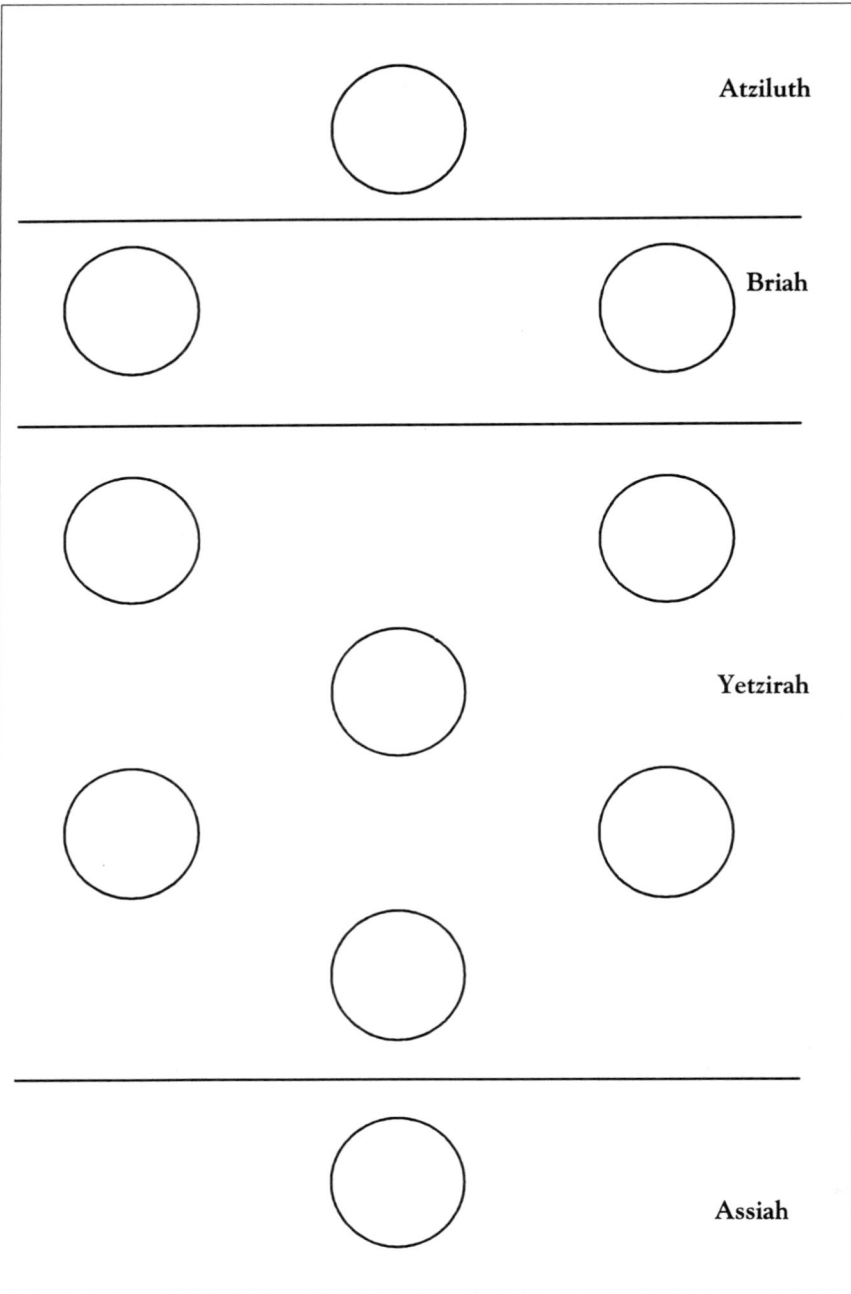

Atziluth

Briah

Yetzirah

Assiah

The Tree of Life in the Four Worlds

of Briah. This is very much the Mental World where things have been brought through and are now down, so to speak, on paper.

The Fourth World is that of **Assiah** and is the Heh Final Force and assigned to the Pentacles Suit of the Tarot. This is the world of the Material or Physical World. Now that the whole mental process of the idea has been assimilated this World now works on the physical plane of action, the end result of the lofty concepts as formulated in Atziluth.

THE VEILS OF NEGATIVE EXISTENCE

Before any understanding is possible of how the Sephiroth function, the primary structure of the way in which the Divine Energy enters the Sephiroth through the three Veils of Negative Existence must be understood. The following lecture on this subject is taken from MacGregor Mathers' introduction to the *Kabbalah Unveiled,* and was considered an unofficial side lecture on the subject to be studied by Golden Dawn Adepti:

34. The idea of negative existence can then exist *as an idea,* but it will not bear definition, since the idea of definition is utterly incompatible with its nature. "But," some of my readers will perhaps say, "your term negative existence is surely a misnomer; the state you describe would be better expressed by the title of negative subsistence." Not so, I answer; for negative subsistence can never be anything but negative subsistence; it cannot vary, it cannot develop; for negative subsistence is literally and truly *no thing.* Therefore, negative subsistence cannot *be* at all; it never has existed, it never does exist, it never will exist. But negative existence bears hidden in itself, positive life; for in the limitless depths of the abyss of its negativity lies hidden the power of standing forth from itself, the power of projecting the scintilla of the thought unto the utter, the power of re-involving the syntagma into the inner. Thus shrouded and veiled is the absorbed intensity in the centreless whirl of the vastness of expansion. Therefore have I employed the term "Ex-sto," rather than "Sub-sto."

35. But between two ideas so different as those of negative and positive existence a certain nexus, or connecting-link, is required, and hence we arrive at the form which is called potential existence, which while more nearly approaching

positive existence, will still scarcely admit of clear definition. It is existence in its possible form. For example, in a seed, the tree which may spring from it is hidden; it is in a condition of potential existence; is there; but it will not admit of definition. How much less, then, will those seeds which that tree in its turn may yield. But these latter are in a condition which, while it is somewhat analogous to potential existence, is in hardly so advanced a stage; that is, they are negatively existent.

36. But, on the other hand, positive existence is always capable of definition; it is dynamic; it has certain evident powers, and it is therefore the antithesis of negative existence, and still more so of negative subsistence. It is the tree, no longer hidden in the seed, but developed into the outer. But positive existence has a beginning and an end, and it therefore requires another form from which to depend, for without this other concealed negative ideal behind it, it is unstable and unsatisfactory.

37. Thus, then, have I faintly and with all reverence endeavoured to shadow forth to the minds of my readers the idea of the Illimitable One. And before that idea, and of that idea, I can only say, in the words of an ancient oracle: "In Him is an illimitable abyss of glory, and from it there goeth forth one little spark which maketh all the glory of the sun, and of the moon, and of the stars. Mortal! behold how little I know of God; seek not to know more of Him, for this is far beyond thy comprehension, however wise thou art; as for us, who are His ministers, how small a part are we of Him!"

38. There are three qabalistical veils of the negative existence, and in themselves they formulate the hidden ideas of the Sephiroth not yet called into being, and they are concentrated in Kether, which in this sense is the Malkuth of the hidden ideas of the Sephiroth. I will explain this. The first veil of negative existence is the AIN, *Ain* = Negativity. This word consists of three letters, which thus shadow forth the first three Sephiroth or numbers. The second veil is the AIN SVP, *Ain Soph* = the Limitless. This title consists of six letters, and shadows forth the idea of the first six Sephiroth or numbers. The third veil is the AIN SVP Avr, *Ain Soph Aur* = the Limitless Light. This again consists of nine letters and symbolizes the first nine Sephiroth, but of course in their hidden idea only. But when we reach the number nine we cannot progress farther without returning to the unity, or the number one, for the

number ten is but a repetition of unity freshly derived from the negative, as is evident from a glance at its ordinary representation in Arabic numerals, where the circle 0 represents the Negative and the 1 the Unity. Thus, then, the limitless ocean of negative light does not proceed from a centre, for it is centreless, but it concentrates a centre, which is the number one of the manifested Sephiroth . . ."

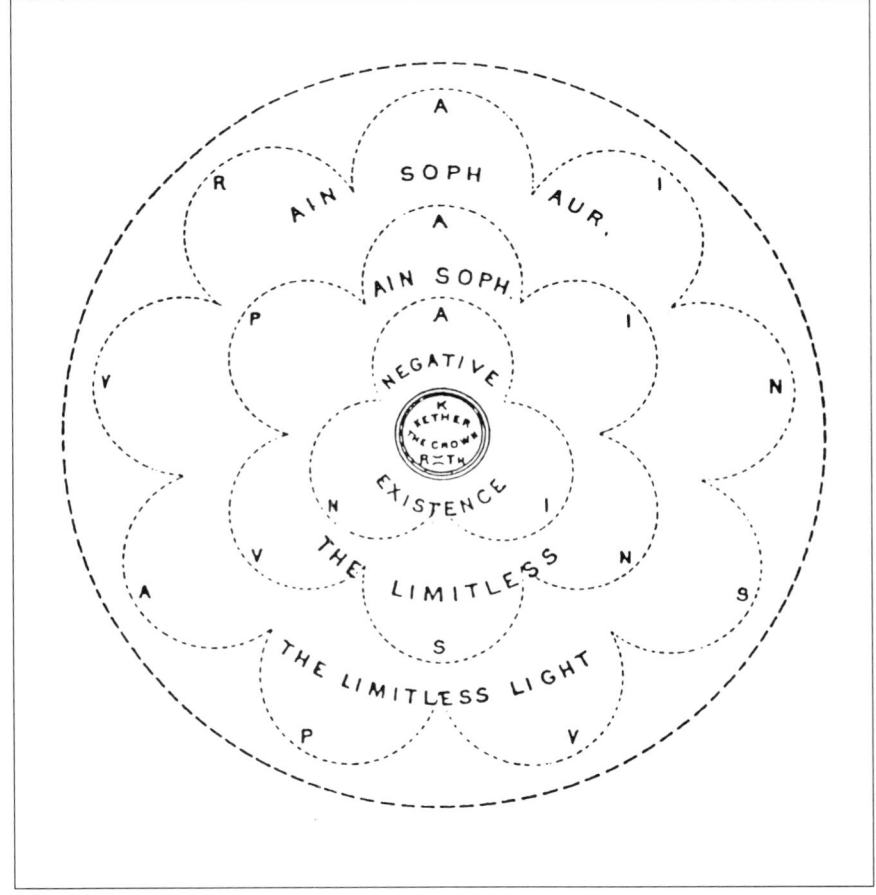

The Three Veils of Negative Existence
The cloud-veils of the Ain formulating the Hidden Sephiroth, and concentrating in Kether, the first Sephira.

THE TEN SEPHIROTH

The actual word Sephiroth is plural and in meaning denotes "spheres" or "emanations" while the word Sephirah is singular. Because the Sephiroth were ten in number, Mathers made the observation that abstract concepts of mathematics could also be applied to the Sephiroth. Within the Sephiroth themselves there are large polarity swings of both genders, but which are still abstract in concept. They develop in varying stages so that when each stage reaches its maximum point a new level is created for the refined energy to go to the next level. The Sephiroth can be observed to be analogous to glass receptacles of varying shapes and quantities. When one is full, then the energy overflows to the next, where it conforms to the shape of the vessel and what that shape represents.

The first three Sephiroth are very important, for many have considered this Supernal triad to be manifested, yet still in a state that is invisible to us. In a modern light it could be likened to a DNA chain or to the formation of basic atoms or molecules that have formed a certain pattern, yet have not yet multiplied enough for visible states of growth.[49]

It should be observed that the Sephiroth are also opened up to the manipulation of negative influences as well as of good ones.

> The Ten ineffable Sephiroth have ten vast regions bound
> unto them; boundless in origin and having no ending: an
> abyss of good and of ill; measureless height and depth . . .[50]

From this we see divided in each Sephirah a positive and negative polarity that can be related to both Spiritual and demonic hierarchies. Since each Sephirah has both positive and negative polarities incorporated in it, then one may assume that there are certain Sephiroth that are grouped under both headings. Once polarity has been established, the neutral polarity must be accepted as well, and certain Sephiroth now fall under this heading, but all in balanced juxtaposition one to each other.

---

[49] See *Superstrings: a Theory of Everything?* P. C. W. Davies and J. Brown (Cambridge University Press, 1988), for a theory of deep formation that can be Kabbalistically applied. Also *Occult Chemistry* by Besant and Leadbeater (3rd ed. 1980), which adds yet other dimension to the formations or stages of growth, applied to the Kabbalah.

[50] *Sepher Yetzirah*, 1.5.

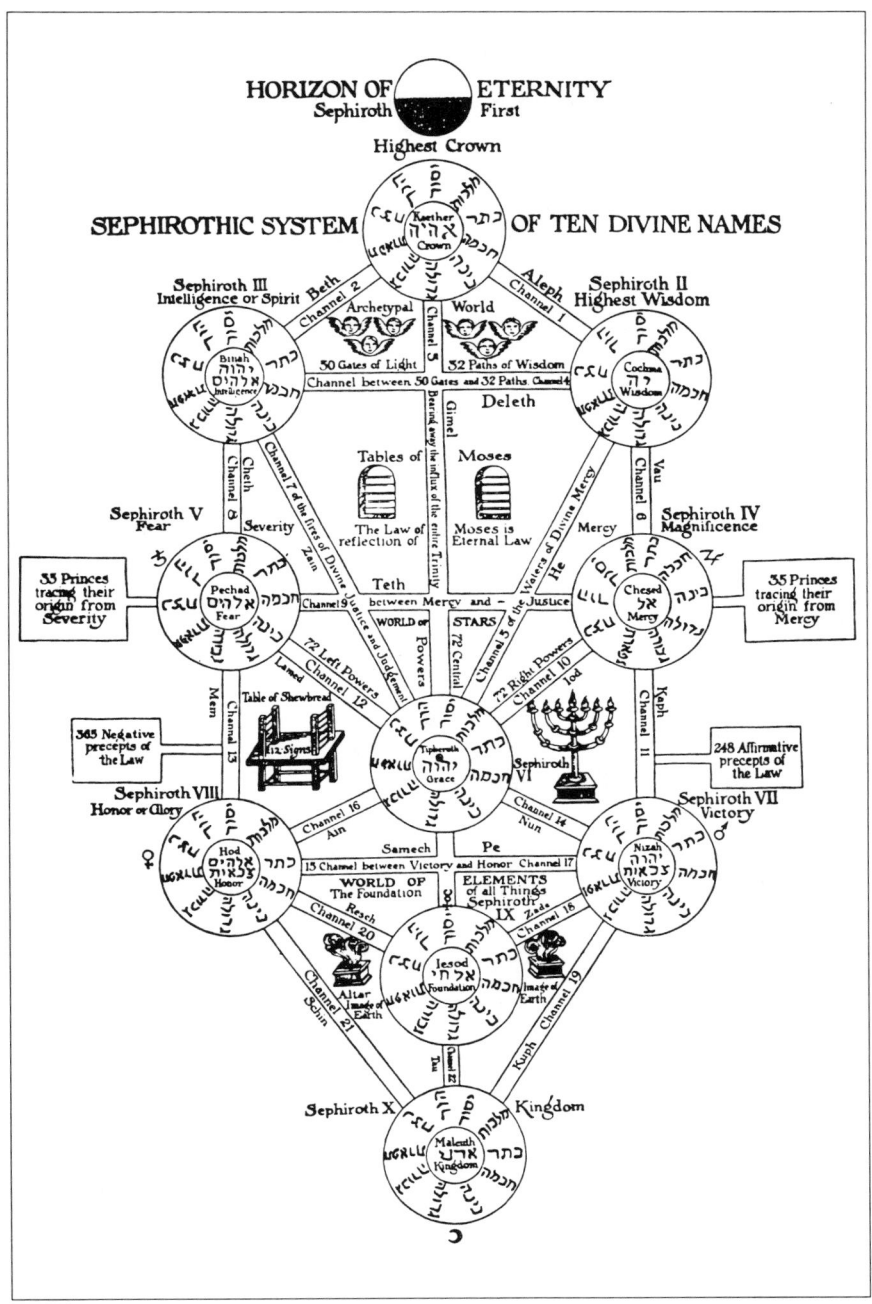

The Tree of Life

The *Zohar* describes the Sephiroth as emanating from each other, a difficult concept to grasp visually (some have used the diagram of concentric circles). Later Kabbalists have considered the Sephiroth as being placed on three pillars (Severity, Middle, and Mercy) while others have used the age-old glyph of the Tree of Life (which has been with us since antiquity) to apply the Sephiroth visually in balanced disposition.

The First of the Sephiroth is called Kether, the Crown, which is the first manifested form and which many have associated with the Hebrew name of God as shown in the letters YHVH,[51] the incomprehensible deity. Kether is often referred to the Godhead as the primal source of manifestation. The Hebrew name associated with this is AHIH,[52] meaning "I am," a simple statement of manifestation.

There are a number of ways to visualize Kether. The first is to view it by way of descent. Here we have a homogeneous force that is perfect in every way except for experience, and that is what it must gain before it can be reunited with itself in Malkuth, the last Sephirah. In many respects, Kether is much like the spirit of man as he arrives on this plane of existence; he must gain experience through the process of trial and tribulation before the re-unification with the Higher Self at death. Any Sephirah, Kether included, can be applied to the smallest speck or atom of this planet and also to the greatest distance in the heavens. This explains the reference in the *Sepher Yetzirah* to the Sephiroth being boundless and having no ending. Looking at Kether by way of ascent here, we have the Godhead on earth, perfection as far as the physical laws will allow. It is something everyone aspires to, for Kether is the absolute ideal, untainted by the fears and worries of this world, for it has risen above them. The Mathers description of the Sephiroth, as given in the *Book of the Path of the Chameleon*,[53] is as given below:

> First are the Feminine colours of the Sephiroth, the Queen's Scale. In Kether is the Divine White Brilliance, the scintillation and corruscation of the Divine Glory— that Light which lighteth the Universe—that Light

---

[51] Exodus 20:2, "I am YHVH thy God."

[52] Exodus 3:14 "I am the first and I am the last and beside me there is no God. And who, as I, can proclaim, let him declare it, and set it in order for me."

[53] This manuscript, called also "Hodos Chameleonis," was issued out in separate parts in the Golden Dawn's Inner Order.

which surpasseth the Glory of the Sun and beside which the light of mortals is but darkness, and concerning which it is not fitting that we should speak more fully. And the Sphere of its Operation is called *Rashith ha-Gil-galium*—the beginning of whirling, the Primum Mobile or First Mover, which bestoweth the gift of life in all things and filleth the whole Universe. And Eheieh is the Name of the Divine Essence in Kether; and its Arch-angel is the Prince of Countenances—Metatron or Metraton, He who bringeth others before the face of God. And the Name of its Order of Angels is called *Chaioth ha-Qadesh*, the Holy Living Creatures, which are also called the Order of Seraphim.

The Second Sephirah is called Chokmah, Wisdom. It shows the establishment of polarity in a balanced and harmonious disposition. The Divine name associated to Chokmah is YH, a derivative of YHVH. In this situation Chokmah is the first break from Kether (by way of descent). The complete unit must now start to separate its component parts from the whole so that each can experience a new dimension of what it is designed for. Although separated, Chokmah still acknowledges that Kether is its superior and that any knowledge coming to it will be through the perfected point. In many ways Chokmah is still under the reflected glory of Kether, for the Wisdom that it utilizes is still far above that of normality, and in many aspects this in itself is something to aspire to.

Since Chokmah is the first separation from Kether, it is the masculine essence or seed and as such still pliable. It is a mixture of both the Wisdom of God and the Wisdom man tries to attain. It is the Sephirah that gives man the chance of attaining what is normally the unattainable through the power of the intellect. The *Zohar*[54] (Temurah, Folio 155a) says:

> YHVH created man in the mystery of Wisdom (Chokmah) and made him with great art and breathed into him the Soul of Life, so that he might know and understand the mysteries of Wisdom to attain His glory.

Wisdom can be ascribed to many different levels and, to make mat-ters extremely complex, it is said that in each Sephirah there are in fact

---

[54] From Whare Ra temple papers, by unknown translator.

ten Sephiroth. The first manifestation of wisdom is, of course, Kether of Chokmah, while the other end of the scale is Malkuth of Chokmah. In terms of the Microcosmos, the areas in between each of these extremes vary according to the type of person one is, which Eastern mystics have considered to be states of satori. The complexity of this is that, while man or woman may be satisfied with one level of Wisdom, it is not unheard of for him or her, during a lifetime, to tap into the other levels as well. On what level and for how long he or she is able to do this, of course, depends on the individual and on what is happening in his or her life during that moment. For some gifted or advanced individuals, this can be done simultaneously with more than one level at a time.

> In Chokmah is a cloud-like grey which containeth various colours and is mixed with them, like a transparent pearl-hued mist, yet radiating withal, as if behind it there was a brilliant glory. And the Sphere of its influence is in *Masloth*, the Starry Heaven, wherein it disposeth the forms of things. And *Yah* is the Divine Ideal Wisdom, and its archangel is *Ratziel*, the Prince or Princes of the knowledge of hidden and concealed things, and the name of its Order of Angels is *Auphanim*, the wheels or the whirling Forces which are also called the Order of Kerubim.[55]

The Third Sephirah is Binah, Understanding, and it shows the establishment of the Triad and the next step after Wisdom. while Wisdom gives us the ability to discern things, Understanding shows us the way to do it. The Divine Name associated to Binah is YHVH ELOHIM which means "Lord my God." The name Binah, in fact, comes from the Hebrew BNYH, Ben, a Son, and YH from Chokmah, showing the Son of Chokmah.

In many respects Binah is the other side of the coin to that which Chokmah represents. The Divine Name Elohim shows that the name Binah is something of a misrepresentation, for the Hebrew linguistic components of Elohim show the combination of both masculine and feminine. While the name in itself is masculine, the Holy name is a mixture of both, showing a very feminine trait underlying this Sephirah. For the

---

[55] From "Hodos Chamelionis."

purpose of this discussion we will concentrate on its masculine impetus, as the feminine side of its nature will be discussed in a later section.

The key word of this Sephirah being "Understanding" shows that it is an energy or form that channels information and compartmentalizes it. Binah brings out the whole pattern of things, to see things in a totality at the top end of the scale, such as Kether of Binah. For those at the lower end of the scale we have an overconcern for trivia, the dissecting of the part taken to the extreme so that the whole is forgotten.

In Zoharistic Kabbalism there is no direct connection of Binah and Kether, as one has to get to Chokmah to get to Kether; but in later schools of Kabbalistic thought, when the Paths were considered in the form of the Tree of Life, Binah actually linked directly to Kether through the Path of Beth. This later appendage of Kabbalism is further complicated due to the fact some schools do not agree on which Path connects with which Sephirah. Beth is considered by some to be the first letter of the Hebrew Alphabet due to the fact that *Bahir* says:[56]

> And what does Beth resemble? It is like Man, formed by YHVH with Wisdom (Chokmah) he is closed on all sides but opened in front.

This shows that there is still a strong connection directly between Binah and Kether through the Path of Beth. Understanding is a very necessary concept to provide the frame for Chokman-Wisdom, for without Understanding, Wisdom cannot be attained or conceptualized.

> In Binah is a thick darkness which yet veileth the Divine Glory in which all colours are hidden, wherein is mystery and depth and silence, and yet, it is the habitation of Supernal Light. There is the Supernal Triad completed. And the Sphere of its Operation is *Shabbathai*, or rest, and it giveth forms and similtudes unto chaotic matter and it ruleth the sphere of action of the planet Saturn. And *Jehovah Elohim* is the perfection of Creation and the Life of the World to Come. And its Archangel is *Tzaphqiel*, the Prince of the Spiritual Strife against Evil, and the Name of the Order of Angels is *Aralim*, the Strong and Mighty Ones who are also called the Order of Thrones. The Angel *Jophiel* is also referred unto Binah.[57]

---

[56] Westcott translation.
[57] From "Hodos Chameleonis."

The Fourth Sephirah is Chesed, Mercy, and the establishment of the Quartenary. This shows Mercy being expressed from Wisdom and Understanding. The Divine Name associated with this Sephirah is AL, which means God. AL is the Holy Spirit that can loosen its grip on the material for those traveling up the Sephiroth of the Kabbalah, thus help-ing them to cross up to Binah. For while we are investigating here the ori-gins and formation of the Kabbalah, the practical use of the Kabbalah must be always kept in mind. It can be used like a ladder for those magi-cians and aspirants ascending it in their endeavor to unite with the God-head in Kether.

In many respects Chesed is a very important Sephirah, for it is the first of the manifested Sephiroth beyond the triad of Kether, Chokmah, and Binah. It is also the first one from which to cross the Abyss (Daath) to get to Binah, by way of ascent. There is no Path connecting Binah and Chesed, and how one travels a route that is not laid out is something of a mystery. It is the area of the shadow Sephirah Daath which cannot be considered a Sephirah proper. A full explanation will be given in the sec-tion on the Tree of Life, before and after the Fall of Man. The Golden Dawn taught that before the so-called Fall there was another Tree in which Daath was a Sephirah proper, connected by two paths. The Gold-en Dawn teaching was that to get up to Binah by way of ascent one must follow the emanation of the old Paths.

Another title for Chesed is "Grace" and this helps us to understand the term Mercy more correctly. Chesed relates to the accumulation of good deeds or efforts in which state forgiveness is given. It is considered one of the finest virtues one can attain. This is achieved through flawless love, of a fraternal nature, for the Understanding of Binah is now con-verted into a state of further receptiveness. By way of ascent on the Tree, Chesed takes the power and activity of the subsequent and severe Sephi-rah of Geburah and has simply consumed or swamped the severe power until it is enveloped with a concept of self love. By analogy it is very much like the cushion absorbing the sharp blow of the rapier until it has extended itself and encloses it with its receptivity.

> In Chokmah is the Radix of blue and thence is there a blue colour pure and primitive, and glistening with a spiritual Light which is reflected unto *Chesed*. And the Sphere of its Operation is called *Tzedek* or Justice and it

fashioneth the images of material things, bestowing peace and mercy; and it ruleth the sphere of the action of the planet of Jupiter. And *Al* is the title of a God strong and mighty, ruling in Glory, Magnificence and Grace. And the Archangel of Chesed is *Tzadkiel*, the Prince of Mercy and Beneficence, and the Name of the Order of Angels is *Chashmalim*—Brilliant Ones, who are also called the Order of Dominions or Dominations. The Sephira Chesed is also called Gedulah or Magnificence and Glory.[58]

The Fifth Sephirah is Geburah, Severity. This is, of course, the polar opposite of Mercy, showing that an extremity has been reached through harsh action. The Divine Name for this Sephirah is ELOHIM GIBOR, meaning "God's wars or battles." This is not an easy Sephirah as it deals with Victory only after trial and tribulations, thereby showing that nothing in its area of influence will come easy. Geburah is the Sephirah of rule and retribution, of trial and tribulation, and it represents the extreme of these.

By way of descent, Geburah has taken the receptivity of Chesed to the extreme, where it cannot give any more and now enforces a strict discipline upon it to circumvent any future actions of this nature. The Divine Name also shows the feminine aspect associated with this Sephirah. This is not the gentle feminine quality but the harsh vengeful quality that is, in many respects, more fierce then any masculine quality and is totally unrelenting. The feminine concept is very much needed in Geburah to receive the Emanations of Chesed and then transform them by way of its masculine counterpart, so that the feminine energy is transmuted to suit the temperament of the Sephirah. These aspects are well illustrated by the following from the Song of Songs (6:10).

> Who is She that looks forth as the dawn, fair as the Moon, clear as the sun, terrible like an army with banners.

By way of ascent, Geburah develops from the Beauty of Tiphareth and becomes proud. The pride, in turn, can become eventually arrogance. The fine line is drawn in this Sephirah between arrogance and discipline.

---

[58] Ibid.

The harshness of this Sephirah spares no one, for here we can meet the hard-core religious fanatic and zealot who would enforce his spiritual beliefs by the point of the sword. We can also meet the mercenary soldier. Both are wading deep in the blood of their fellow man, yet each with his own preconceptions of why he is acting like he is. In the *Zohar* we are told of how both David and Jacob were to face the Lord over their transgressions, not so much for punishment but due to separation from YHVH. Jacob felt he had no need for Geburah and longed for the Mercy of Chesed because it was closer to YHVH. Geburah, though, is a very necessary Sephirah, for (by way of ascension) one has to have the extreme of Mercy to temper the Severity of one's nature.

> In Binah is the Radix of Red, and therein is the red colour, pure and scintillating and flashing with flame which is reflected unto *Geburah*. The Sphere of its Operation is called *Madim* or violent rushing Force and it bringeth fortitude, and war and strength and slaughter, as it were the flaming Sword of an avenging God. And it ruleth the Sphere of Action of the Planet Mars. And *Elohim Gibor* is the Elohim, Mighty and Terrible, judging and avenging evil, ruling in wrath and terror and storm, and at whose steps are lightning and flame. Its Archangel is *Kamael*, the Prince of Strength and Courage, and the Name of the Order of the Angels is *Seraphim*—the Flaming Ones who are also called the Order of Powers. The Sephirah *Geburah* is also called *Pachad*—Terror and Fear.[59]

The Sixth Sephirah is Tiphareth, Beauty. This Sephirah stands directly below Kether on the Middle Pillar and the emanations that flow from it are then mixed with those of Geburah and Chesed so that a perfectly balanced, radiant polarity for the whole Tree of Life is found. Its title is directly related to the emanations of Kether that bind it to harmonizing those of Geburah and Chesed thereby achieving that perfection which the Kabbalists often call "perfection." The Divine Name of this Sephirah is YHVH ELOAH VE DAATH which roughly translated means "God's knowledge," showing the direct link with the Godhead in Kether.

---

[59] Ibid.

Beauty is a word that well describes Tiphareth because, by virtue of its placement directly under Kether through the Path of Gimel, it reflects the glory of the Godhead in Kether. By ways of descent, Tiphareth breaks away from the martial Geburah and stops halfway on its trip to the other side of the Tree in the Pillar of Mercy to its station in Netzach-Victory. Severity, when taken to yet another extreme and stopped in the Middle Pillar as Tiphareth, creates a whole new approach, for the aggressiveness is tempered by Kether's Glory, creating the Beauty of what one is seeking. For some it can be said in the American expression "the brass ring," meaning the whole of one's wants and desires in one package, an ideology delivered. It is a time of rebirth and for a change of values.

> Kether is the Radix of a Golden Glory and thence is there a pure, primitive and sparkling, gleaming golden yellow which is reflected unto *Tiphareth*. Thus is the *first reflected triad* completed. And the Sphere of its operation is that of *Shemesh*, the Solar Light, and bestoweth Life, Light and Brilliancy in metallic matter, and it ruleth the sphere of action of the Sun. And *Yhvh Eloha va-Daath* is a God of Knowledge and Wisdom, ruling over the Light of the Universe; and its Archangel is *Raphael*, the prince of Brightness, Beauty and Life. And the name of the Order of Angels is *Melechim* or *Malakim*, that is Kings or Angelic Kings, who are also called the Order of Virtues, Angels and Rulers. The Angels Peniel and Pelial are also referred unto this Sephira. It especially rules the Mineral world.[60]

The Seventh Sephirah is Netzach, Victory, which relates to the end of the emanations from the Pillar of Mercy which has successfully won through. The Divine Name for this Sephirah is YHVH TzBAOTH, which means "Lord of Hosts," and relates to one of the Seven Archons who created the Universe.

Netzach takes the Beauty of Tiphareth and distributes it towards a desired end. The operative word for this Sephirah is "desire," something that relates strongly to Netzach. The brightness of Kether that is reflected through Tiphareth is now channeled into a format that can control it, for while Beauty remains on the Middle Pillar it becomes a center of sorts,

---

[60] Ibid.

with little control or direction to it, yet when it is transformed into Netzach, the tremendous amount of energy it has is now focused, and that is
where Victory comes in. This focus point can barely contain the beauty
and power of Tiphareth yet it does so by fine tuning it to the point that
no one or no thing can stand up to its burst.

The energy of the Creator, through its link from Kether directly
above it, knows no defeat and its energies overcome all obstacles. Since
beauty and radiance have their limitations that energy must be harnessed
into something progressive, and this is where Netzach is formed. Geburah
at the other end of the scale shows power, but this is not directed, whereas Netzach performs this function with the help of the divine interven-
tion of Kether.

> The beams of Chesed and of Tiphareth meet in *Netzach*
> and thence arises a green, pure brilliant liquid, and
> gleaming like an emerald. And the Sphere of its Opera-
> tions is that of *Nogah* or External Splendour, producing
> zeal, love, harmony, and it ruleth the Sphere of Action
> of the Planet Venus and the nature of the vegetable
> World. And *Jehovah Tzaboath* is a God of Hosts and of
> Armies, of Triumph and of Victory, ruling the Universe
> in Justice and Eternity. And its Archangel *Hanial* is the
> Prince of Love and Harmony, and the Name of the
> Order of Angels is *Elohim* or Gods who are also called
> the Order of Principalities. The Angel *Cerviel* is also
> referred unto this Sephira.[61]

The Eighth Sephirah is Hod, Splendor. This Sephirah like its opposite number, Netzach, is the last in the Pillar of Severity, showing that the
energies of this dynamic Pillar are now at their strongest. The Divine
Name for Hod is ELOHIM TzABOATH meaning "God's Hosts" (or
armies) and relates to the martial aspect of God's works as the end result.

The term "Elohim," with its hidden feminine concept, is applied
here as well, and this shows that the Victory of Netzach has reached the
point where the competition or pushing now stops. The divine energy of
that Victory is converted into the pomp and glory that creates Splendor.
In many ways Splendor is the victory celebration after the battle

---

[61] Ibid.

celebration is over. Since Splendor is on the Pillar of Severity, the pomp and circumstance of Hod now takes the celebration to the extremity and it becomes an issue all in itself. The Bhagavad-Gita says:

> The Splendour of the sun, which dissipates the darkness
> of this universe, is due to me. And the Splendour of the
> moon and the splendour of fire are also from me.

This verse shows how all the opposites that eclipse the universe emanate from the same source no matter how things may swing one way or the other. Eventually the Universal balance is attained.

> The beams of *Geburah* and *Tiphareth* meet in *Hod* and
> thence arises in *Hod* a brilliant and pure flashing orange
> tawny. And the Sphere of its Operation is that of *Kokab*,
> the Stellar light, bestowing elegance, swiftness, and sci-
> entific knowledge and art, and constancy of speech, and
> it ruleth the sphere of the action of the planet Mercury.
> And *Elohim Tzabaoth* is also a God of Hosts and of
> Armies, of Mercy and of Agreement, of Praise and Hon-
> our, ruling the Universe in Wisdom and Harmony. And
> its Archangel is *Michael*, the Prince of Splendour and of
> Wisdom, and the Name of the Order of Angels is *Beni
> Elohim*, or Sons of the Gods, who are also called the
> Order of Archangels.[62]

The Ninth Sephirah is Yesod, Foundation. This is the Sephirah on the middle path that now tapers the two completed forces of Splendor and Victory into Foundation. Yesod is a basic building block on which further developments can be built. In many respects this Sephirah is much like the foetus in the Womb, fully formed but not yet grown to full maturity. The Divine Name of this Sephirah is SHADDAI EL CHAI which means "Mighty Living One" and is concerned with the creation of Life on a new level.

The Splendor of Hod is now transformed into the building blocks or foundation of a new beginning, just as the Victory of Netzach has vanquished the opposition. A new era now begins and the old is no more. Kether, through the influence of Tiphareth, has pushed its rays down the central pillar to Yesod so that they stabilize the celebration of

---

[62] Ibid.

Hod into something more than a momentary high, but something concrete and lasting.

> The beams of Chesed and Geburah meet in *Yesod* and
> thence arises in *Yesod* a brilliant deep violet-purple or
> puce, and thus is the third triad completed. And the
> sphere of its operation is that of *Levanah*, the Lunar
> beam, bestowing change, increase and decrease upon cre-
> ated things and it ruleth the Sphere of Action of the
> Moon and the nature of mankind. And *Shaddai* is a God
> who sheddeth benefits, Omnipotent and Satisfying, and
> *Al Chai* is the God of Life, the Living One. Its Archangel
> is *Gabriel*, the Prince of Change and Alteration. And the
> name of the Order of Angels is *Kerubim*, or Kerubic Ones
> who are also called the Order of Angels.[63]

The Tenth Sephirah is Malkuth, Kingdom. Malkuth is the final
Sephirah where an emergence of a vast and complete cosmic cycle has
been completed. Apart from the emanations of Yesod placed above, it is
now time for the emanations from Hod and Netzach to blend in together and to give additional impetus to the form. The Divine Name applied
here is ADONAI HA ARETZ, meaning "Lord of Earth." This concerns
the stabilization of matter through the influence of the Spirit in Kether
which Malkuth is a reflection of, in a much deeper form.

> And from the Rays of this Triad there appear three
> colours in *Malkuth* together with a fourth which is their
> synthesis. Thus from the orange tawny of Hod and the
> green nature of Netzach, there goeth forth a certain
> greenish "citrine" colour, yet pure and translucent withal.
> From the orange tawny of Hod mingled with the puce of
> Yesod there goeth forth a certain red russet brown, "rus-
> set" yet gleaming with a hidden fire. And from this green
> of Netzah and the puce of Yesod there goeth forth a cer-
> tain other darkening green "olive" yet rich and glowing
> withal. And the synthesis of all these is a blackness which
> bordereth upon the Qlippoth. . . . In Malkuth, *Adonai
> Ha-Aretz* is God, the Lord and King, ruling over the
> Kingdom and Empire which is the Visible Universe.

---

[63] Ibid.

And *Cholem Yesodoth*—the World of the Elements, is the name of the Sphere of the Operation of Malkuth which is called the Sphere of the Elements from which all things are formed, and its Archangels are three:— *Metatron*, the Prince of Countenance reflected from Kether, and *Sandalphon*, the Prince of prayer (feminine), and *Nephesch Ha Messiah*, the Soul of the Reconciler for Earth. And the Order of Angels is *Ashim* or Flames of Fire, as it is written "Who maketh his Angels Spirits and His Ministers as a Flaming Fire," and these are also called the Order of Blessed Souls, or of the Souls of the Just made Perfect.[64]

THE THIRTY-TWO PATHS OF WISDOM

This particular text is appended to Westcott's translation of the *Sepher Yetzirah* and was translated from the Hebrew Text of Joannes Stephanus Rittangelius in 1642. It is also found in Kircher's *Aedipus Aegyptiacus*[65] of 1653. The actual origin of the original work that both texts were based on is obscure, though it formed a very important part of the Golden Dawn teachings. It was mainly used in the Tarot descriptions[66] of the 22 Trumps and utilized in the rituals of the Golden Dawn proper, the Alpha et Omega and the Stella Matutina, to help describe the Paths of the Tree of Life. In many respects this little document is the mainstay of Kabbalistic teaching within the Order and also outside of it. The first ten "Paths" as they are called relate to the Sephiroth themselves and the next 22 relate to the Paths proper of the Kabbalah.[67]

> The Thirty-two Paths of Wisdom issue forth from Chokmah, the Father of Wisdom, the Yod force of our nature for this showeth the spirit of the Theoretical Kabbalah, before the Dew of Wisdom hath implanted its seed into Adam.[68]

---

[64] Ibid.

[65] Kircher said "The 32 Paths of Wisdom are the luminous roads by which holy men of God, through long usage, long experience of divine things and long meditation upon them, can attain the hidden centers."

[66] See forthcoming *The Magical Tarot of the Golden Dawn* by Pat and Chris Zalewski for an explanation of how this is applied.

[67] A very thorough analysis is given in the Golden Dawn Correspondence Course.

[68] This quote is from a notation by Mathers which was the lead paragraph to my copy of this document. The document itself is a copy of what is appended to Westcott's *Sepher Yetzirah*.

The First Path is called the Admirable or the Hidden Intelligence (the Highest Crown): for it is the Light giving the power of comprehension of that First Principle which has no beginning; and it is the Primal Glory, for no created being can attain to its essence.

The Second Path is that of the Illuminating Intelligence: it is the Crown of Creation, the Splendour of the Unity, equalling it, and it is exalted above every head, and named by the Kabalists the Second Glory.

The Third Path is the Sanctifying Intelligence, and is the basis of foundation of Primordial Wisdom, which is called the Former of Faith, and its roots are Amn; and it is the parent of Faith, from whose virtues doth Faith emanate.

The Fourth Path is named Measuring, Cohesive or Receptacular; and is so called because it contains all holy powers, and from it emanate all the spiritual virtues with the most exalted essences: they emanate one from the other by the power of the Primordial emanation. (The Highest Crown.)

The Fifth Path is called the Radical Intelligence, because it is itself the essence equal to the Unity, uniting itself to the Binah, or Intelligence which emanates from the Primordial depths of Wisdom or Chokmah.

The Sixth Path is called the Intelligence of the Mediating Influence, because in it are multiplied the influxes of the emanations, for it causes that influence to flow into all the reservoirs of the Blessings, with which these themselves are united.

The Seventh Path is the Occult Intelligence, because it is the Refulgent Splendour of all the Intellectual virtues which are perceived by the eyes of intellect, and by the contemplation of faith.

The Eighth Path is called Absolute or Perfect, because it is the means of the primordial, which has no root by which it can cleave, nor rest, except in the hidden places of *Gedulah*, Magnificence, which emanate from its own proper essence.

The Ninth Path is the Pure Intelligence, so called because it purifies the Numerations, it proves and corrects the designing of their representation, and disposes their unity with which they are combined without diminution or division.

The Tenth Path is the Resplendent Intelligence, because it is exalted above every other head, and sits on the throne of *Binah* (the Intelligence of the Third Path). It illuminates the splendour of all the lights, and causes a supply of influence to emanate from the Prince of countenances.

The Eleventh Path is the Scintillating Intelligence, because it is the essence of that curtain which is placed close to the order of the disposition, and this is a special dignity given to it that it may be able to stand before the Face of the Cause of Causes.

The Twelfth Path is the Intelligence of Transparency, because it is that species of Magnificence called *Chazchazit*, which is named the place whence issues the vision of those seeing apparitions. (That is the prophecies by seers in a vision.)

The Thirteenth Path is named the Uniting Intelligence, and is so-called because it is itself the Essence of Glory. It is the Consummation of the Truth of individual spiritual things.

The Fourteenth Path is the Illuminating Intelligence, and is so called because it is that *Chashmal* which is the founder of the concealed and fundamental ideas of holiness and of their stages of preparation.

The Fifteenth Path is the Constituting Intelligence, so called because it constitutes the substance of creation in pure darkness, and men have spoken of these contemplations; it is that darkness spoken of in Scripture, Job xxxviii.9, "and thick darkness a swaddling band for it."

The Sixteenth Path is the Triumphal or Eternal Intelligence, so called because it is the pleasure of the Glory, beyond which is no other Glory like to it, and it is called also the Paradise prepared for the Righteous.

The Seventeenth Path is the Disposing Intelligence, which provides Faith to the Righteous, and they are clothed with the Holy Spirit by it, and it is called the Foundation of Excellence in the state of higher things.

The Eighteenth Path is called the House of Influence (by the greatness of whose abundance the influx of good things upon created being is increased), and from the midst of the investigation the arcana and hidden senses are drawn forth, which dwell in its shade and which cling to it, from the cause of all causes.

The Nineteenth Path is the Intelligence of the secret of all the activities of the spiritual beings, and is so called because of the affluence diffused by it from the most high blessing and most exalted sublime glory.

The Twentieth Path is the Intelligence of Will, and is so called because it is the means of preparation of all and each created being, and by this intelligence the existence of the

Primordial Wisdom becomes known.

The Twenty-first Path is the Intelligence of Conciliation, and is so called because it receives the divine influence which flows into it from its benediction upon all and each existence.

The Twenty-second Path is the Faithful Intelligence and is so-called because by it spiritual virtues are increased, and all dwellers on earth are nearly under its shadow.

The Twenty-third Path is the Stable Intelligence, and it is so-called because it has the virtue of consistency among all numerations.

The Twenty-fourth Path is the Imaginative Intelligence, and it is so called because it gives a likeness to all the similitudes which are created in like manner similar to its harmonious elegancies.

The Twenty-fifth Path is the Intelligence of Probation, or is Tentative, and is so called because it is the primary temptation, by which the Creator trieth all righteous persons.

The Twenty-sixth Path is called the Renovating Intelligence, because the Holy God renews by it all the changing things which are renewed by the creation of the world.

The Twenty-seventh Path is the Active or Exciting Intelligence, and it is so called because through it every existent being receives its spirit and motion.

The Twenty-eighth Path is called the Natural Intelligence; by it is completed and perfected the nature of all that exists beneath the Sun.

The Twenty-ninth Path is the Corporeal Intelligence, so-called because it forms every body which is formed beneath the whole set of worlds and the increment of them.

The Thirtieth Path is the Collective Intelligence, and is so-called because Astrologers deduce from it the judgment of the Stars, and of the celestial signs, and the perfections of their science, according to the rules of their resolutions.

The Thirty-first Path is the Perpetual Intelligence; but why is it so-called? Because it regulates the motions of the Sun and Moon in their proper order, each in an orbit convenient for it.

The Thirty-second Path is the Administrative Intelligence, and it is so called because it directs and associates in all their operations the seven planets, even all of them in their own due courses.

THE FOUR COLOR SCALES
OF THE GOLDEN DAWN

One of the most intriguing set of teachings within the Golden Dawn was the application and use of the Four Color Scales as placed on the Four Trees of Life. Without any understanding of both the theory of these scales and how they are used in practical magic, one cannot expect to make much progress as a magician in the Golden Dawn system. The symbolic importance of the color lies behind virtually every aspect of the work undertaken in both the First and Second Orders.

When Mathers created this color system he took it from 22 systems of color theory with no two colors being exactly identical, sometimes the separation between colors being only a slight shade lighter or darker. This subject was indeed one of the most complex among the Order's teachings and due to the difficulty of painting the colors correctly many adopted their own set of scales. What I have presented here is what was originally in the Golden Dawn and the following set of color scales was taken from a very early manuscript, later altered a number of times by various temples over the years. This manuscript also had a set of very well-preserved, painted scales, and although I have had the advantage of adding the odd piece of modern color terminology when I felt it needed it, I have resisted tampering with it.

There are some interesting differences when these scales are compared with those of Crowley's *777*. I note that in these, Binah in the Queen Scale is given the correct coloring of Blackish Red, whereas Crowley gives it as Black, altogether ignoring its Red Root. Since the Crowley Scales are readily available, I have decided to give this version which I obtained from the papers of a former Chief of Whare Ra Temple. Having said that I would add that either the Crowley Scales or the ones given here can be used and the choice is ultimately up to the reader as I am unsure which is the earlier version. The truth of the matter is that there are so many versions of the Color Scales (even Mathers altered his own on a number of occasions) that to give a completely authoritative version is almost impossible.[69] The scales are numbered from 1 to 32. The first

---

[69] Oral tradition at Whare Ra temple has it that the original scales were partly unusable when they were applied to the coloring of the Tarot Trumps. An example of this is the 18th scale for each of the Four Trees which relates to the Tarot Trump the "Chariot," as given in the Crowley scales. A comparison with these scales will show the difference, though this is only one example of some of the changes. It would be a fair comment to say that the color scales were altered from the originals to fit in with the Tarot cards.

ten numbers relate to the Sephiroth, while the rest are concerned with the Paths. The association of the 22 Trumps to the scales actually starts at Number 11, which is the first Path after the ten Sephiroth.

In the Golden Dawn there were two theories of color mixing. The first was to have bright colors that gradually darken with the mixing, so that some colors achieve a type of color that is not easy to identify. The second approach is to make the colors translucent or very watery, and when one reaches the colors of the Prince and Princess Scale, for instance, the original root color can be identified. When my old mentor from Whare Ra Temple taught me the scales he made me use both methods when painting the Four Trees; by doing the former, then watering it down somewhat around the dark colors so that these appeared like a glow or hue on both the Sephiroth and Paths. The reason for the dark and light transparent colors became obvious when I started painting the Tarot Cards which used the Four Trees as a basis for coloring.[70]

THE FOUR COLOR SCALES

	KING	QUEEN	PRINCE	PRINCESS
1	Brilliance	Brilliance	Brilliance	White-flecked Gold
2	Pure Soft Blue	Light Gray	Blue Pearl Gray	White-flecked Red, Blue, Yellow
3	Crimson	Blackish Red	Dark Brown	Gray-flecked Pink
4	Deep Violet	Dark Blue	Deep Purple	Deep Azure-flecked Yellow
5	Bright Orange	Scarlet Red	Bright Scarlet	Red-flecked Blackish-Red
6	Clear Pink Rose	Yellow Gold	Rich Salmon	Gold Amber
7	Light Amber Gold	Light Emerald	Bright Yellow Green	Olive-flecked
8	Violet Purple	Tawny Orange	Red Russet	Yellow-Brown flecked White
9	Indigo	Violet Purple	Very Dark Purple	Citrine-flecked Azure

[70] In the forthcoming *The Magical Tarot of the Golden Dawn*, the same set of scales will be given, but I have used modern color terminology and corrected the odd mistake made in color generation.

	KING	QUEEN	PRINCE	PRINCESS
10	Bright Yellow	Citrine, Russet, Black	As Queen but with Yellow	Black rayed with Olive, Bright Yellow
11	Bright Pale Yellow	Pale Blue	Grayish Green	Yellow-Green flecked Yellow
12	Primrose-Yellow	Light Purple	Light Gray	Light Indigo-rayed Violet
13	Pale Silver Blue	Silver	Cold Pale Blue	Silver-rayed Sky Blue
14	Emerald Green	Sky Blue	Spring Green	Bright Rose-rayed Pale Green
15	Blood Red	Dark Rose Red	Rich Red	Crimson
16	Red Orange	Maroon	Lake Red	Rich Brown
17	Marigold-Orange	Pale Mauve	Brownish Orange	Reddish-Gray hue to Mauve
18	Dark Amber	Deep Blue-Purple	Rich Bright Russet	Dark Greenish-Brown
19	Greenish-Yellow	Deep Purple	Medium Gray	Reddish-Amber
20	Yellowish-Green	Indigo	Green Gray	Plum
21	Violet	Purple-tinged Blue	Bright Purple	Bright Blue-rayed Yellow
22	Grass Green Blue	Sea Blue	Aquamarine	Pale Green
23	Deep Blue	Sea Green	Deep Olive-Green	White-flecked Purple
24	Green-Blue	Dull Brown	Very Dark Brown	Livid Indigo Brown
25	Deep Blue Hidden Red	Yellow Slate Gray	Pale Gray Blue	Red Gray to Mauve
26	Dark Indigo	Yellow	Light Pale Gray	Dark Greenish Brown
27	Deep Scarlet	Elemental Red	Venetian Red	Bright Red-rayed Azure or Emerald
28	Amethyst	Dove color	Bluish Mauve	White-tinged Purple
29	Ultra Violet Crimson	Warm Golden Brown	Light translucent Pinkish Brown	Stone
30.	Golden Yellow	Maize Yellow	Rich Amber	Amber-rayed Red
31	Glowing Orange Scarlet	Vermillion	Scarlet-flecked-Gold	Vermillion-flecked Crimson and Emerald
32	Very Light Indigo	Dark Indigo	Blue Black	Black-rayed Blue

CHAPTER SIX

An Extra Dimension of the Tree

Up to this point we have looked at the Sephiroth as formed in a Tree. Now we come to another dimension of the Kabbalah where instead of Ten Sephiroth we have a series of figures or Partsufim (Countenances). Like the Sephiroth, the Partsufim are included in the *Zohar* proper, mainly in the "Book of Concealed Mystery," "Greater Assembly," and "Lesser Assembly" which Mathers translated from the Latin of *Kabbala Denudata*, and published under the title *Kabbalah Unveiled*. For many within the Golden Dawn, this Mathers' work was a source of study in the Partsufim theory, yet it is barely mentioned in the Order's Knowledge lectures.[71] Apart from the official Knowledge lectures of the Order, there were a number of papers handed around on the subject that seemed to come from two sources. The first is from an early English translation of the *Zohar* from Levi's *Book of Splendours* (dated 1897), and the second from a series of papers that have come from Rosenroth's *Kabbala Denudata*, which included three explanations of diagrams and quotes from the text (which Mathers translated). These were placed together in a section of scattered notes called the "Book of the Long Face." The introduction to

---

[71] It comprises mainly the Fifth Knowledge Lecture.

this section is missing, though Taylor remembers it being taught in the early 1930s at Whare Ra. Attached to this were also translations of portions of Franck's work on the Kabbalah and that of Ginsburg and Jellinek. These were done in the Golden Dawn proper, and not the Stella Matutina, according to Taylor. I have taken the liberty of expanding the skeletonic framework of these notes, that were given out in lecture form, and combining it with other Golden Dawn lectures to form the basis of this section of the book.

To call these papers unofficial may be misleading, as there were a number of very valuable documents that Mathers translated and that were circulated among Golden Dawn Adepti which could be termed unofficial, yet still were studied widely. Regardie, I feel, was the one who perpetrated this mistaken type of thinking about Golden Dawn papers. What one Temple deemed official another Temple did not, hence the apparent confusion over the status of certain documents. I have in my possession a number of notes made by Mathers on the Tarot that were classed as official by Whare Ra tutors and students alike, yet were never shown nor published in collections of Golden Dawn material. These notes were not classed as Knowledge Lectures but "side lectures," and are not to be confused with the Flying Rolls.

In certain of the Golden Dawn papers there are some very subtle theories which can only have come from the Partsufim concept, though they have never been acknowledged openly as such. For example, within the Golden Dawn Tarot scheme, all the Court Cards are based on the Partsufim theory. A failure to understand the Partsufim theory will prevent the gaining of understanding, not merely of the Court Cards and their formation, as used within the Order, but also of many Kabbalistic concepts.

One of the things that has often amazed me about this Partsufim section is that it is largely ignored by students of the Kabbalah in favor of the Sephirotic system despite being of equal importance. In fact, it is an additional dimensional and crucial concept of Kabbalistic study. It is for this reason we are going to devote a great deal of space to it.

In order to understand the concept of creation, before, during and after the Fall of Man, the heavens were mapped out in the form of a face or countenance of Man, which was said to reflect God's image. Each part of this face has a certain significance and is applied to Kabbalistic thought. The Ten Sephiroth are included as a type of extension of it, for the *Zohar* discusses the concealed Adam (or first Adam) who encompasses the Ten Sephiroth. The Partsufim scheme tried to incorporate the Sephirotic development and actually take it a step further, and give a huge overview of the varying stages of development, and show how the varying Trees of Life are incorporated in its vast theory. The Golden Dawn tried to simplify this in a single diagram, showing the main divisions of the Partsufim theory by grouping various Sephiroth together.

To a certain extent the Partsufim theory continues where the Sephirothic emanations leave off. At this juncture in the *Zohar* we are faced with what could be described as a fifth world of the Kabbalist, made up of four divisions, AB, SAG, MAH, and BEN. These divisions are derived from a permutation of the letters YHVH, sometimes called in each of the Four Worlds. Within the Golden Dawn papers (in the 4=7 ritual and associated papers) however, Mathers opted for the four traditional worlds and thus applied these to the Partsufim theory.

The next phase is the grouping of the ten Sephiroth through seven stages. From this point there is a further negative space, or Abyss. This is not to be confused with the Ain Soph Aur, but an area of what one would call Negative Space, which is then reformed into the Second primordial Adam, for the *Zohar* says:

> He spoke firstly of the Kings who ruled over Edom before the arrival of the King of Israel, symbols of the unbalanced powers which manifested themselves at the beginning of the Universe, before the triumph of harmony. "God" said he, "when he wished to create, threw over his radiance a veil, and in its folds, he cast a shadow. From this shadow there arose Giants who said: 'We are Kings' but they were nothing more than phantoms. They appeared because God had hidden himself by creating Night within Chaos; they disappeared when there was brought forth from the east that Luminious Head, that glowing head that humanity gives itself by proclaiming the existence of God, the sun, governor of our aspirations and our thoughts.
>
> "Gods are mirages made of shadow, and God is the synthesis of splendours. Usurpers fall away when the

King mounts his throne, and when God appears, the
Gods are banished."[72]

What we have here, by analogy, is the fact that the previous chaos
is not nothingness nor negativeness, but simply a state of imbalance that
is corrected by the shining light of the sun sweeping away the darkness,
and the formation of a new archetypal face. For we are told:

> The Divine Image is a double one. There are heads of
> light and shadow, the white ideal and the black ideal, the
> upper head and the lower. One is the dream of the Man-
> God and the other is the invention of the God-man.
> One represents God the wise, and the other, the idol of
> the lowly.[73]

The restoration of Adam by YHVH shows that in the single head,
called the Attik Yomin or the Ancient of Days,[74] are three further heads
and these are but a reflection of the Supernal Triad. Each head comprises
a Tree of Life of Ten Sephiroth which has been reflected through and
down by the emanations of the First Adam. The first head is Concealed
Wisdom, the second is Hidden Wisdom, while the third head is Remaining Wisdom. The diagram of the head is broken down into seven parts:

(1) The cranium or skull has no beginning but the emanations
reflected on its surface are said to have received the input from 400
worlds. This figure is arrived at through the fact that each of the ten
Sephiroth contains ten Sephiroth(for example Malkuth of Kether, Yesod
of Kether, etc.) and this situation is reflected in each of the Four Worlds
of Atziluth, Briah, Yetzirah, and Assiah—thus $10 \times 10 \times 4 = 400$. It is also
the numerical value of Tau, the last letter in the Hebrew Alphabet for,
while it has no beginning, it has an end or limit to its size. The *Zohar* tells
us that the skull is the residual place of knowledge and is the residence
not only of the Son but of the 32 Paths and 50 gates.[75]

---

[72] Idra Suta.

[73] Ibid.

[74] He is called the Ancient of Days because Daniel said that he had seen the Thrones of Life giving
Fire overturned and the Ancient of Days sit down so that he can renew the world around Him.
(Daniel 7:9)

[75] The section on the 50 Gates will be discussed later in the alchemical section of the book.

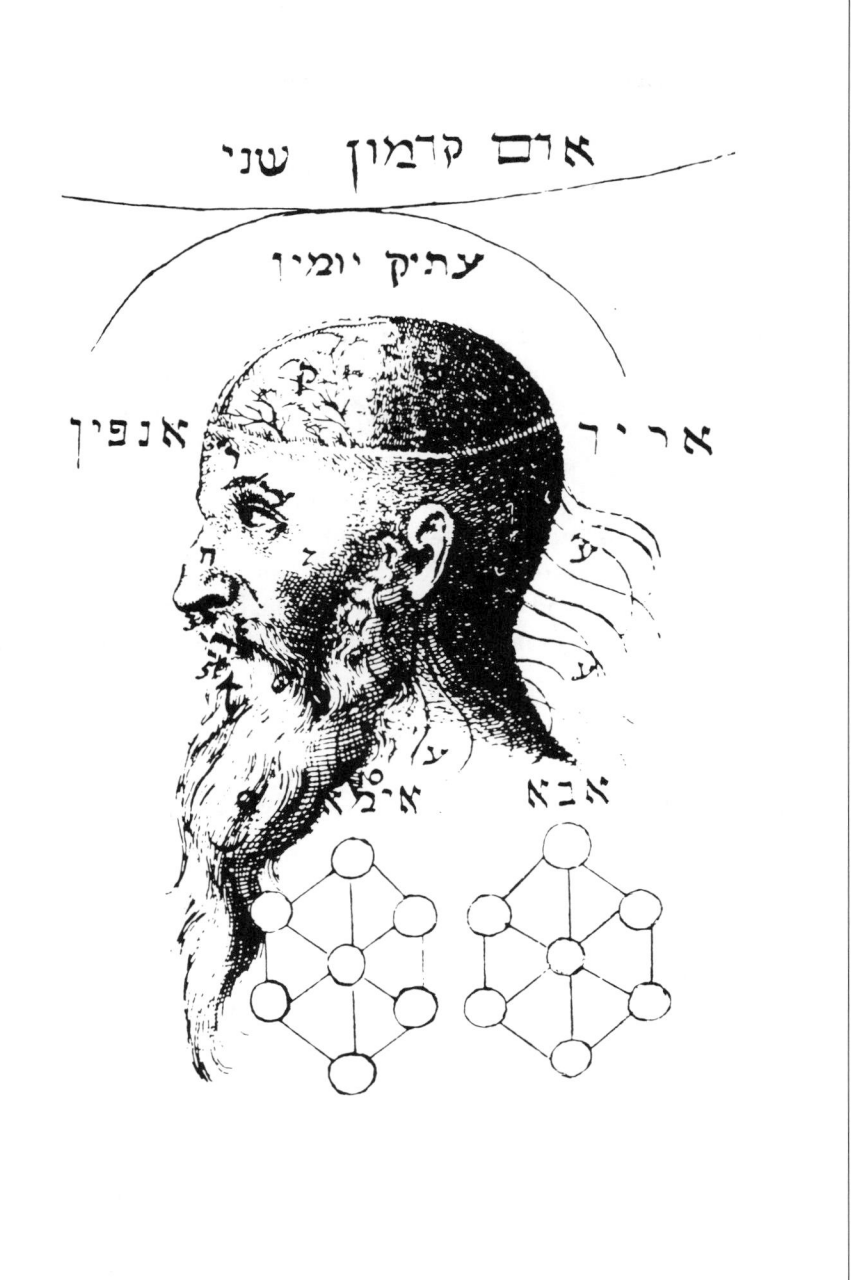

The Face of the Second Adam

(2) The dew from the head comes through the Chokmah of the Hidden or Concealed Adam:

> ... The Most Holy and Ancient one is Hidden and concealed, and in that skull is the Supernal Wisdom concealed[76] ... Genesis 27:27; "And Elohim shall give thee from the Dew of Heaven.

(3) The forehead (sometimes referred to as the brain) has 370 worlds. This applies to Grace and to the benefits of remaining true to the religious feasts and philosophy in general and not deviating from these. Such is said to be the Will of the Law. It is also called the Fountain of Benevolence where blessings are found. From it the Light goes forth in 32 directions.

(4) The eyes have no eyelashes or eyebrows[77] for the figure never sleeps and represents the vigilance of Israel. The Eyes, Skull, and forehead represent the Yod force, as a combined unit. The eyes have three emanations from them and this is from the Supernal triad reflected therein. Their colors change from black to white, depending on the influence at the time.

(5) The nose is the gateway for the spirit of life, the breath, to enter and exit. It represents the Heh force. Within the Zoharic text great importance is placed on the number of breaths, for example four quick breaths are said to come from YHVH.

(6) The beard is divided into 13 parts and describes the Word of God, for the 13 parts of the white beard shows perfection of the Word. There are 31 curls of the beard and 390 hairs, for Psalms says: "The perfume of the supreme head is poured out of the beard of the father, and from there, on to the beard of Aaron." The black beard, of course, is the negative aspect of the white, yet both are a homogeneous part of the same whole. The beard itself hides the Supernal Triad of Kether, Chokmah, and Binah, or three heads which are held together by the letters YHVH. It extends to the pit of the chest of the Arik Anpin or Macroprosopus— Vast Countenance.

---

[76] "Idra Zutra," Mathers translation.
[77] This is disputed in French translations of this section of the *Zohar*.

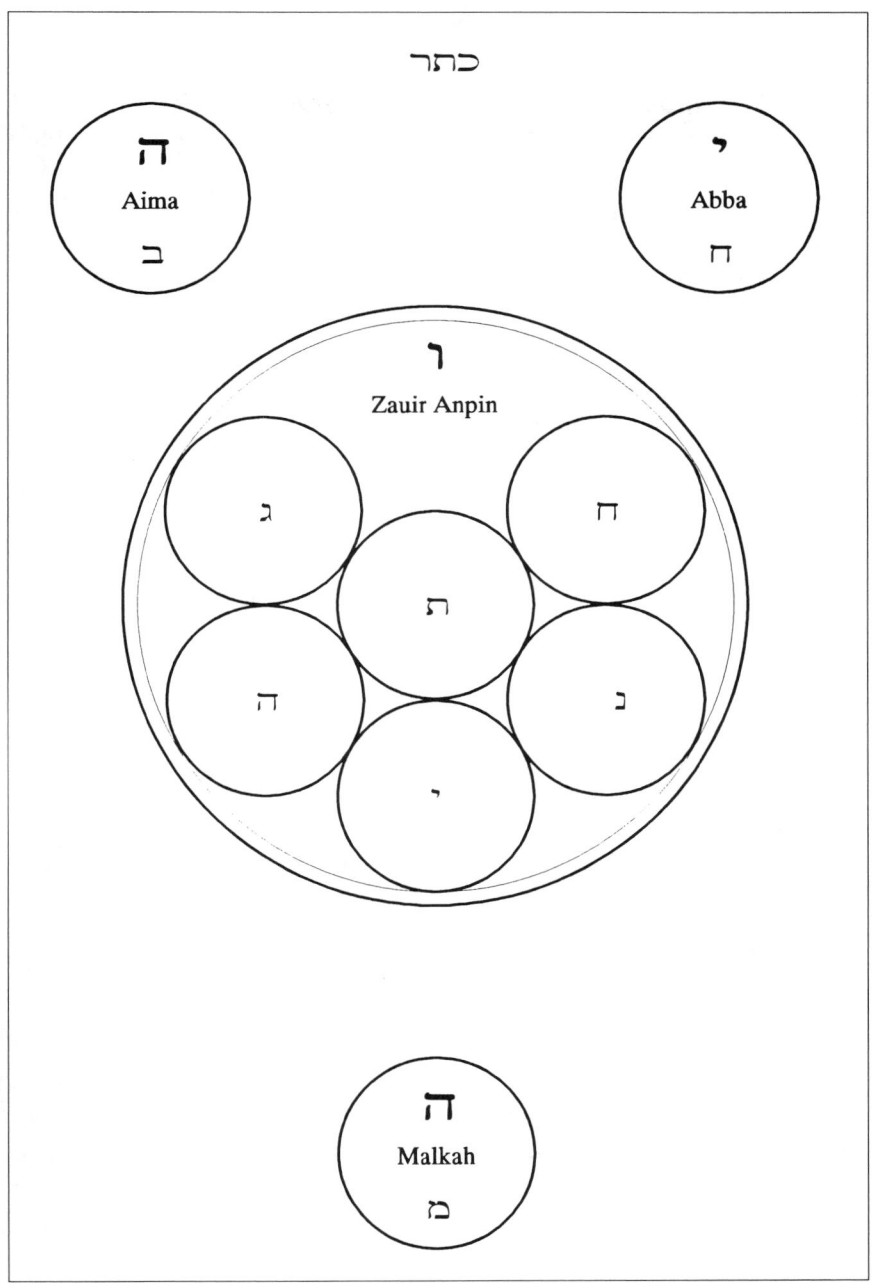

**The Four Letters applied to the Countenance
or Partsufim Theory**

(7) The Father (ABBA), and Mother (AIMA are concealed within the beard and are united by the 8th and 13th parts. The fact that they are hidden shows that they are produced from this level to form in the lower area of the Macroprosopus (where the beard finishes covering the length of the whole body), for the Father and Mother are analogous to Chokmah and Binah of the Sephirotic system. The names of Ishrael and Tebunah (which some have considered as Chokmah and Binah), however, are in fact an outer covering for these forces, yet still distinct from them. They cover the area of the Arik Anpin, for these are the direct emanations that enter the brain of the Zauir Anpin.

(8) From the Father and Mother the Son is produced, and he is called the Zauir Anpin, or Lesser Countenance, which relates to the letter Vau. The Lesser Countenance equates with the Sephiroth Chesed to Yesod of the Sephirotic system.

(9) The Bride of the Microsrosopus (Malkah), representing the Heh (final) force, goes through a period of changes of personality at varying stages or times. Mathers says:[78]

> The conception of the Microprosopus is more properly under the name of Jacob, whose wife is Rachel; and his cognomen, is Israel, whose wife is Leah.[79]

Applied to the figure, Leah is the area from the neck to the pit of the chest, where she then joins Rachel's head. The wombs of both produce the five loves and five powers.

Up to this point, some students of the *Zohar* have considered that the world of Atziluth is being discussed, and that anything below this point now disperses into the world of Briah. This belief, to a certain extent, contradicts the extra dimension theory (which the Golden Dawn have tended to ignore in favor of the Atziluthic system, as advocated by Rosenroth). Because of the confusion and complexity of this section with the Sephiroth system, some Kabbalists have considered that each section of the Figure can be broken down into ten Sephiroth and

---

[78] "Siphra Dtzenioutha," Mathers translation.

[79] On the night of the nuptials Leah was substituted for Rachel, unbeknown to Jacob.

also representing a Sephirah in the greater scheme. This theory is highly complex and will not be discussed here, for it quite often contradictory, as Rosenroth tried to show in his *Kabbla Denudata*. The Golden Dawn initiates also realized the complexity of this theory and opted for the simplistic diagram of the dispersion of the Sephiroth as applied to the Macroprosopus and the Microprosopus.

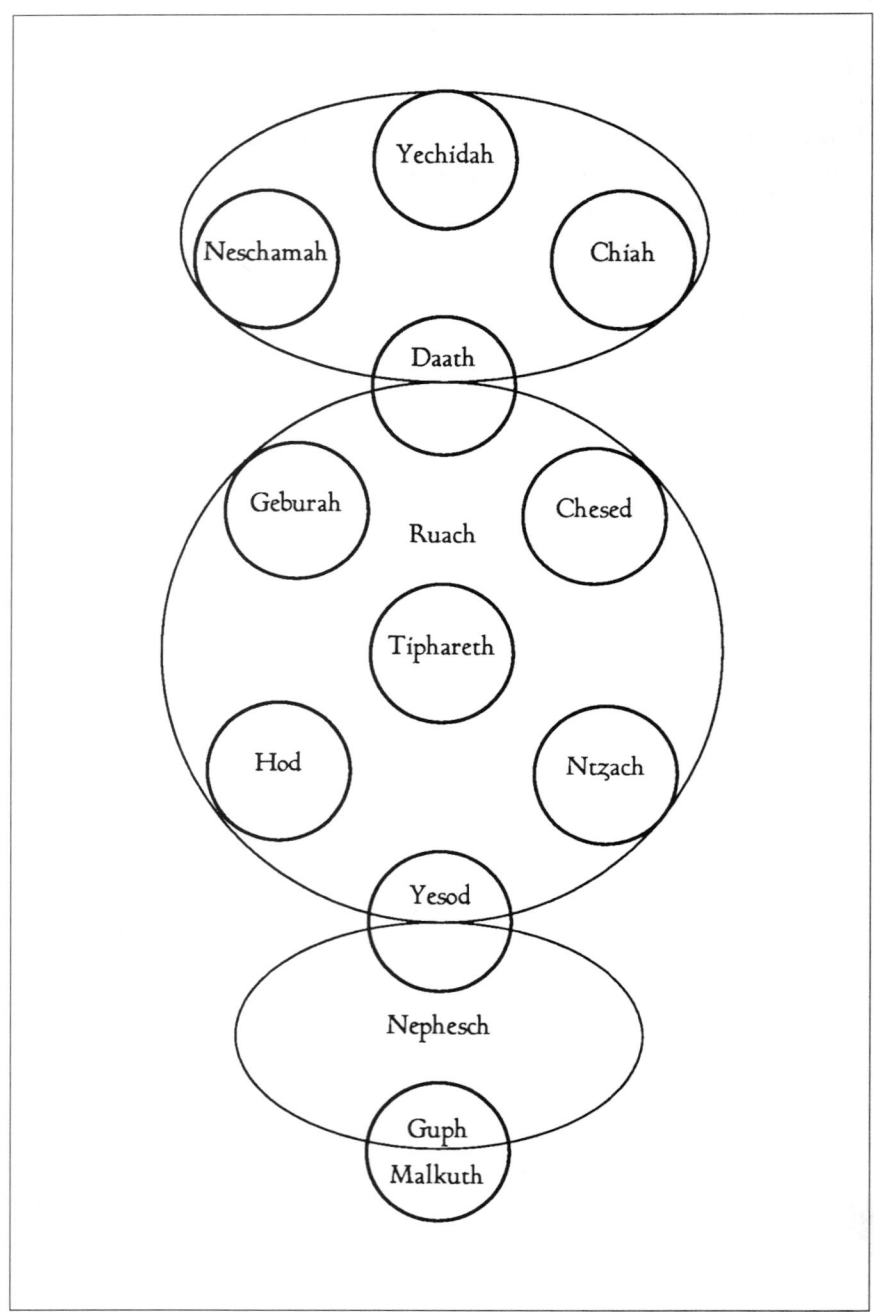

The Soul of the Kabbalah

CHAPTER SEVEN

The Soul of the Kabbalah[80]

THE PRE-EXISTENCE STATE

Before one can accept the pre-existence state of the Soul one must first believe in the state of reincarnation in which the soul sends forth its emanations into various lives, then retracts itself after each life so that the lessons of each life can be studied and learned from. With this type of pre-existence concept the soul is, to a certain extent, contracted and devoid of its extensions into the realm of mankind. The *Bahir* refers us to the meaning of "generation to generation" (as given in Ecclesiastes 1:4) yet Rabbi Akiba tells us bluntly that a generation has already came or been before, stating that it is the same people and yet of another generation.

---

[80] The quotes from the *Zohar*, as given in this chapter, were taken from a series of lectures given at Whare Ra temple in New Zealand, on the Kabbalistic Soul, from 1919–1921. I found these translations in an old notebook with various books and folio references of the *Zohar* given. Many of these translations pre-date previous English publications and no indication was given of who actually translated them into English. Some are taken from Mathers' *Kabbalah Unveiled*. Some have been taken from the French translation of the *Zohar* by Pauly, others from *The Kabbalah* by Franck. There are some parts that I have been informed must have been taken directly from the Hebrew version of the *Zohar*.

This is expounded upon in the system of Isaac Luria and Chaim Vital.[81]
The *Zohar* states:[82]

> If all dead bodies are risen from the dust, what will
> become to the bodies that have shared the same soul?

Rabbi Jose tells us that these do not count and it is the last body
that one has shared that will rise again at resurrection. The entire concept relates to the Biblical book of Genesis, where it is said that something is created in physical form then returned to God on the final day.
Of the actual creation itself, the *Zohar* says:[83]

> As the body is made in this world from the combination of
> the four elements, the spirit (soul) is made in the Gar-
> den[84] from a combination of the four winds that are there
> and the spirit in them shaped in the shape of the body.

This tells us that when the soul is first fashioned it is in empathy
with the body. The effect of its shaping in the Garden through the four
winds is analogous to the four elements on earth. In fact, one could
assume that the soul is reshaped in the Garden before any re-entry into
man or woman. The *Zohar* says:[85]

> Blessed are the just, whose NShMThHVN, souls are
> drawn from that Holy Body which is called Adam, which
> includeth all things; the place, as it were, wherein all the
> Crowns and Holy Diadems are associated together,
> arrayed in equilibrium and balance.

This concept shows that all souls were created together, even
though the vast majority took their time before entry into mankind.

On the question of polarity of the Soul, with the continual reference to the male Adam, the *Zohar* says:

---

[81] See *Sepher Ha-Gilgalim* or Book of Transformation.
[82] Vol. 2, folio 131a.
[83] Vol. 3, folio 13b.
[84] This is possibly the Lower Garden of Eden and not the Upper.
[85] Lesser Holy Assembly.

Every form in which the male and female principle is not to be found is not a superior or complete form. The Holy One, blessed be He, does not establish His abode where these two principles are not perfectly united; the blessing comes down only where this union exists, as we learn from the following words: "He blessed them and called their name (Adam) on the day they were created (Genesis 5:2) for the name of Man can be given only to a man and a woman who are united into one being."

We are told in the *Zohar*[86] that the world of Earth is a reflection of the upper World of spirit, echoing the words of Hermes Trismegistos who says in the Emerald Tablet:

In truth certainly and without doubt, whatever is below is like that which is above, and whatever is above is like that which is below, to accomplish the miracles of one thing. Thus this little world is created according to the prototype of the great world.

The *Zohar* further states that when Adam was created he gathered the earthy materials from all over the world and made him from it, on earth. The soul is a compound of three grades or degrees. The lowest is the Nephesch, while the next is the Ruach, and the highest is the Neschamah. Each of the two lowest functions, or levels of the Soul, relies on the energies of the one above it, so that the body of man can exist with the spirit therein. It is the function of the lowest to try and unite with the highest while man is still in material form.

DIVISIONS OF THE SOUL

Guph

Although the Nephesch is the lowest form of the Soul, in one sense there is another form even lower, Guph, the physical body. This is the clothing vehicle for the next level, the Nephesch. The *Zohar* says of this:[87]

---

[86] Vol. 2, folio 205b.

[87] Vol. 3, folio 76a, from Job 10:11 "Thou hast clothed me with skin and flesh, and hast fenced me with bones and sinews."

Do not think that man is but flesh, skin, bones and veins; far from it! What really makes man is his soul; and the things we call skin, flesh, bones and veins are but a garment, a cloak; they do not constitute man. When man departs this earth, he divests himself of all veils that conceal him. Yet, the different parts of the body conform to the secrets of the supreme wisdom. The skin represents the firmament, which extends every-thing and covers everything like a cloak. The flesh recalls the evil side of the universe (the purely external and tangible element) The bones and veins represent the celestial chariot, the forces that exist within, the ser-vants of God. However, all this is but a cloak; for the deep mystery of celestial man is within. Celestial Adam is as spiritual as terrestrial man, and everything happens below as it does on high. Therefore it is written in scrip-tures: "And God created man in His own image" yet, different figures formed by the stars and planets in the firmament that envelops us betoken hidden matters and profound mysteries—so do the figures and lines on the skin which encompasses the human body and are the body's stars and planets. All these signs have a hidden meaning and are the objects of attention of wise men who know how to read the face of man.

Following the lead of the above paragraph, we find that in the *Zohar*[88] there are some very rigid rules of what is now called physiognomy, or the study of one's physical features to determine one's worth or charac-ter. Apart from this, there is also a discourse on palmistry.[89] Within the Golden Dawn and later Alpha et Omega temples under Mathers the lec-ture on palmistry which is taken from the *Zohar*. The astrological break-down of man, as given from a Golden Dawn tabulation,[90] and as applied to the Kabbalistic Paths, is as shown on the following page.[91]

---

[88] Volume 3, folios 70b-75b.

[89] Vol. 3, Folio 78a

[90] This is from a document called "Book of General Correspondences," which was published by Crowley as *777*.

[91] For a more detailed tabulation see *Rulership Book* by Rex E. Bills.

Astrological Breakdown of the Body

Path	Astrological Influence	Body Part
11	Air	Respiratory Organs
12	Mercury	Cerebral and Nervous System
13	Moon	Lymphatic System
14	Venus	Genital System
15	Aries	Head and Face
16	Taurus	Shoulders and Arms
17	Gemini	Lungs
18	Cancer	Stomach
19	Leo	Heart
20	Virgo	Back
21	Jupiter	Digestive System
22	Libra	Liver
23	Water	Organs and Nutrition
24	Scorpio	Intestines
25	Sagittarius	Hips and Thighs
26	Capricorn	Genital System
27	Mars	Muscular System
28	Aquarius	Kidneys and Bladder
29	Pisces	Legs and Feet
30	Sun	Circulatory System
31	Fire	Organs of Circulation
32	Saturn \ Earth	Excretory System

In his book *Garden of Pomegranates*, Israel Regardie made the observation that:

> In their analysis of man, the Qabalists found that hand in hand with the physical body man had an automatic- or habit-forming or desire-consciousness, which gave him impetus and volition in certain directions. It took care of the functions of his organism to which conscious attention was seldom directed, such as the circulation of the blood, the beating of the heart, and the involuntary motions of the diaphragm resulting in the inspiration and expiration of breath. They also noted the faculty of

reason and criticism, the power whereby a man proceeds from premises to conclusion. And above and beyond this was the Spiritual entity who used this body, who used this desire and rational consciousness.

Nephesch

The Nephesch is part of the Soul that directly feeds the human organism for it is said:[92]

> She giveth meat to her household (body) and an appointed portion of labour to her maidens (limbs).

To understand this more completely, we have to turn to Indian culture and the subtle body that is called the Etheric Body, which is analogous to the Nephesch. The Etheric Body can be seen clairvoyantly like a series of streams or rivers covering the human body. These are called nadis, or channels, in which the energy flows from the seven chakras. Within the Order of the Stella Matutina, or in the New Zealand Temple Whare Ra at the very least, the Etheric Body was discussed almost in the same breath as the Nephesch. This eastern perspective gives new dimensions to the concept and opens up insights into some very cryptic Biblical passages that are quoted in the *Zohar*, like the one above. The *Zohar* tells us that the Nephesch has no light of its own and can only conform to the influence of Spiritual Light (of Metatron) above it. In many respects, this is a very accurate description of the Etheric Body, for the *Zohar* states that the abode of the Nephesch is in the Physical Body, and not in another dimension, such as the other component parts of the soul.

Since the Nephesch is in the physical, the question may be asked, why can't we see it. The answer to this is that a number of people *can* see it. It has been mapped by both Indian and Chinese mystics within the formulae for Acupuncture. It can also be measured scientifically as the skin cells along the various pathways of energy differ in structure electrically. So, in every respect, the Nephesch is the identical twin of the physical body.

A careful study of the *Zohar*[93] will show some reference to the Nephesch actually walking around and this is explained by a distinction

---

[92] Prov. 31:15.
[93] See Volume 3, Folios 142b–143a.

made between the two different concepts of the Nephesch. Again, drawing an analogy with eastern theology, this is separated into the Etheric Body and the Astral Body, which is a body subtle anatomy seemingly classed by the Kabbalists in the form of the Nephesch. For the *Zohar* says:[94]

> For there is a certain Nephesch which does not rest and there is a Nephesch which is not cut off from the body.

The *Zohar* clearly states that there are both higher and lower forms of the Nephesch, with the lower form being equated with the Etheric Body, which exists in every living creature, and the higher Nephesch, which equates with the Astral Body and which has the ability to journey from one place to the next, both with and without the knowledge of the body to which it is attached. Such traveling can involve actual physical distances or psychic dimensions. The Astral Body can do both. So much has been written on this subject that there is no requirement to repeat it here.

The Astral Body, or Higher Nephesch as some prefer to call it, is in fact also a plasmic body in its own right. As such, it has a certain amount of freedom. The Astral Body feeds on both pleasure and pain, and in some instances, when the individual is at either end of the spectrum, a distortion can occur where either pleasure or pain can be the main impetus into this body. The Astral Body then sends down its impulse through the Etheric Body and its Seven centers to the Physical Body. Distortion at this level alters the balance of the seven centers and can cause both physical and mental ill health and is the major cause of disease. Any form of stress build-up carried through to the Astral Body will cause it to release energy through the Solar Plexus center in the Etheric Body to the Physical Body, resulting in problems concerned with the area this center governs. In some cases, where extreme karma is called for, the energy or impetus is then brought to bear on the Astral Body from the next level up (the Mental Body). This can be in conflict with what the Astral Body is experiencing at the moment. It may be that the Astral Body is having a very good time of it through the experiences of the physical, and all of a sudden a command comes down to change direction. As a result conflict can occur, which in turn results in disease in the physical.

---

[94] Volume 3, Folio 142b.

Apart from the Astral Body of the individual human being, we also have the Astral Body of various other energies that can equally affect us. One example is the Astral Body formed through groups of people and their emotions. Another is the Astral Body of the Planet Earth itself. A contributing factor here is the energies from the Zodiac which are Astral in emanation. In group Astral energy we have the effect of various religious organizations and Hermetic Orders, such as the Golden Dawn, which generates a great deal of power on the Astral level. It is this energy that is tapped through ritual and pushed through to the Etheric bodies of the groups or of individuals involved in ritual work. Equinox is a particularly good example, where contacts with energies and thought-forms are done through the Astral Body of the Order as a whole. This also opens the doors to individual contact.

Another example of Astral energy at work through the individual is the Banishing Ritual of the Pentagram, which can be done either on the Etheric or Astral level, depending on the degree of competence of the operator. A good rule of thumb is that if one wishes to do either a Pentagram or Hexagram ritual in the Astral, that is, without physical movement, the Astral level is then tapped and utilized.

Another example of the Astral in ritual is the Vault of the Adepti in which no invocations or banishing can be done due to the fact that the Vault functions on the Astral level. To bring any form of mundane physical movement into the Vault would reduce the interior energy to function on the Etheric level. When in the Vault, the Adept must be able to reach and work from the Astral level so that the higher energies can be tapped. The Etheric energies do, however, exist in the Vault by virtue of its color scheme, but this is merely a web that uses the colors to draw down the Astral power. Once again, to achieve this successfully depends on the Will of the Temple Officers or Adepti and for the Etheric level is never utilized directly within the Vault.

The next level to consider is the use of the Astral Body on the physical plane of the Earth. By this I mean the ability to astrally travel to any part of the globe, return and give an accurate account of what is happening there, whether it be next door or the next country. The Astral Body will, during sleep, shock, or direction, actually vacate the physical body at certain times with an attachment of a silver cord to the solar plexus center of the Etheric Body. This type of voyaging with the Astral Body can be induced by hard work, though in a number of instances it occurs involuntarily as an escape mechanism, when the force of the Mental Body is too great. This results in the Astral Body vacating its function as a form of distraction, so that it will not have to obey the higher Mental Body which governs it.

We now come to the complete opposite of the situation outlined in the previous paragraph, where we deal with the subject of "Inner Space," a rather glib piece of terminology for psychological experiences within the psyche. "Inner Space" is a descriptive term that implies falsely that all the experiences one has are internal, and hence psychological, and have nothing whatever to with the Astral Body on the astral planes. The astral planes are the level on which the Astral Body functions and travels. The astral planes are numerous, and many experiences of the mystics relate entirely to the experiences of the Astral Body. A good example of this is given in *Flying Roll Number 4*, by Florence Farr and Elaine Simpson, who did what could be described in today's terms as a Pathworking where a group vision is given to one or more members simultaneously from a tarot archetype. Flying Rolls numbers 11, 25, 32, and 33 also give examples of traveling and utilizing the astral planes in the Astral Body. This area also covers the animal, mineral, and vegetable kingdoms where the Astral Bodies of various animals (and people), vegetables, and minerals can be clairvoyantly contacted. The alchemists of old worked on these levels, and a very good example of this can be found at the beginning of the ancient alchemical text, the *Mutus Liber*.

One of the dangers for the Astral Body is its overuse with the technique of astral projection. This can, and has, caused mental problems, including unwelcome hallucinatory effects for some adepti. If the Astral Body has not had the chance to recover from its journey into the astral planes, then it can be overstimulated. This results in a congestion of the Etheric Body, which is unable to adjust to the new vibratory pitch that the energy and direction from the Astral Body that is being poured into it. Such congestion of this body leads, of course, to disease, whether it be physical or mental. If the Astral Body is given a chance to adjust once back in its correct environment, then one can continue with astral exploration of the astral planes. The Astral Body does, however, need rest and replenishment, as does any other plasmic-energy body.

Astrology can affect the Astral Body and the Astral planes as well, and this is one of the reasons that the rituals are timed astrologically so that the negative energies are not putting pressure on the various auric bodies, particularly the Etheric and Astral Bodies. The emotions are one of the most obvious aspects affected by the various astrological influences and which, in turn, influence the energy variance through the Etheric Body. One must, therefore, be careful to be in harmony with these factors through calculation before any real occult work can begin in earnest.

The Nephesch, in terms of Sephirotic reference, corresponds to the Sephirah of Yesod. For Mathers says:[95]

> The Automatic Consciousness, as it is called, is in Yesod, and has to do with the lower passions and desires. Being automatic, that is, moving of itself, it can hardly be said to be Will. Now this is the danger which threatens the man who yields to the temptations of the lower desires.

The two component parts of the Nephesch, according to eastern tradition, are linked by the seven chakras. In the Golden Dawn these were never directly referred to, though in western literature the planetary influence, or whirls as they were called on the body, are well documented. It is unfortunate the Golden Dawn tended to ignore them. In the Stella Matutina, however, they were studied (within the New Zealand Temple, Whare Ra, that is), and my own training under Taylor involved a very detailed study of what these centers represented. This is an area that Mathers could have done much with; however those he taught who went into the Stella Matutina adopted it with much vigor. The bulk of the following section is taken from a paper called the "Sphere of Sensation" which I wrote some years ago for the Thoth Hermes Temple in New Zealand. I feel it takes a more balanced approach toward the Etheric Body or Lower Nephesch, and in some instances approaches it from a completely different level than given in this section.

---

[95] *Flying Roll 22.*

THE SPHERE OF SENSATION[96]

The Etheric Body or Lower Nephesch

Within the Outer Order the subject of the Kabbalistic Soul and its component parts was first discussed. The next phase of study for the Grade of Adeptus Major is that of the Subtle Anatomy of Man and its links to the Kabbalistic Soul. The Sphere of Sensation, or under its common name, the aura, is very intricate in its nature and functions. The number of auras around the body of man has been and is always a debatable point, but the Order teachings show that there are in fact seven in number. Of that seven there are four that are tangible (including the physical body) and three that are intangible to psychics, which correspond to some aspects of Eastern teachings as well. In the ritual of the 5=6 grade we are told:

> And being turned, I saw Seven Golden Lightbearers, and in the midst of the Lightbearers, One like Ben Adam, clothed with a garment down to the feet, and girt, with a Golden Girdle.

There are the manifestations of the aura, each one distinct from the other that manifests from the body, shown as the empty pastos within the Vault.

The first Auric Body that encloses itself around Guph, the physical body, under the power of the Nephesch, is the Etheric Body. Its function on a basic level is to keep the vital flows of energy that it receives from its next highest level (the Astral Body) and transmit them directly into the various energy points throughout the body, of which there are many. On one level it stimulates the seven major centers and the 21 senior centers, as well as the 49 subcenters. From this it stimulates the energy flows through the various meridians of body, which in turn are categorized as both major and minor influences. From this combined influence, every organ and structure of the body has its own vibrational pitch that the Etheric Body stimulates in harmony with each other.

---

[96] For a full understanding of some of the terminology used in this paper see *The Golden Dawn* by Israel Regardie (Llewellyn Publications).

Within the technique of the Middle Pillar exercise we tend to charge up the Etheric body by altering its polarity, and also tend, through the help of the Kabbalistic Cross, to polarize the aura, so that the bodily centers are in fact aligned correctly in each of the Subtle Body centers. This, of course, differs from some of the Eastern teachings which advocate altering these centers directly through tone vibrations on a mantram effect.[97] While the Etheric body concentrates on passing this energy on to the physical, the Nephesch has the function of sustaining this energy through instinctive urges such as hunger, thirst, sex, and self-preservation.

The Etheric Body is much like an electronic grid map that is placed on the physical body and must have a clear flow of energy to pass on to the physical body. Where this flow is interrupted, mainly by congestion, diseases are then forced through into the physical body, because the vibrational pitch of energy that keeps a tissue, cell, or organ manufacturing harmoniously is then prevented from achieving its range of output. Its direct links to the physical body are extremely important.

The Etheric body is the regulator which must not pass too much energy into the Physical Body. This would cause the psychic channels to overload and produce overstimulation. This can manifest in many different forms of stress, particularly on the nervous system and the endocrine glands, which can, in turn, produce many blockages on the physical level. The formulation of the energy from these areas to each other (etheric body, nervous system, and glands) is the same field of energy impression that works from the Ain, Ain Soph, and Ain Soph Aur.

The Etheric Body functions under the Kabbalistic World of Yetzirah (Yetzirah comes from the Chaldee ITzR, meaning to "form or "make"). It is the world of the unconscious that also relates to the dream states of man. The main function of the Etheric Body is to receive and pass on information and energy. This applies not only from the view of a down-

---

[97] Technically speaking, the Golden Dawn version of the Middle Pillar groups the smaller or sub-chakras together so that they handle the energy in ten divisions, but these divisions do not interfere directly with the seven chakras.

Here the Kabbalistic meditation uses the subcenters only, which then, through the spleen center, alter the major ones indirectly. My teacher in Tantra, the late Vivandatta, nearly a quarter of a century ago in India, informed me that Westerners were better advised to approach the chakras indirectly, that is through the subcenters, as a safe method of chakra balancing. He could psychically see the centers in Westerners were more in tune to the indirect approach, due to a different psychic anatomical makeup. He made the point that some races had differences in the Etheric Body structure and alignment with the physical.

ward motion, but from the view of ascent as well. Our experiences in daily life are then manifested in dream states that are passed on to the Etheric Body, where they are sometimes amalgamated, refined, and passed on to the next Astral Body.

The psychological terminology that is analogous with the Etheric Body is the libido. From here the energy must be separated into a form of polarity, so both progression and regression can occur through a state of regular interaction. The Jungian concept of the libido, which we refer to here, goes beyond the original Freudian concept, which associated it with sexuality. Jung considers that it refers to "psychic energy" in general and warned against trying to define it too rapidly.

The energy flow from the Etheric Body into the physical body relies primarily on two aspects (1) a daily flow rate which is divided into the five major Tattvic divisions,[98] and (2) the energy effected by the astrological influences (the other effects of disease and karmic influences are not included here). The first such influence is the Akasha Tattva which is the encompassing tubular linkage (space) for the energy to flow through. Its main principle is to "connect." The next division is the Vayu Tattva, which provides the pulse for the energy to flow, much in the same vein as the heartbeat of the body. The Tejas Tattva produces a stronger flow rate while the Apas Tattva provides the control mechanism that reduces the flow of energy. The Prithvi Tattva is the one that resists the flow rate of energy when the various centers of the body are full of energy, and this helps to produce overstimulation.

During the process of initiation either directly or indirectly into a group, or by an individual into a different field of awareness, the Etheric Body is the one that is first stimulated. In forms of ritual magic we have the temple officers slowly stimulating your Etheric Body by carefully altering its vibrational rate so that it becomes more receptive to the external stimuli of the Higher Self.

This stimulation can, in some cases, produce what is called in alternative medicine a "healing crisis," in which the transition state that the Etheric Body goes through does not immediately settle on one vibrational pitch but alters until it finds its own correct accord within a new range or

---

[98] The Tattwas are located in the Chakra centers and control the flow rates of energy going to and from it. See *Natures Finer Forces* by Rama Prasad for a full indepth study of them. The Knowledge lectures on the Tattwas in the Golden Dawn were based on Prasad's book.

pitch. If the Etheric Body is blocked or the energy is not coming through in its proper course, then the sudden alteration will cause the release of energy that can precipitate a "healing crises" while all the dammed-up energy finds a release.

In the case of individuals, going through the grades, who have hidden psychological disorders, it can take in some cases years to rectify. We then have the negative aspect when the Temple Officers are performing correctly and they can cause a lowering of the vitality rate which can cause psychological problems and cut off any clairvoyant ability. This has happened in the past and no doubt will happen in the future.

The sexual teachings of the Golden Dawn tell us that the Etheric Body is the vehicle of attraction, for this is instinctive. When two physical bodies attract each other, one often uses the phrase that they are on the "right wavelength" and this is true to a certain extent. This "wavelength" is the same vibrational pitch of both your and your partner's Etheric Bodies, which form a magnetic attraction. However, if this is just magnetic attraction, then it can sometimes be short-lived, for the pitch of the Etheric Body does not always remain the same, and when this alters then the attraction one first felt can also alter. This is because the individual you are attracted to, or even you, yourself, are undergoing constant changes in the Etheric Body due to the day-to-day stimuli it constantly faces. Karmic ties enter here, for they can override the attraction of two individuals or individuals to a group because the Higher Self has dictated that there are other things one must yet perform.

In cases of one individual feeding off the energy of another, from the Etheric Body, one will find connections or shells forming from this person to the next. This is mainly because more power is available to the stronger, on the Etheric level, than the other. When one does the Pentagram Ritual in the physical (as opposed to the Astral version) or the Hexagram Ritual, then one uses the energy of the Etheric Body, and this is one of the reasons why the Pentagram has to be drawn daily to be charged for any real effect. When we have performed group ritual, or coming away from a concert, we go away feeling "charged," and this is due to our Etheric Bodies adjusting to the tone vibrations and being very receptive to them. The effect of color on the individual, from a colored room, and also from color therapy, is done through the Etheric Body. A stay in the Vault of the Adepti is a good example of this, but in the case of Vault ritual or meditations, then one progressively works through the Etheric Body to the next level which pushes forth the True Will of the Adept.

Earlier I briefly touched on the aspect of attraction to members of the opposite sex, or the same sex, for that matter. Now we come to the realm of sex magic and its effect on the level of the Etheric Body. The orgasm and the foreplay of the sex act produce energy, and this energy can and does interfere with the flow rate of energy into the Physical Body from the Etheric Body. In most cases this burst of energy is welcomed, for it can release certain blockages and keep tension down to a minimum. In other areas it can make the energy pattern of the Etheric Body jump into the physical and become blocked, a term which Reich has termed "armor."[99]

> The total defence apparatus of the organism, consisting of the rigidities of the character and the chronic spasms of the musculature, which functions essentially as a defence mechanism against the breakthrough of the emotions— primarily anxiety, rage, and sexual excitation.

When the orgasm occurs there is a vast increase in energy flow and tempo which washes through the various centers and circuits that lead into the physical body. Once the blockages that Reich mentions are cleared, then the energy flow is more pronounced and one is more at harmony with the self. When the Etheric Bodies of two people engaged in intercourse have simultaneous orgasm, then the two bodies interconnect with the energy going through both circuits and forming, for a brief instant, one super-circuit that produces a tremendous amount of Etheric energy.

In sexual magic there are two main variables. The first is for both partners to reach orgasm at the same time and concentrate this energy up through the next auric body for a desired result, as a combined unit. The second is where one partner, whether it be male or female, uses the other's Etheric energies, and then directs these through his or her Etheric Body for the desired result. Where blood, semen, and any other bodily part is used in sex magic, then it is the Etheric Body that is being manipulated

---

[99] See Wilhelm Reich, *Selected Writings* (Farrar, Straus and Giroux, New York, 1951).

to supply the energy needed. In some forms of sex magic, and indeed some forms of ritual magic, Elementals, that is, artificially created ones, can be made and invested with Etheric energy, even though their lifespan is only for a few hours at best. While part of this formula is included in the Golden Dawn's papers on talismans, it is barely the tip of the iceberg, because animals can be created, whether they be real or imaginary. The limit to their powers is with the operator, with his or her Etheric Body supplying their energy needs.

Another aspect where the Etheric Body is utilized directly is in Spiritualism, especially in cases where an ectoplasm is found. This phenomenon can, in fact, protrude a number of meters out of the physical body. In any form of magnetic healing, whether it be direct from another individual or from a machine to stimulate the currents, then the Etheric Body is the one being utilized. Passes, with the hands or an elemental weapon, made over the body then work directly into the Etheric Body and create the "wash" effect of energy stimulating the various meridians. In acupuncture one uses this type of situation, and in forms of Taoism the deeper psychic channels are also used. These are likened to rivers of energy, where the acupuncture meridians are analogous to streams. In magical works, such as in talismanic rituals, it is the energy of the Etheric Body that impregnates itself into the talisman. A good example of this in ritual is the use of the "Sign of the Enterer" and the "Sign of Silence." The first stimulates the flow of the Etheric energy, while the second cancels it and is used as a checking device. The Grade Signs of the Outer Order are all working from the Etheric energy; the only difference between them is vibrational pitch and flow rate.

Similarly, in color healing one has a process where the Etheric Body can be categorized into as many divisions as there are colors, though for the most part a seven- or twelve-division is normally used. These colors are closely allied with planetary and zodiac energies. It is also during ritual initiation that varying grades can be shown in the division of the Etheric Body and color and planetary energies can be considered a yardstick on this.

The next important aspect of ritual work and the Etheric energy is in the theory of God-form assumption. When the astral shells are created in

---

[54] From Whare Ra temple papers, by unknown translator.

group ritual the outline of these shells are from the Etheric Body, directed by the Will of the Adept. while the outline, color, and shape are all taken from the Etheric Body, the actual power it gives one is on a higher plane. This will be discussed in other papers relating to other auric bodies later, though for the present the basic foundation of their creative form is Etheric energy or energy directed from the Etheric Body. It is this energy that is felt and sometimes seen by those clairvoyant enough during ritual.

THE SEVEN CENTERS

The Seven centers of man, commonly called chakras (from the Sanskrit meaning "wheel"), are indicated on the floor of the Vault as the seven-headed dragon. Here are all the ills of man, manifested through these seven centers. By symbolically standing on them, we, in fact, control the potent and negative energies that they can introduce. On the Altar table there are the four images of the Calf, Man, Lion, and Eagle, which represent the four lower centers. Because they are still on the floor, yet raised above it, they are the lower natures of man which have been exalted so that a form of realignment or changing of their vibrational pitch occurs, which brings them into higher contact with our Higher Nature. Each of these four centers relates to an element and to the elemental grades the Adept has gone through, which in theory have also stimulated each of these four centers. The Altar itself represents what could be called the "Eight center" and is associated to the spleen, the energy vortex from which the energy flows, so that it can be transmitted to the seven centers on the back. The "Eight center," as the Altar, is the control point for this energy. The 49 petals of the Rose and Cross at the head of the pastos (normally placed below the Altar) relate to the 49 minor centers that are under control through the four major lower centers as portrayed on the Altar. On the ceiling of the Vault we have the seven centers at their highest point and on the floor the seven centers at their lowest, with man standing in the middle trying to aspire to the highest through the influences of the Seven Rays—the vault walls.

Each of these chakras, save the spleen, manifests in the four auric bodies. In the Physical Body we have the seven major gland areas that act as a type of receptor for these energies. In the Etheric, Astral-Emotional, and Mental Body there is a certain amount of sympathetic reaction to the seven centers as well. In the Etheric Body, these centers directly stimulate the physical body and receive impetus from it as well. In the next two bodies, the Astral-Emotional and Mental, the centers still remain, but here they are nothing but connective links to the body above and below them, with the connective links being, of course, two-way.

The chakras in the Etheric Body directly relate to the Physical Body, with the psychic ramifications caused by manipulation of these centers appearing in the other auric bodies. The adept is warned against trying to place a definite planetary correspondence with each chakra, as in each center there are the influences of all of the planets and these change according to the development of each individual. The same principle also applies to color and to the centers as well. Now, as to the exact body position of these centers, they form a vortex both on the front and on the back of the body, hence the confusion of placement. The description of the Shadow Chakras which follows shortly is formed from the same underlying principles of everything in the subtle body having a counter-part of either a higher or lower vibrational level.

Base Chakra

This is the lowest chakra and is situated at the base of the spine (and not at the front of the body as some have indicated). Its receptors are the adrenal glands, which also relate to the kidneys, the spinal column, and part of the automatic nervous system. This chakra is made of four major vortices of energies which have been seen by some Eastern mystics as petals. In many ways this center is the control valve for the other centers for it is here that additional energy can be prematurely released through the other centers. This could result in Etheric damage, especially to the nervous system. The link is through the adreno-medullary and extra-medullary distribution of chromaffin tissue along the sympathetic nerve chains, which incidentally are the links between chakras in the physical body. Generally speaking the nervous system is the first that is stimulated directly by the Etheric energies. These in turn work the endocrine system of glands, then the blood, and from this to the various organs concerned. This center is not associated to any other particular center but, in fact with all of the others, in a primary support role.

This center corresponds to the Earth element and the Biblical imagery of this is the Calf (from Revelation).

Sacral Chakra

This center has six vortices associated with it, and governs the reproductive system and the gonads. Its overstimulation can cause sexual problems. It controls the organs of elimination. Its corresponding chakra is the Brow Chakra. It is associated with the Water element and the Biblical imagery is humankind itself.

Solar Plexus Chakra

This center has 10 vortices associated with it and relates to the pancreas (liver and stomach). Overall it controls nutrition and the function of energy extraction from it. In layman's terms it is the function of this center to break down all the food processed in the body into component parts that can be correctly assimilated by the body. The corresponding center that this is associated to is the throat center. The solar plexus center is associated with the Fire element and the Biblical imagery of the Lion.

Heart Chakra

This center has 12 vortices associated with it and relates to the thymus gland and also controls the circulatory system of the body. The Biblical imagery is the Eagle, and the Air element is associated here.

Throat Chakra

This center has 16 vortices associated with it and relates to the thyroid gland and controls the respiratory system.

Brow Chakra

This center has two major vortices associated to it and 96 smaller ones. The Brow Chakra controls the pineal gland, the sympathetic nervous system which is represented in the skull by the medulla oblongata and controls the sense organs. This also controls the entire endocrine system.

Crown Chakra

This center has 1,000 vortices associated with it and represents the pituitary gland and the volitional nerve system.

Shadow Chakras

Situated above the head there are, in fact, five more centers. These are shadow representations of the lower five or their etheric counterparts. In other words they function at a much higher level of the Etheric Body, which some have considered the thermal area of it. Their functions, like the lower five, are in fact more fluid and are the ones which tend to be the first manifestations of things before being sent down to the lower five. Some call these seam centers, because they have to keep the subtle bodies polarized so the lower main centers can function correctly.

RUACH

The term "Ruach'" means breath. The Ruach in fact rests not only on the Nephesch but within it, and rules over it. In the previous section you have seen how the Nephesch, in both its higher and lower form, is closely allied with the body, the Higher Nephesch being in fact likened to a transmission set of sorts. This is still very much the instinctive process which has to be directed through the mental or thinking process of the Ruach.[100] It has been allied with the Sephiroth of Chesed to Hod and some have considered that the influences of those planets attributed to those Sephiroth are also analogous but this is something of an understatement. The Ruach is in many ways the sum total of the individual before he has sent the actions of his thoughts and reason down through the Nephesch to the Guph.

From the psychological viewpoint, the Ruach is, of course, the collective components of the Psyche. Jung breaks down the Psyche into sensation, thinking, feeling, intuition, memory, subjective functions, effects, and invasions, which are all allied to the Ruach. I have always thought that the Ruach is in many respects more psychological than Spiritual, though the spiritual direction it takes must not be ignored. While one function of the Ruach is to digest the emanations from above that are woven into some type of karmic destiny, the other part also digests the information the individual experiences through the senses and thinking process. In many respects this is a two-way communication system, for its function is to assimilate the experience of life itself.

---

[100] Vol. i, folio 287b, Appendix 2.

The *Zohar* informs us[101] that the Ruach actually leaves the body at the New Moon and feast days, then returns to its place. This suggests a very interesting astrological influence on the soul of man, as generally most of the Hebrew festivals are based on astrological events. The soul is said to leave the body on the Sabbath as well, which, apart from its religious significance, shows that it must be continually replenished every seven days.

The subtle anatomy that is allied to the Ruach is the Mental Body. It is in this area that the scattered mental thoughts flow and group themselves into various subdivisions which are separated yet again, forming in the Astral-Emotional Body. It is here that the universal energies have to adapt to suit themselves to the vibration and pitch of the lower bodies and make sure that the energy that is incoming will not disrupt or burn out the lower layers, especially the end result on the physical body.

The Mental Body is the home of the abstract concept, where it is "conditioned" briefly before it goes down to the Emotional level. There it is subdivided according to the personality. More than any other level, we try to "discover the cause of ignorance" through the pulsation vehicle of the soul and the lesser formulations that govern the Mental Body. Its function is to try to control the pulsation system; it feeds the Astral-Emotional Body which tends sometimes to be a law unto itself due to the day-to-day reactions it has to deal with. In short, one of the main functions of the Mental Body is to "control" the Astral-Emotional Body, and, as a result, a continuous battle emerges, which will continue to carry on unabated until the Mental Body has properly aligned the Astral-Emotional Body and is in full control of it.

Meditation is one such way that the Mental Body tries to get its way and in many instances succeeds, though meditation, however, should be an ongoing thing, for if there is a brief respite before the Astral-Emotional Body will try to seek dominance. Initiation is yet another way that the Mental Body seeks control. Here the self is opened up to Higher Energies that must be rationalized correctly through the Mental Body, or a type of burnout will occur. In this way the Astral-Emotional Body is cornered and must submit to the Higher Mental Body.

In the Mental Body, the Thought Forms that occur are completely on the subconscious level, and because of this some thought forms, due to

---

101 Volume 3, folio 141b.

polarity, can manifest negativity which can cause many mental problems. Thought forms come to us in three fundamental directions. The first is from the Higher Self, which dictates our life's journey and the karmic destinies to be carried out. The second is the influence of other thought forms, group or otherwise, that can also influence this body. Finally, there is impetus that is received from the Emotional Body which is gained from our life experiences and which can slightly alter the initial frequency the Mental Body puts out. Normally the first takes predominance, while the second and third are limited in their input.

Within occultism the first and second aspect are considered most, for here things are done on an entirely unconscious level—a level which gives the barest hint to the conscious mind. "Purity," that word which is debated so much, relates to the purity of mind, and that means the purity of all the other bodies. Unfortunately the seat of daily life on the conscious level is in the Astral-Emotional Body, and this has more often than not got in the way of the Higher thought forms filtering through when the bodies are not in alignment. Carl Jung once stated that the main purpose of psychology is to bring the unconscious under conscious control, and in essence this is the goal of auric body alignment and of the unification of the varying stages of the Kabbalistic Soul.

Neschamah[102]

This is the highest of three levels of the soul and in it there are three divisions (counting the Neschamah itself). Mathers says:

> Neschamath is either plural of Neschamah, *defectively written*, or else shows that Neschamah is *in regimene* to Chiim, and evidently means the united higher souls of *both Adam and Eve conjoined in one body.*[103]

The Neschamah is analogous to pure spirit and can be likened to the Jungian approach of the anima (corresponding to the Neschamah) and animus (corresponding to the Chiah). Applied Kabbalistically to the Partsufim theory, the anima is the Great Mother or Heh Force and

---

[102] The spelling of this seems to differ considerably in the Golden Dawn, with people like Mathers spelling it a number of different ways. I have opted for this spelling throughout this text, except where direct quotes are involved.
[103] Notes to the "Greater Holy Assembly," page 228, from the *Kabbalah Unveiled.*

the animus is the Father or Yod Force. There is also some contradiction in the application of the Chiah and the still higher form of the Yechidah to the Kabbalistic Soul, and the two latter phases of the soul are mentioned only in the "Faithful Shepherd" portion of the *Zohar*.[104] The confusion exists because the Chiah and Yechidah have also been associated with the Ruach. The Golden Dawn, however, opted for the five parts of the soul.

The Higher Mental body is the Neschamah, the Chiah is the Causal Body, with the Yechidah as the highest point or Spirit. The three bodies mentioned here are in reality separated by a type of gulf from the four lower bodies and this type of analytical approach is very difficult in these areas as the *Zohar* has very little, if anything on them.

The Soul and Death

Before we discuss the actual function of the three degrees of the Soul at and after death, the spirit or channel that binds the soul should also be looked at. This is called the Zelem, and its shape is said to resemble that of the body, or Nephesch. The Zelem, according to the Loriahian concept, has three parts, one is the main energy force and the other two are similar to auric envelopes which are called Makifim. Before the appointed time of death both of the Makifim of the Neschamah withdraw from the body and go to their appointed place, then the Ruach and Nephesch, over a 30-day period. This Zoharic teaching is similar to that of Edgar Cayce, the great American psychic, who stated on more than one occasion that those people he saw who died a short time later had no visible aura. Not only Cayce but other psychics, such as Arthur Ford, have also made similar statements that seem to parallel the teachings of the *Zohar* with the term "aura" being used instead of the word "soul." The time scale of the withdrawal of the Zelem of the Neschamah depends on the individual. Some people have, well before the time of death, allowed the Ruach to withdraw into the Neschamah. In very highly evolved individuals this has the effect that both Ruach and Neschamah are one (this would make the withdrawal a lot less than 30 days). In this instance the Nephesch is clearly very highly evolved, and after the death of the body there is no decomposition. The *Zohar* tells us:[105]

---

[104] Part 2, folio 158b.

The body of Joseph was never under the power of the
impure spirit although his soul (Neschamnah and
Ruach) had left him when he had not yet entered the
Holy Land.

Besides the example of the body of Joseph, we also have hard physical evidence of this situation occurring in some Catholic saints, where
decomposition does not occur. The soul, or shell of it, remains (for us
mere mortals) in the body till the moment of death for this is the sum
total of the personality and it must have the three phases functioning correctly for it to function at all. Since the Zelem has gone, the energy for
this is drawn from the shell of the Neschamah, which has stored power
prior to the death just for this purpose, before the Zelem withdraws.
Without it, the body would not be able to function through any of the
senses. In the Talmud are listed in excess of 900 different kinds of death,
from the easiest to the most painful.

The Yechidah has, before death, certain functions to carry out and
these are done in the world of Briah. Some of these functions are prepara-
tory and depend on the type of life lead by the individual. The Yechidah
must also find a place for the Ruach, and this level or place is determined
by the Ruach's actions during the previous life on earth. For we are told
in the *Zohar*[106] that if the Neschamah is prevented from attaining the
place set aside for it, then the Ruach and Nephesch cannot enter the
Garden of Eden. It must then roam the various planes and experience further suffering by observation until the Most High has considered that it
can then enter its abode, which of course opens the door for the Ruach,
as well, to rest in the world of Yetzirah. Although the *Zohar* is not clear on
this point, the three phases of the soul can be considered to occur in the
Gehinnon (a type of Hell associated with the Catholic concept of Purga-
tory). It is in cases like this that supernatural occurrences of the most
unpleasant kind occur. For Job 25:22 says:

But flesh upon him shall have pain and his soul within
him shall mourn.

---

[105] Vol. 3, folio 141b.
[106] Vol. 3, folio 141a.

At the moment of death the Nephesch, in its lower form as the Etheric Body, ceases to exist and disintegrates and this is the decomposition state. The Nephesch in its higher form as the Astral Body is then cut loose from its ties of the physical body. Since it now has a Ruach to give it impetus, it ends up in what might be called a wandering state. Some have considered that the Gehinnon is merely a state away from the Most High and hence the Nephesch, along with the Ruach and Neschamah, wanders until it meets with the Yehudiam, or angelic messenger, who takes it to the Garden of Eden where is reunited with its source.

ADAM KADMON AND HIS SOULS[107]

Thou shalt know that the whole Sphere of Sensation which surroundeth the whole physical body of a man is called "The Magical Mirror of the Universe." For therein are represented all the occult forces of the Universe projected as on a Sphere, convex to the outer, but concave to man. This sphere surroundeth the physical body of a man as the Celestial Heavens do the body of a Star or Planet, having their forces mirrored in its atmosphere. Therefore its allotment or organisation is a copy of the Greater World or Macrocosm. In this "Magical Mirror of the Universe," therefore, are the Ten Sephiroth projected in the form of the Tree of Life as in a solid sphere.

A man's physical body is within the Ten Sephiroth projected in a Sphere. The divisions and parts of the body are formed from the Sephiroth of the Tree of Life, thus.[108]

Kether is *above* the Crown of the Head, and represents a crown which indeed is powerful, but requires one worthy to wear it. In the crown of the head is placed the faculty of Neschamah, which is the power of Aspiration unto that which is beyond. This power of Neschamah is especially attributed

---

[107] This document was originally called 'Microcosm-Man" and issued in the Golden Dawn (and was the basis for Israel Regardie's book *The Middle Pillar*) at the Zelator Adeptus Minor level. It concerns much of the above information in relation to the body of man and different to the above texts as far as format goes but is nevertheless an interesting document that is to a certain extent based on the work of de Leiningen.

[108] This view of a Tree of Life on both the front and back of Man differs from the Regardie association as given in the "Middle Pillar" and falls in with the diagrams of Westcott as given in his papers "The Tree of Life in the Celestial Heavens Projected as if in a Solid Sphere." A color representation of this correct rendition is given in Robert Wang's book "Qabalistic Tarot," on the back cover of his book.

unto the Supernal Triad in Assiah, of which there are three manifestations which are included in the general concept, Neschamah.

From Chokmah and Binah are formed the sides of the brain and head. Therein exist the intellectual faculties of Wisdom and Understanding, shining into and illuminating their inferior, the Ruach. They are the mansions of the practical administration of the intellect, whose physical shewing forth is by reflection in Ruach. In the Magical Mirror of the Universe, or the Sphere of Sensation, Man is placed between four pillars of the Tree of Life as projected in a sphere. These keep their place and *move not.*

But the Man himself places in his Sphere of Sensation that point of the zodiac which ascended at the moment of his birth and conception (for the same degree of the Zodiac ascendeth at both, otherwise the birth could not take place).[109] That is to say that at those times the same degree of the Zodiac is ascending in the East of the Heavens of the Star whereon he is incarnated. Thus doth he remain during that incarnation facing that particular point in his sphere of sensation. That is to say this sphere *doth not revolve* about the physical body.

From Chesed and Geburah are formed the arms. Therein exist the faculties of operative action, wherefore at their extremities are the symbols of the Four Elements and the Spirit, thus:

Thumb — Spirit

Third Finger — Fire

Index Finger — Water

Little Finger — Air

Second Finger — Earth

The arms are the manifestors of the executive power of the Ruach and therein are the faculties of touch strongly expressed.

From Tiphareth is formed the trunk of the body, free from the members, and therein as in a receptacle of influences are situated the vital organs.

---

[109] For a full descriptive process of this statement one could do no better than study Alice Bailey's *Esoteric Astrology,* which seems to amplify what Mathers was trying to say here.

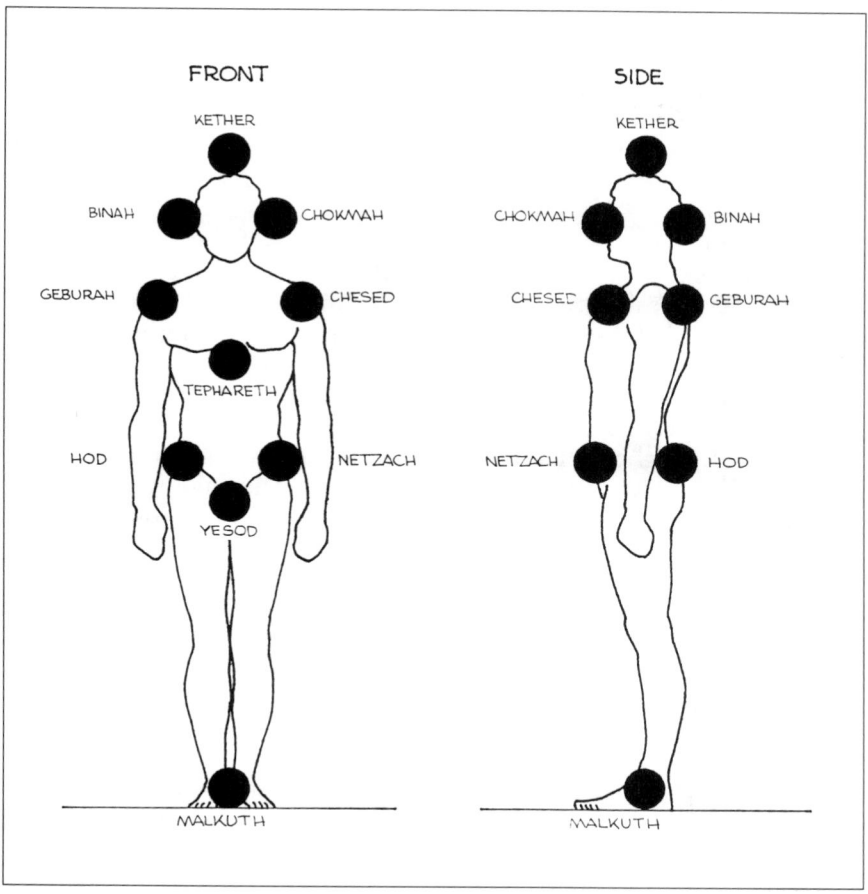

FRONT

KETHER

BINAH CHOKMAH

GEBURAH CHESED

TEPHARETH

HOD NETZACH

YESOD

MALKUTH

SIDE

KETHER

CHOKMAH BINAH

CHESED GEBURAH

NETZACH HOD

MALKUTH

The Kabbalah and Man

The blood is Spirit mingled with and governing the watery principle. The lungs are the receptacles of Air which tempereth the blood as the wind doth the waves of the sea—the mephitic impurities of the blood in its traversal of the body requiring the dispersing force of the Air, even as the sea, under a calm, doth putrify and become mephitic.

The heart is the great centre of the action of Fire, lending its terrible energy as an impulse unto the others. Thence cometh from the fiery nature the red colour of the blood.

The part above the heart is the chief abode of the *Ruach*, as there receiving and concentrating the other expressions of its Sephiroth. This part is the central citadel of the body and is the particular abode of the lower and more physical will. The higher will is in the Kether of the body. For the higher will to manifest, it must be reflected into the lower will by Neschamah. This lower will is immediately potent in the lower membranes and thus, in the region above the heart, is the lower will seated like a King of the body upon its throne.

The concentration of the other faculties of the *Ruach* in and under the presidency of the Will, at the same time reflecting the administrative governance of Chokmah and Binah, is what is called the human consciousness. That is, a reflection of the two creative Sephiroth under the presidency of the Four Elements, or the reflection of *Aima* and *Abba* as the parents of the human Jehovah. But the human Neschamah exists only when the higher Will is reflected by the agency of aspiration from Kether into the lower body, and when the flaming letter Shin is placed like a crown on the Head of Microprosopus. Thus only doth the human will become the receptacle of the higher Will and the action of Neschamah is the link therewith. The lower will is the human Jehovah—an angry and jealous God, the Shaker of the Elements, the manifestor in the life of the body. But illuminated by the higher Will, he becometh Yeheshuah, no longer angry and jealous, but the self-sacrificer and the Atoning and Reconciling One.

This as regards the action of the more physical man.

Unto this *Ruach* also are presented the reflections of the Macrocosmic Universe in the Sphere of Sensation. They surround the *Ruach* which, in the natural man, feeleth them but vaguely and comprehendeth them not. The faculties of the Earth are shown forth in the organs which digest and putrify, casting forth the impurities, even as the Earth is placed above the Qlippoth.

Thou wilt say, then, that the Ruach cannot be the reasoning mind, seeing that it reflecteth its reason from Chokmah to Binah—but it is the executive faculty which reasoneth, which worketh with and combineth the Principia of Chokmah and Binah so that the parts of Chokmah and Binah which touch the Ruach are the initiators of the reasoning power. The reason itself is a process and but a simulacrum of the action of the higher Wisdom and Understanding. For Air is not the Light—only the translator of the Light. Yet without the Air, the operations of the Light could not so well be carried out. The word *Ruach*, Spirit, also meaneth Air. It is like a thing that goeth

out thou knowest not whither, and cometh in thou knowest
not whence.

The wind bloweth where it listeth, and thou hearest
the sound thereof, but canst not tell whence it cometh
nor whither it goeth. So is every one that is born of the
Spirit.

This Air, the *Ruach*, permeateth the whole physical body
but its concentrated influence is about the heart. Yet, were it
not for the boundary force of Chokmah and Binah above, of
the sphere of sensation surrounding it, and of Malkuth below,
the *Ruach* could not concentrate under the presidency of the
Name, and the life of the body would cease.

Thus far concerning the Ruach as a *whole*, that is, the
action of the Will in Tiphareth.

From Netzach and Hod are formed the thighs and legs,
and they terminate in the symbols of five, as do the arms; but
they are not so moveable, owing to the effect of Malkuth. In
them are placed the faculties of support and firmness and balance; and they show the more physical qualities of the
Ruach. They are the affirmation of the Pillars of the Sephiroth, as answering to the passive, the arms more answering to
the two pillars which are Active. They are the columns of
the Human Temple.

From Yesod are formed the generative and excretory
organs, and therein is the seat of the lower desires, as bearing
more on the double nature of, on the one hand, the rejection
of the Qlippoth, and on the other hand the simulacrum of
the vital forces in Tiphareth. It is the special seat of the automatic consciousness. That is, not the Will, but the *simulacrum*
of the Will in Tiphareth. Yesod is the lowest of the Sephiroth
of the Ruach, and representeth "Fundamental Action." It
therefore governeth generation. In Yesod is therefore the
automatic consciousness or simulacrum of the Will. This
automatic consciousness is to the Nephesch what the *Daath*
action is to the *Ruach*. Thus, therefore, there being a simulacrum or reflection of the heart and vital organs in the parts
governed by Yesod, if the consciousness of the Tiphareth be
given unto this wholly, it shall pave the way for disease and
death. For this will be a withdrawing of the vital forces of the
Name, which are in the citadel of Tiphareth, to locate them
in Yesod, which is a more easily attacked position. For the

automatic consciousness is the translator of the Ruach unto the Nephesch.

From Malkuth is formed the whole physical body under the command and presidency of the Nephesch. The Nephesch is the subtle body of refined astral Light upon which, as on an invisible pattern, the Physical Body is extended. The Physical Body is permeated throughout by the rays of the Ruach, of which is the material completion. The Nephesch shineth through the material Body and formeth the Magical Mirror or Sphere of Sensation. This Magical Mirror or Sphere of Sensation is an imitation or copy of the Sphere of the Universe. The space between the physical and the boundary of the sphere of Sensation is occupied by the ether of the astral world; that is to say, the container or recipient of the Astral Rays of the Macrocosm.

The Nephesch is divided into its seven Palaces, combining the Sephirotic influences in their material forms. That is, the world of passions dominated by the Ruach, or by the world which is beyond. That is, its Sephiroth are passionate, expressing a passionate dominion. Thus its three Supernal Sephiroth, Kether, Chokmah and Binah, are united in a sense of feeling and comprehending impressions. Its Chesed is expressed by a laxity of action. Its Geburah by violence of action. Its Tiphareth is expressed by more or less sensual contemplation of beauty, and love of vital sensation. Its Hod and Netzach, by physical well-being and health. Its Yesod, by physical desires and gratifications. Its Malkuth, by absolute increase and domination of matter in the material body.

The Nephesch, is the real, the actual body, of which the material body is only the result through the action of the *Ruach*, which by aid of the Nephesch, formeth the material body by the rays of *Ruach*, which do not ordinarily proceed beyond the limits of the Physical Body. That is to say, in the ordinary man the rays of Ruach rarely penetrate into the sphere of Sensation.

Shining through infinite worlds, and darting its rays through the confines of space, in this Sphere of Sensation is a faculty placed even as a light is placed within a lantern. This is a certain sense placed in an aperture of the upper part of the *Ruach* wherein act the rays from Chokmah and Binah which govern the reason—*Daath*. This faculty can be thrown downwards into the Ruach, and thence can radiate into the Nephesch. It consists of seven manifestations answering to the

Hexagram, and is like the Soul of Microprosopus or the Elohim of the human Tetragrammaton. Therefore in the head, which is its natural and chief seat, are formed the seven apertures of the head. This is the Spiritual Consciousness as distinct from the human consciousness. It is manifested in seven as just said or in eight if *Daath* be included. The Father is the Sun (Chokmah). The Mother is the Moon (Binah) The Wind beareth it in his bosom (Ruach). Its nurse is the Earth (Nephesch). The power is manifested when it can be vibrated through the Earth.

The following is the true attributions of the seven apertures of the head:

Right Ear — Saturn

Left Ear — Jupiter

Right Eye — Sol

Left Eye — Luna

Mouth — Mercury (who is the messenger of the Gods)

Right Nostril — Mars

Left Nostril — Venus

These latter represent here the sonoriferous sense. The right and left eye, the luminous sense, as the Sun and Moon are the luminaries of the Macrocosm. The right and left nostrils through which the breath passes, giving strength to the physical body, are under Mars and Venus. The mouth is under Mercury, the messenger and the Speaker.

This spiritual consciousness is a focus of the action of *Neschamah*. The lower will-power should control the descent of this spiritual consciousness into the Ruach, and thence into the *Nephesch*, for the consciousness must descend into the *Nephesch* before the images of the Sphere of Sensation can be perceived. For it is only the rays of this consciousness permeating the *Ruach* that can take cognizance thereof. This faculty of the spiritual consciousness is the seat of Thought. *Thought* is a Light proceeding from the radiation of this spiritual consciousness, traversing the *Ruach* as Light traverseth Air, and encountering thereafter the symbols reflected in the sphere of Sensation, or magical mirror of the Universe. These symbols are by its radiation of (i.e., that of the Thought) reflected again into the Spiritual Consciousness where they are subjected unto the action of the *Reasoning Mind* and of the *Lower Will*. That is, in the ordinary natural man when awake, the thought acteth through the *Ruach*, subject when there to the action of the Lower Will, and submitted to the reasoning power derived as foresaid from Chokmah and Binah.

But in the ordinary man when sleeping, and in the madman, the idiot, and the drunkard, the process is not quite the same. In the sleeping man, the concentration of the *Ruach* in his heart during the waking time hath produced a weakening of the action of the *Ruach* in its subsidiary Sephiroth in the Physical Body. To preserve the salutary conjunction of the *Ruach* with the *Nephesch* in the physical body (whose limits are fixed by the Sephiroth of the Ruach) it is necessary to weaken the concentration in Tiphareth to repair the strain which is produced by the concentration of the *Ruach* therein during the waking state. This reflux of the *Ruach* into its subsidiary Sephiroth produceth naturally a weakening of the Lower Will; and the *Ruach*, therefore, doth not reflect so clearly the Reasoning Faculty. Wherefore, the thought of the spiritual consciousness reflecteth the image in a confused series, which are only partially realized by the Lower Will. (This is as regards the ordinary natural man in sleep.)

In the madman, as considered apart from obsession (thought-obsession is frequently the accompaniment of mania and still more frequently its cause), the thought and lower will are very strongly exercised to the detriment of the reasoning faculty. That is, that there is an alliance between the two former which overpowereth the action of Chokmah and Binah in the latter.

Monomania is shown in the consideration of only one certain symbol which is too attractive to the Will. A chain of thought is simply a graduated vibration arising from the contact of a ray of thought with a symbol. If controlled by reasoning power and licensed by the Will, such vibrations will be balanced and of equal length. But if uncontrolled by the Lower Will and the Reason, they will be unbalanced and inharmonious. (That is, of uneven length.)

In the case of the drunkard, the equilibrium of the Sphere of Sensation and consequently of the Nephesch, is disturbed. In consequence the thought rays are shaken at each vibration, so that the sphere of sensation of the Nephesch is caused to rock and waver at the extremities of the physical body where the *Ruach* action is bounded. The thought therefore is dazzled by the symbols of the Sphere of Sensation, in the same way as the eyes can be dazzled in front of a mirror if the latter be shaken or waved. The sensation therefore then conveyed by the thoughts is that of the Sphere of Sensation oscillating and almost revolving about the physical body, bringing giddiness, sickness, vertigo and the loss of idea of place and position. Nearly the same may be said of Seasickness, and the action of certain drugs.

Restoration of the equilibrium of the Sphere of Sensation after this naturally produceth a slackening of the concentration of the Ruach in Tiphareth, whence sleep is an absolute necessity to the drunkard. This is so imperative that he cannot fight against the need. If he does so, or if this condition be constantly repeated, the thought rays are launched through the Sphere of Sensation so irregularly and so violently that they pass its boundary without either the Lower Will or the Reasoning Power or even the Thought itself consenting thereto; and the latter is therefore without the protection of the will. Thence arise the conditions of delirium tremens, and an opening is made in the Sphere of Sensation which is unguarded, and through which hostile influence may enter. But this latter cometh under the head of obsession.

All thought action in the spiritual consciousness originateth in radiation, and radiation is as inseparable from the spiritual consciousness as it is from Light.

The Spiritual Consciousness is the focus of the action of the *Neschamah*. The spiritual consciousness is, in its turn, the Throne or Vehicle of the Life of the Spirit which is *Chiah;* and these combined form the Chariot of that Higher Will which is *Kether.* Also it is the peculiar faculty of the *Neschamah* to aspire unto that which is beyond: The Higher Will manifests itself through *Yechidah.* The *Chiah* is the real Life Principle, as distinct from the more illusionary life of the Physical Body. The Shining Flame of the Divine Fire, the *Kether* of the Body, is the Real Self of the Incarnation. Yet but few of the sons of men know or feel its presence. Still less do they belong in or comprehend those Higher Potencies—Angelic, Archangelic or Divine, of which the manifestation directly touching *Yechidah* is the Higher Genius.

This *Yechidah* in the ordinary man can but rarely act through the spiritual consciousness, seeing that for it to do so the King of the Physical Body, that is the Lower Will, must rise from his Throne to acknowledge his superior. That is the reason why, in some cases, in sleep only doth the Higher Will manifest itself by dream unto the ordinary man. In other cases it may be manifested; at times through the sincere practice of religious rites, or in cases where the opportunity for self-sacrifice occurreth. In all these cases the Lower Will hath for a moment recognized a higher form of itself, and the YHVH of the man hath reflected from the Eternal Lord of the Higher Life. This *Yechidah* is the only part of the man which can truly say—EHEIEH, I am.

This is then but the Kether of the Assiah of the Microcosm, that is, it is the highest part of man as Man. It is that which toucheth, or is the manifestation of a higher and greater range of Being. This Yechidah is at the same time the Higher Human Self and the Lower Genius, the God of the Man, the Atziluth of his Assiah, even as Chiah and Neschamah from his Briah, and Ruach his Yetzirah. This is the Higher Will and the Divine Consciousness, as Daath is the Spiritual Consciousness, Tiphareth the Human Consciousness, and Yesod the Automatic Consciousness.

It is the Divine Consciousness because it is the only part of man which can touch the All-potent forces. Behind Yechidah are Angelic and Archangelic Forces of which Yechidah is the manifestor. It is therefore the Lower Genius or Viceroy of the Higher Genius which is beyond, an Angel Mighty and Terrible. This Great Angel is the Higher Genius, beyond which are the Archangelic and Divine.

Recall the Tiphareth clause of an Adeptus Minor: "I further solemnly promise and swear that with the divine permission I will from this day forward apply myself unto the Great Work which is so to purify and exalt my spiritual nature, that with the Divine Aid I may at length attain to be more than Human, and thus gradually raise and unite myself to my Higher and Divine Genius, and that in this event, I will not abuse the great power entrusted unto me."

Note that this clause answereth unto Tiphareth, seeing that it is the Lower Will that must apply itself unto this work, because it is the King of the Physical Man. All the Shining Ones (whom we call Angels) are microcosms of the Macrocosm Yetzirah, even as Man is the microcosm of the Macrocosm of Assiah. All Archangelic forms are microcosms of the Macrocosm of Briah, and the Gods of the Sephiroth are consequently the Microcosms of the Macrocosm of Atziluth. Therefore apply this perfecting of the Spiritual Nature as the preparation of the Pathway for the Shining Light, the Light Divine.

The evil persona of a man is in the Sphere of the Qlippoth, and the devils are the microcosms of the Macrocosm of the Qlippoth. This evil persona hath its parts and divisions, and of it the part which toucheth the Malkuth of the Nephesch is its Kether. Tremble therefore at the evil forces which be in thy own evil persona. And as above the Kether of a man are his Angelic and other forms, so below the Malkuth of the Evil Persona are awful forms, dangerous even to express or think of.

SHEKINAH[110]
THE FEMININE FACE OF GOD

Possibly one of the most confusing theories within Kabbalistic teaching is that of the Shekinah. Within the Golden Dawn's Outer Order the Shekinah, or more simply the female aspect of the deity, is only briefly mentioned. A number of the Order's critics have often felt that the Order was too patriarchal. This applies, if at all, however, only to the levels up to the Inner Order, for the rituals of the 6=5 upwards are under the guidance of the Shekinah or Matrona as it is sometimes called, and the apparent patriarchal aspect is then reversed.

To describe the function of the Shekinah is very difficult because many of the mystics, who recorded seeing the Shekinah, found that it appeared on many different levels and this is the point of confusion. The Shekinah is very closely allied, though not identical with the soul, both on individual and group levels. Its relationship with the soul is close and strong, not unlike that between womb and fetus, for the Shekinah is the aspect of God that cradles and nurtures the soul. It is also called Eden (the Upper Eden). In the *Zohar*[111] we are introduced to the Shekinah in the feminine word "mihalekh," which is the voice of God heard in the Garden of Eden "in the coolness of the day."[112] When applied to the tribes of Israel, the Shekinah guided them in Exodus 13:21. A reference to this guidance is also found in Psalms (85:13) where it states that "the Just One goes before him and shall deliver him from his steps," which also

---

[110] This word refers to something dwelling within.
[111] Part 1, folio 76a.

relates to Exodus. The first separation of the Shekinah occurred during the Deluge. The Lesser Hecaloth text tells us that the first generation denied the Lord and went to idol-worshipping, and the only man worthy of being saved was Enoch,[112] who was taken up into the heavens with the Shekinah. Once removed from the earth, then the destruction began, and man had to begin all over again. The Shekinah in man in the second generation was a separate entity in itself and divided. The Four Kerubs are the Throne on which the Shekinah rests.

This notion of the cleaving of the Spirit associated with the Shekinah is not confined to its active part in guiding the Tribes of Israel. It can also be found in the association of the Shekinah and the Torah which was was written under her influence. Once the Torah is truly understood then one is in direct contact with the Shekinah.

At this point we have the Shekinah manifesting on two levels. The first is the higher echelon or upper level of Eden, and the second is the influence of the Law. The experience of the Shekinah manifesting as guide during Exodus actually comes through the understanding of the Torah. At this point there is not really a separation from the masculine concept of deity, for God is Elohim, both masculine and feminine, and the Shekinah shone through and led them through the Torah.

There are some early references to the Shekinah in Kabbalistic texts but the first one of any substantial importance is in the *Bahir* where the analogy is with the Matrona in the King's chamber, who could not be seen by her children, for she was hidden. The analogy here is considered by some to be the development of the Sephiroth, with the Shekinah being allotted to Binah, while the children are the seven lower Sephiroth, who are cut off from the Mother by the Abyss. We are told in the *Zohar*[114] that the Lord God Jehovah is plural, for he is also called Elohim, showing up the feminine source within. On a more personal level, the Shekinah is often referred to as an angel. She was the angel that appeared to Moses,[115] although to Jacob[116] she appeared as Rachael,[117] and to Abraham she was Adonai.[118] The *Zohar* states[119] that the Shekinah abides in all women, and man can come to know the Shekinah through a wife, but fails if he has none. For in all true matrimonial unions the

---

[112] Genesis 3:8.
[113] Both Enoch and Metatron are considered the same in some texts.
[114] Part 2, folio 161b–162a.

Shekinah hovers overhead between husband and wife.[120] The Shekinah is also the Union of Metatron (the male) and Sandalphon through the central pillar of the Tree of Life. Some Kabbalistic authors, such as Waite, have ascribed the Middle Pillar to the Shekinah, but this I feel is an error. The Middle Pillar is a sheath that allows the energies of the Shekinah to unite so Elohim is formed.[121] A good analogy here is with Kundalini Yoga. The spine for the Shekinah is aligned with Shatki, the energy that resides in the base of the spine, and closely allied with Malkuth. This energy then works its way up the spine through two channels, Ida and Pingala, releasing her energy at various stops or chakras and striving for the union in the godhead.[122]

The Talmud informs us that man and his Shekinah were separated when Adam left Eden "enthroned above a cherub under the Tree of Life, her splendour being 65,000 times greater than the sun." The Shekinah then followed Adam and will continue to do so until he has achieved his rightful place back in the Garden of Eden.

---

[115] Part 5, folio 187a.
[116] In Genesis 48:16 we are told "the angel which redeemeth me from evil," uttered by Jacob.
[117] See the Countenance section to fully explain this.
[118] Who was said to have descended from the second heaven.
[119] Part 2, folio 228b.
[120] Talmud Shabbath 55b; Bereshith Rabba 98,4 etc.
[121] I must agree with Shuster in his book *Crowley's Apprentice*, page 121, where he gives a description of the dual polarity in the Middle Pillar, a point Francis King feels is not valid in his *Tantra For Westerner*.
[122] See *The Serpent Power* by Arthur Avalon.

The Garden of Eden before the Fall

CHAPTER EIGHT

The Garden of Eden

In the Golden Dawn Practicus Grade, associated with the Sephirah of Hod, the candidate is shown a diagram of the Garden of Eden before the Fall and the following explanation is given by the Hierophant:

> Before you is represented the symbolism of the Garden of Eden. At the summit are the Supernal Sephiroth, summed up and contained in Aima Elohim, the Mother Supernal, the Woman of the 12th chapter of the Apocalypse clothed with the Sun and the Moon under her feet and upon her head a crown of 12 stars, Kether. And whereas the name Tetragrammaton is joined to the Elohim, when it is said Tetragrammaton Elohim planted a Garden Eastward in Eden, so this represents the power of the Father joined thereto in the Glory from the Face of the Ancient of Days. And in the Garden were the Tree of Life, and the Tree of Knowledge of Good and Evil, which latter is from Malkuth, which is the lowest Sephirah between the rest of the Sephiroth and the Kingdom of the Shells, which latter is represented by the Great Red Dragon coiled beneath, having seven heads (the seven infernal Palaces) and 10 Horns (10 averse Sephiroth contained in the seven Palaces). And a River Nahar went

forth out of Eden (namely the Supernal Triad) to water the Garden (the rest of the Sephiroth) and from thence it was divided into four heads in Daath, whence it is said; "In Daath the depths are broken up and the clouds drop down dew."

The first head is Pishon which flows into Geburah "where there is gold," it is the River of Fire. The second head is Gihon, the River of Waters, flowing into Chesed. The third is Hiddekel, the River of Air flowing into Tiphareth. And the fourth river which receiveth the virtue of the other three is Euphrates which floweth down upon Malkuth the Earth. This river going forth out of Eden is the River of the Apocalypse, of the Waters of Life, clear as crystal, proceeding out of the Throne of God and the Lamb, on either side of which was the Tree of Life bearing 12 manner of fruit. And thus do the Rivers of Eden form a Cross, and on that Cross the great Adam the Son who was to rule Nations with a rod of iron is extended from Tiphareth and his arms are stretched out to Gedulah and Geburah. And in Malkuth is Eve, the completion of All, the Mother of All, and above the Universe she supporteth with her hands the Eternal Pillars of the Sephiroth."

The Golden Dawn approach, from this description, is a combination of the traditional Judaic and the Christian. The *Zohar*[123] tells us that God planted Man, as Israel, in the Lower Garden of Eden,[124] from which man was formed from the Middle column, along with Eve, as two distinct entities from the single source that would never be separated, the branches of the Tree being the purity and guardians of YHVH's teaching. Only when the teaching is accepted by mankind (as Israel) will the knowledge and benefits of the fruits of knowledge, being born in Malkuth at the base of the Tree of Life, benefit everyone, as from this fruit all will eat, from the one Tree.

As shown by the diagram on page 126, Metatron (or Enoch) came down from the Supernal Eden to the Lower Eden to protect it from the Qlippoth who were trying to climb to the source of Light. The problem was that the vessels of the Sephiroth were formed from Chaos or Tohou and were imperfect, and could not hold the light emanating from above.

---

[123] Part I, folio 25a–26b, was the basis of this Mathers explanation of the Garden of Eden before the Fall.

[124] The Garden is the Shekinah on earth while Eden is the Supernal Mother, two levels of the Shekinah in one form.

In many respects, it could be said that since the vessels[125] were the androgyny of Adam and Eve, that they were made imperfect. Therefore they could not mate to perpetuate the species. It appears that they could have carried on their own existence though this would have got mankind itself nowhere fast. The separation of the female from the male was the force that shattered the vessels and also prevented them from knowing God as they once did when they were a complete form. This was the banishment, the lack of knowledge with God that they once had, that was the Fall of Man, for they left the Garden of Eden through a lack of communion with the Divine. This did not happen overnight, nor in the 42 days as given by Jacob Boehme, but over a period of time.

Going to a completely different type of approach, it appears that man, in the beginning, had control of the shaping of his body, or was not yet quite flesh. In Genesis we find Adam saying[126] "This is now bone of my bones and flesh of my flesh." Psychics such as Edgar Cayce have stated that man in this early time was much aligned to semi-matter, and once the flesh was formed so was the urge to procreate, and the sexual urge between Adam and Eve began to polarize.[127] The Qlippoth that Metatron[128] had to protect them from was in fact the pull of the earth and its desires in the material form, for this pull made them more dense, and as such, they lost their state as energy or semi-energy. Metatron was a man who could rise above the power of the material and could guide the others to follow in his footsteps. The *Zohar* states that Adam and Eve ate from the vine and suggests procreation attempts that were made were unsuccessful[129] at first. It may be, however, that they were simply not ready for it, for they themselves had not yet fully formed, let alone could they procreate themselves.

---

[125] The Torah considers these vessels the Kings of Edom, though this theory will be dealt with in the Garden of Eden after the Fall.

[126] Genesis 2:23

[127] See *Edgar Cayce's Story of the Old Testament* by Robert Krajenke (Edgar Cayce Foundation, 1973).

[128] Who is also associated with Adam or a form of him.

[129] Part 1, folio 192a.

The Garden of Eden

THE GARDEN OF EDEN

The Golden Dawn description of this diagram is as follows:

> The outer circle is the enclosing Paradisiacal Wall guard-
> ed by the Kerubim and the Flame, and the seven Squares
> are the Seven Mansions thereof, or the Seven Spheres,
> wherein Tetragrammaton Elohim planted every Tree
> which is pleasant and good for food, symbolized by the
> Palm Trees on the Veil of the Tabernacle, and the Door

of the Holy of Holies in the Temple. But in the midst is the Tree of Life, the Throne of God and the Lamb. Twelve are the Foundations and Twelve are the Gates,[130] shown by the entrances in the drawing. the four streams rising from one central fountain are the Rivers of Eden, referring to the four elements proceeding from the Omnipresent Spirit.

The Garden of Eden in this instance refers to the Supernal Bride as received by the Bride below, and they are given the Seven Benedictions so that the union will be complete.[131] These are all needed to form and nurture the Tree of Life in Eden. In the Seventh Benediction we are told that it represents the ten created worlds and ten aspects of joy.

GARDEN OF EDEN AFTER THE FALL

The Golden Dawn concept of the Garden of Eden after the Fall[132] does not follow the continuity of the Garden of Eden before the Fall. The problem that Mathers faced was that there were a number of different Zoharic viewpoints of it.[133] Prior to the Fall he used a combination of two different concepts and did the same with that of "after the Fall," which primarily came form the Idra Sutra.[134] As Mathers explains it:[135]

Ere the Eternal instituted the Formation, Beginning and End existed not. Therefore, before Him, he expanded a certain

---

[130] Refer to the section of the Kabbalah and Astrology for a fuller explanation of this meaning.

[131] Part Four, folio 169b.

[132] On my original copy of this diagram Mathers made the following notes: "The first head, Daath, represents King Bela (son of Beor) from Dinhabh, and the three Dukes, Timnah, Alvah and Jetheth. The second head in Chesed, is King Jobab (son of Zerah) from Bozrah, and the Duke Aholibamah. The third head is in Geburah and is King Husham from the Temani, and Duke Elah. The fourth head is in Tiphareth and is King Hadad (son of Bedad) and is from Avith, with Duke Pinon. The fifth head in Netzach is King Samlah from Masrekah, with Duke Kenaz. The sixth head is in Hod and is King Saul from Rehoboth by the River, and with Duke Teman. The seventh head is in Yesod and is King Baal-hannan (son of Achbor) with Dukes Mibzar and Magdiel. The eight head is in Malkuth and is King Hadar from Pau (wife of Mehetabel, daughter of Matred, daughter of Mezahab) with Duke Eram.

[133] In Part 1, folio 31b, the *Zohar* refers to the three sinful generations of man: Enoch, the Deluge, and the Tower of Babel, which Mathers tried to incorporate into one concept.

[134] You will note that in the former, the Edomite Kings are not mentioned, as they are in the latter.

[135] The quotes are taken from the Philosophus Ritual from a number of sections and have been amalgamated together into a cohesive pattern so that the aim of this ritual, or at least one layer of it, is quite clear in its teaching about the Fall, which is mainly Isaac Luria's viewpoint.

veil, and therein He instituted the Primal Kings. And these are the Kings who reigned in Edom before there reigned a King over Israel: but they subsisted not when the earth was formless and void. Behold, this is the reign of Edom; and when Creation was established, lo this is the reign of Israel. And the Wars of the Titanic Force in the Chaos of Creation, lo these are the Wars between them. From a Lightbearer of insupportable brightness proceeded a radiating Flame, hurling forth like a vast and mighty hammer whose sparks were the Primal Worlds. And these sparks flamed and scintillated awhile, but being unbalanced they were extinguished. Since lo, the Kings assembled, they passed away together. They themselves beheld, so were they astonished, they feared, they hasted away. And these be the Kings who reigned in Edom, before there reigned a King in Israel . . . [136]

The Dukes of Edom were amazed, trembling took hold of the Mighty of Moab. Lord when Thou wentest out of Seir, when thou marchedst out of the field of Edom, the earth trembled and the Heavens dropped, the Clouds also dropped water. Curse ye Meroz said the angel of the Lord, curse ye bitterly to the inhabitants thereof, because they came not to the help of the Lord, to the help of the Lord against the Mighty. The river Kishon swept them away, that ancient river, the River Kishon.

O my Soul, thou hast trodden down strength! He bowed the Heavens, also, and came down and the Darkness was under His Feet. At the brightness that was before Him, the thick clouds passed, hailstones and flashings of Fire. The Lord thundered through the heavens and the highest gave forth his Voice, hailstones and flashings of Fire. He sent out his arrows and scattered them: he hurled forth His Lightnings and destroyed them.

Then the channels of the Waters were seen and the Foundations of the World were discovered. At Thy rebuke, O Lord, at the blast of the Breath of Thy nostrils, the Voice of Thy thunder was in the heavens and Thy Lightnings lightened the World. The Earth trembled and shook. Thy way is in the sea

---

[136] Mathers explains this more simply in the Introduction to *The Kabbalah Unveiled*: ". . . According to the Qabalah, before the complete form of the Heavenly Man (10 Sephiroth) was produced, there were certain primordial worlds created, but these could not subsist, as the equilibrium of balance was not yet perfect, and they were convulsed by the unbalanced force and destroyed. These primordial worlds are called 'Kings of ancient time,' and the 'Kings of Edom who reigned before the monarchs of Israel.' In this sense, Edom is the world of unbalanced force, and Israel is the balanced Sephiroth (Gen. 26:31). This important fact, that the worlds were created and destroyed prior to the present creation, is again and again reiterated in the *Zohar*."

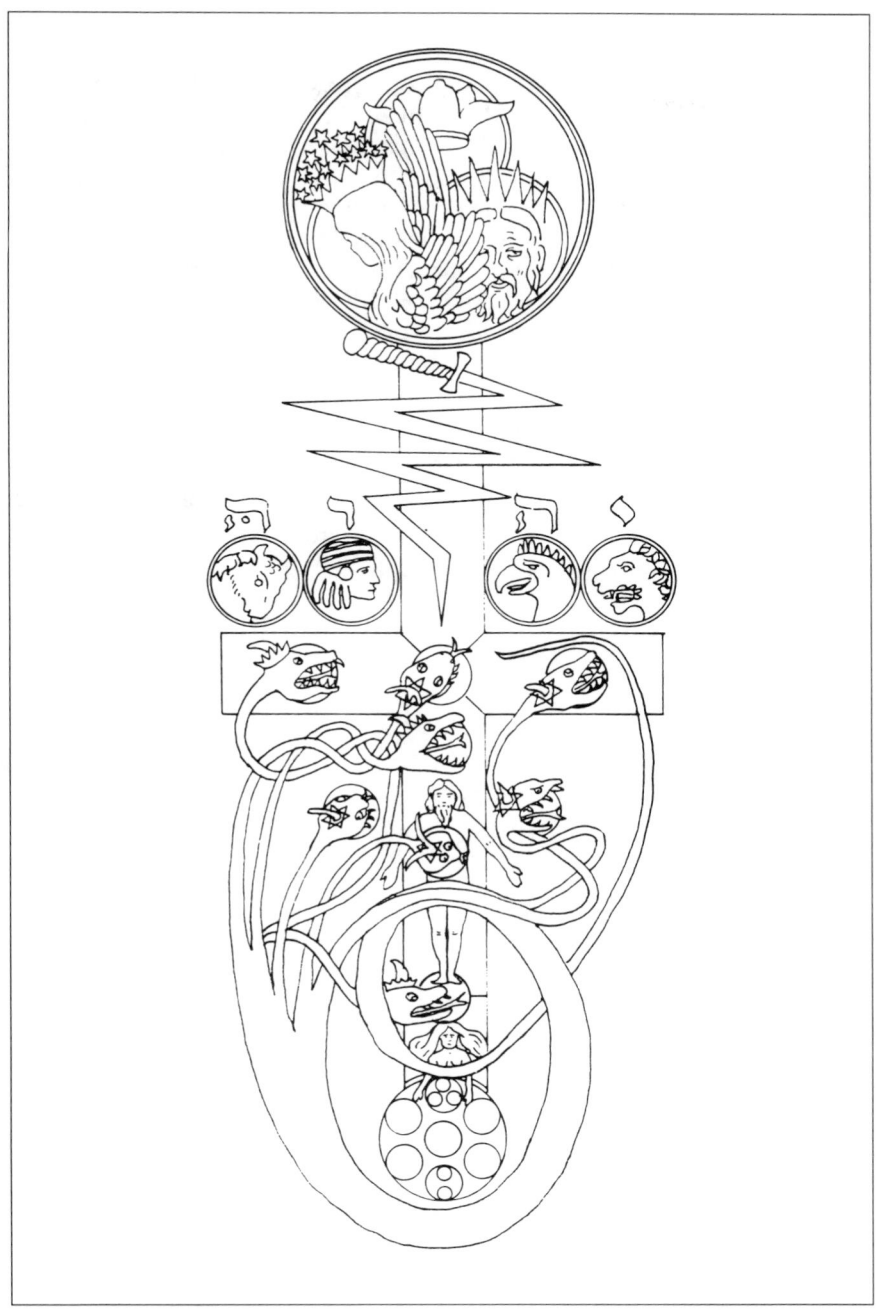

The Garden of Eden after the Fall

and Thy Path in the Great Waters and Thy Footsteps are not known . . . [137]

. . . Eloah came from Teman of Edom and the Holy One from Mount Paran. His Glory covered the Heavens and the earth was full of His praise. His brightness was as the Light. He had Karmaim in His hands and there was the hiding of His Power. Before Him went the pestilence and flaming Fire went forth at His feet. He stood and measured the Earth. He beheld and drove asunder the Nations. And the Everlasting Mountains were scattered, the Perpetual Hill did bow; His ways are everlasting. I saw the tents of Cushan in affliction and the curtains of the land of Midian did tremble . . .

The *Zohar* gives us further information on Adam and Eve, noting that they were separated for 130 years. Apparently during this time both had intercourse with creatures,[138] and from this demons and elementals were formed. None could return to the Garden of Eden, which was guarded by a Cherub with a Flaming Sword.

---

[137] The Golden Dawn also adapted the Tarot Trump "Blasted Tower" to this theme.
[138] Part 1, folio 54–55a.

CHAPTER NINE

THE QLIPPOTH[139]

These be they who are Unclean and Evil, even the Distortion and Perversion of the Sephiroth; the fallen restriction of the Universe; the rays of the Coils of the Stooping Dragon. Eleven are their classes, yet Ten are they called; seven are the heads and yet an eighth head arises. Seven are the Infernal Palaces, yet do they include Ten.

In the Tree of Life, by the Waters of the River, in the Garden of Wisdom, is the serpent of the Paths; it is the Serpent of the Celestial Eden. But the Serpent of the Temptation is that of the Tree of Knowledge of Good and Evil; the antithesis and opposer of the other: the Red Coiled Stooping Dragon of the Apocalypse, the Serpent of the Terrestrial Eden.

Regard thou therefore the Celestial Serpent as of Brass, glistening with green and gold, the colours of vegetation and of growth. Banish thou therefore the evil and seek the good, thou who wouldst know the Life of Ages, thou who would fol-

---

[139] This paper, of which Mathers was the author, was given out at 4=7 level and is an amalgamation of the statements on the Qlippoth forces made during the Outer Order rituals.

low in the footsteps of our Master, O Brother of the Order of the Golden Dawn. For as Moses lifted up the Serpent in the Wilderness, even so must the Son of Adam must be lifted up, raised through the balance of Strife and of Trial, to the pathway of the Eternal Life. And when like our master, thou art extended on the Tree through suffering and through pain, let thy countenance be raised up towards the Light of the Holy One to invoke the Divine Brightness, not for thyself, but for those who have not yet attained unto the Pathway, even though they be thy tormentors. Balanced between the spiritual and the Material, the type of the Reconciler, remember the symbol of the Brazen Serpent.[140] Mark thou well the difference between the two Serpents, for before the Serpent of Brass of numbers, the Serpent of Fire could not stand.

But at the Fall, the Serpent of Evil arising in the Tree surrounded Malkuth, and linked her thus unto the Outer and the Qlippoth, for this is the Sin of the Fall, even the separation of the Material Plane from the Sephiroth through the interposition of the Coils of the Stooping Dragon.

Thus therefore must Malkuth be cleansed and this is the Redemption to come. For also Christ expiated not Sin till after he had overcome the Temptation. But surely all things in the Creation are necessary, seeing that one existeth not without the other. And the evil also helpeth the Work, for thus the greater and more intense the darkness, by so much the more doth the Light become bright by contrast and draweth, as it were, increased force from the Blackness.

INFERNAL HABITATIONS[141]

The *Zohar* tells us[142] that while God took six days to create the world, the infernal regions of man were created at night in the mirror image of the world above them. At the point where both day and night merge the elements were mixed and unsettled, forming a division in the waters (of the first day). Due to this imbalance between the first and second day, the third was created to finish the work of the second.

---

[140] This will be discussed fully later in the text.

[141] The original text in this section consisted of little more than what was given in the Ritual. I have taken the liberty of rewriting this part of the paper with a more fuller explanation.

[142] Part I, folio 46a–47a.

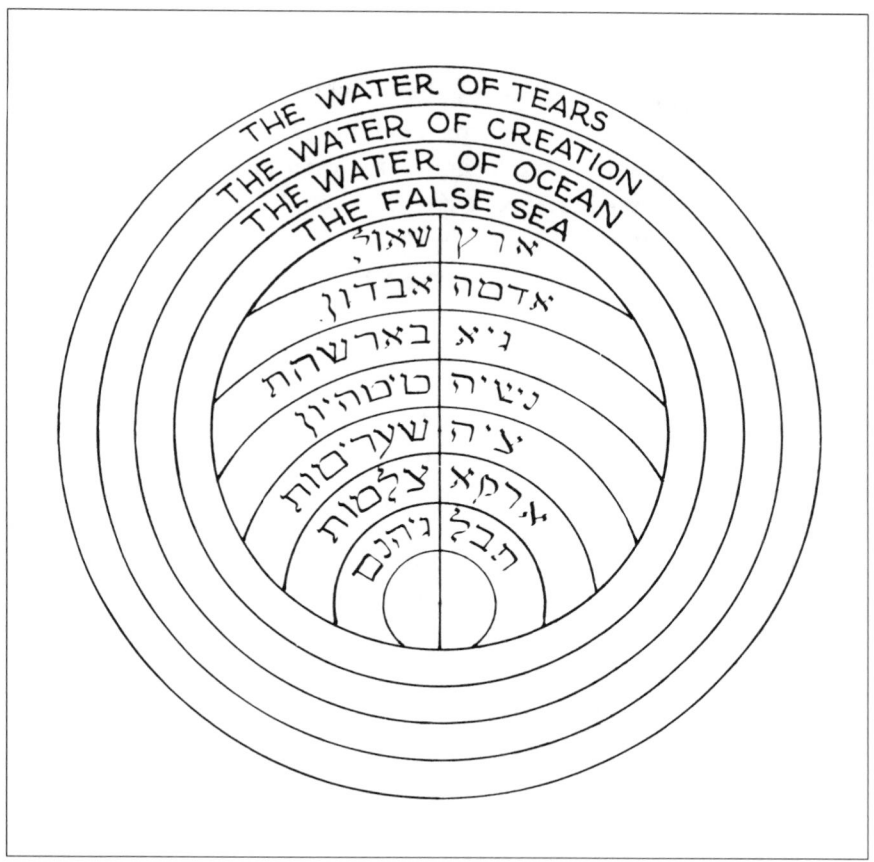

Infernal Habitations[143]

In the diagram above, the first circle shows the Water of Tears, for the tears are the separation from the Light after the Fall. It is the cry of Adam separated from the first Adam and the loss of the Shekinah. The second circle shows the Waters of Creation. This represents Creation away from the Light. It is the creation of the Shells of the Qlippoth and the creation of man from Adam. The third circle shows the Waters of the Ocean which team with living creatures, both Good and Evil, and it is from this that the serpent issues forth. The fourth circle is

---

[143] All the diagrams in this section on the Qlippoth were adapted by the Golden Dawn (as were the explanations) almost verbatim from Rosenroth's *Kabbala Denudata*.

the False Sea and is the Astral World, the place where deception and reflection are confused. The Four Seas are also reflections of the Four Rivers from the Garden of Eden (and also the Four Worlds), for it is they who must nourish the seven Infernal Habitations.

On the right side of the diagram, the lesser circles represent the 7 Earths. Though these circles are referred to as earths they should be called states for they are states of awareness or consciousness that envelop man at different times. They are also reflections of the Sephiroth and are part of the Garden that man inherited that he could aspire to, for these were left with man when he was banished from the Garden of Eden. In many respects these were the shells of the Kingdoms of Edom which had been destroyed by their imperfect ability to accept God's Light, and are but shadows of their former glory. The entire concept here is to show the falsity of matter over the spirit. For the earths represent the material side of man, his passions and desires, which eventually crumble with time as shown by Aretz, the earth furtherest away from the present. Some consider the seven earths' periods of time or evolution to start with the present, Thabel, considered the most perfect of them all, and lead to the less perfect worlds, and to the final crumble and decay of Aretz.

1. Aretz — Dry crumbling Earth

2. Adamah — Reddish mould

3. Gia — Undulating ground, like the side of a valley

4. Neschiah — Pasture or meadow land

5. Tziah — Sandy or desert land

6. Areqa — Earth

7. Thebel or Chaled — Mitrd earth and water

On the left-hand side of the diagram are the seven Infernal Habitations. These are the experiences one will have passing through the seven imperfect earths, as described above. Some of the names on the left are of the angelic guardians (except the last), after whom these experiences have been named. The guardians prevent anyone from leaving his or her allotted area before the designated time.

1. Sheol — Depths of the earth

2. Abaddon — Perdition

3. Titahion — Clay of Death

4. Bar Shasketh — Pit of Destruction

5. Tzelmoth — Shadow of Death

6. Shaari Moth — Gates of death

7. Gehinnon — Hell

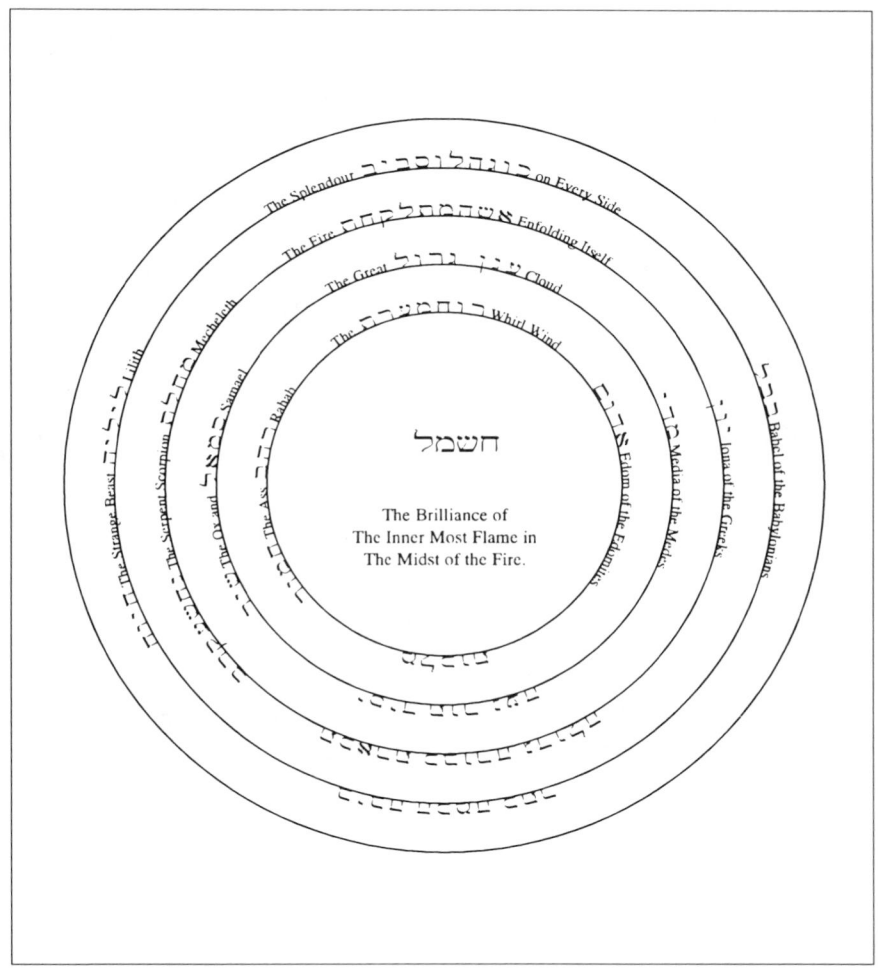

Adverse Powers at the Feet of the Cherub

THE EVIL AND ADVERSE POWERS BENEATH THE
FEET OF THE FOUR CHERUBS

Sephiroth	Spirit	Kingdom	Qlippoth
Kether	Lilith	Babel	Splendor
Chokmah	(strange-		
Binah	(beasts)		
Gedulah	Machaloth	Greeks	Whirling Fire
Geburah	(serpent)		
Tiphareth			
Netzach	Samael (ox)	Medes	Great Cloud
Hod			
Yesod			
Malkuth	Rahab (ass)	Edom	Whirlwind

In the Mercavah vision of Ezekiel it is written: "And I looked and behold a whirlwind came out of the North, a great cloud, and Fire enfolding itself, and a Splendour on every side, and Chasmal, the brilliance of the inner-most flame in the midst of the Fire.

These are the Four Kerubic expressions of Force, and the Evil and Adverse Powers broken beneath their feet are:

1. Rahab, whose symbol is a woman riding upon an ass.

2. Samael, whose symbol is a terrible demon leaping upon an ox.

3. Machaloth, a form compounded of a woman and a serpent, and she rideth upon a serpent-scorpion.

4. Lilith, a woman outwardly beautiful but inwardly corrupt, and putrefying, riding upon a strange and terrible beast.

To these four are attributed the Four Kingdoms, and they are also classed under the Sephiroth as shown.

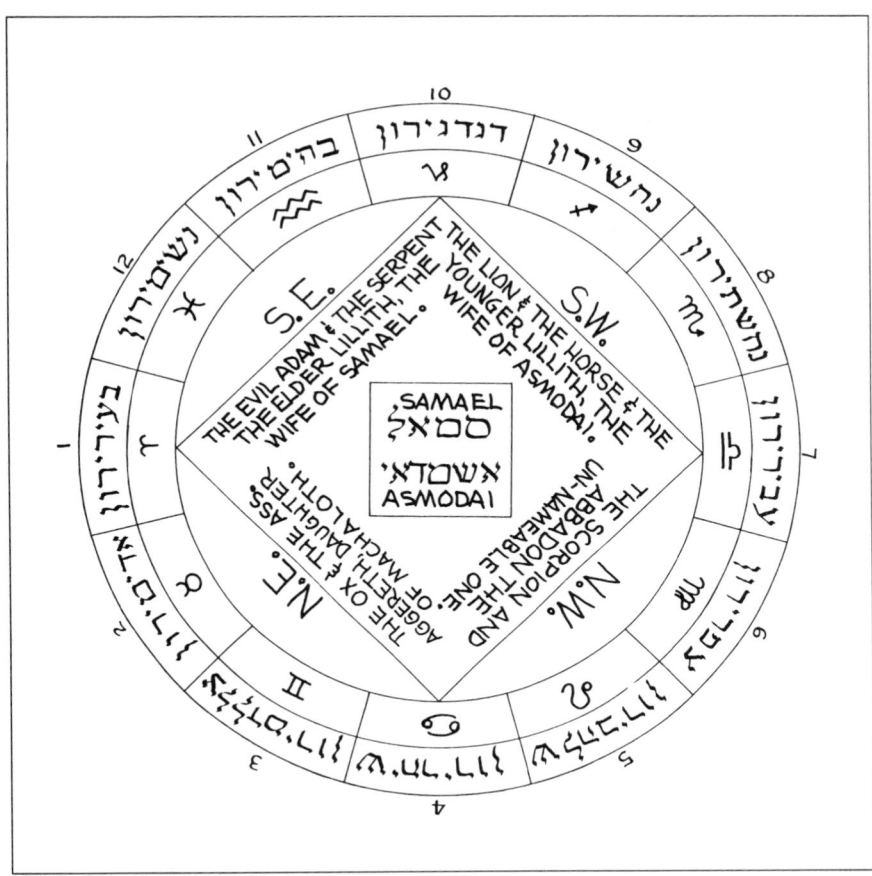

The Twelve Princes of the Qlippoth

THE TWELVE PRINCES OF THE QLIPPOTH
WHO ARE THE HEADS
UNDER THE MONTHS OF THE YEAR

These are the names of the Twelve Princes and Tribes of the Qlippoth who are the heads of the months of the year.

1. BAIRIRON — so called because they are derived from the Fourth Evil Force; viz, Samael the Black. Their colors are dull and black; and their form is that of a Dragon-Lion.

2. ADIMIRON — whose colors are like dam[144] blood, mixed with water and dull yellow and gray. Their form is that of lion lizards.

3. TzELLADIMIRON — whose colours are like limped blood, tzelil,[145] bronze and crimson. They are like savage triangular-headed dogs.

4. SCHECHIRIRON — whose colors are black, and their form blended of reptile, insect and shell-fish, such as the crab and the lobster, yet Demon-faced withal.

5. SHELHABIRON — whose colors are fiery and yellow and their form like merciless wolves and jackals.

6. TZEPHARIRON — whose colors are like those of earth, and their form is partially living yet decaying corpses.

7. OBIRIRON — whose colors are like clouds and their form like gray bloated Goblins.

8. NECHESHETHIRON — whose color is like copper, and their forms like that of a most devilish and human headed insects.

9. NACHASHIRON — whose colors are like serpents, and their form like dog-headed serpents.

10. DAGDAGIRON — whose colors are reddish and gleaming, and their form like vast and devouring flat-shaped fishes.

11. BEHEMIRON — whose arms are derived from Behemoth, and their colors are black and brown, and their forms like those of awful beasts, like hippopotamus and an elephant, but crushed flat, or as if their skin was spread out flat over the body of a gigantic beetle or cockroach.

12. NESHIMIRON — whose colors are of a stagnant gleaming watery hue, and their forms like hideous women, almost skeletons, united to the bodies of Serpents and Fishes.

In the midst of the circle are placed Samael and Asmodai. The symbolic form of the former is somewhat like that of the Devil of the Tarot, but colossal and attenuated; that of Asmodai is that of a bloated and bestial man, but in a crouching position.

---

[144] This is the title of the blood from the last of the ten plagues of Egypt.
[145] This relates to a ringed formation of colors.

At the *Southeast Angle* are placed the Evil Adam, a goat-headed, skeleton-like giant, and the thousand- headed Hydra serpent; and the Elder Lilith, wife of Samael, a woman with an ever-changing and distorted countenance.

At the *Northeast Angle* is Aggereth, the daughter of Machaloth, a fiendish witch with serpent hair, enthroned in a chariot drawn by an ox and an ass.

At the *Northwest Angle* is a gigantic Scorpion with a fearful countenance, but standing upright as it were and formed of putrefying water. After him cometh the unnameable one, Abbadon, and his appearance and symbol are of a closely-veiled, black, gigantic figure covered with whirling wheels, and in his hand is a vast wheel whence come as it whirls, multitudes of cat-like demons. Behind him cometh Maamah, like a crouching woman with an animal's body crawling along the ground and eating the earth.

And at the *Southwest Angle* are a winged lion and a winged horse drawing in like a chariot the youngest Lilith, the wife of Asmodai. She is dark, a woman to the waist, and a man below it, and she appears as though dragging down, with her hands, small figures of men into Hell.

OF THE THREE EVIL FORCES BEFORE SAMAEL

1. This is Qematiel, whose form is that of a vast black-headed Dragon-serpent and he uniteth under him the force of Kether of the Internal and Averse Sephiroth.

2. This is Belial, a black, bloated Man-dragon. He who denied God; and he that uniteth the force of the averse Chokmah.

3. This is Othiel or Gothiel, a black bloated man-insect horrible of aspect; his breadth greater than his length; and he uniteth the force of the averse Binah.

4. This is Samael the Black. All of these are of gigantic stature and terrible aspect.

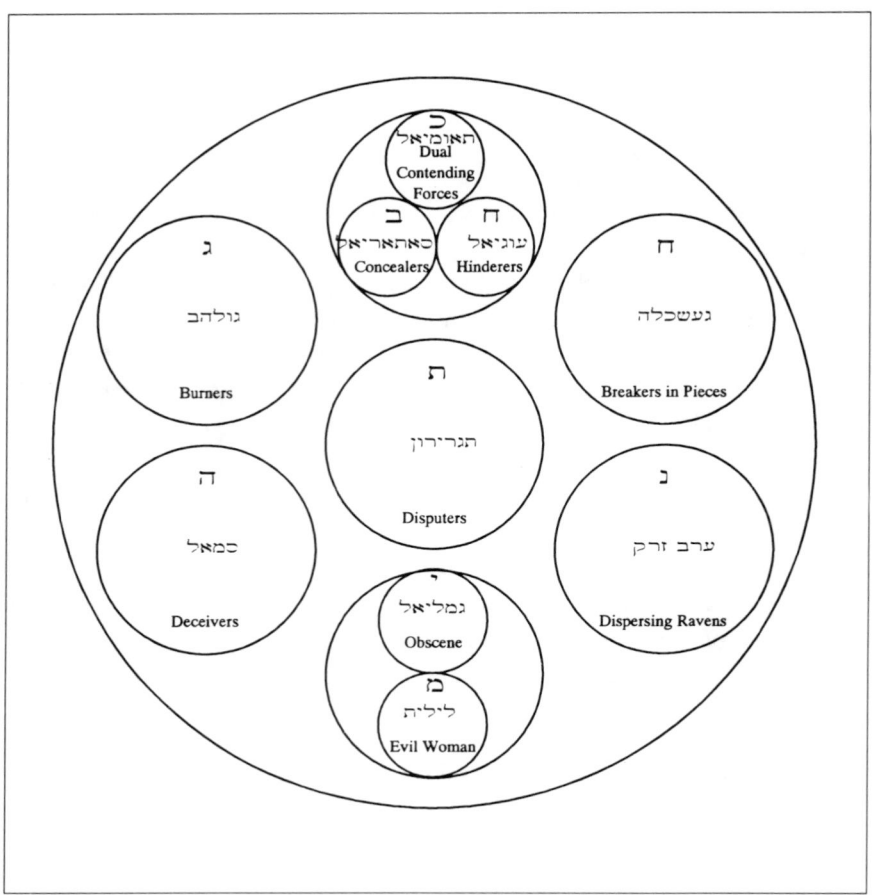

The Evil and Adverse Tree

THE EVIL AND AVERSE
SEPHIROTH

These be the Evil and Averse Sephiroth, contained in the Seven Palaces, and these Sephiroth have their place from behind the holiness of the World of Assiah. And Samael the Evil, surroundeth the whole Evil Sephiroth who are thus eleven instead of ten.

There are eleven letters in the Hebrew word for "Lieutenant Governor:" Esther 9:3; 11 days from Horeb, Deut.1:3;

11 curtains; The Hebrew word AY,[146] were the curses of Ebal; 11 were the Dukes of Edom, and so forth.

In the Evil Palaces the first containeth Kether, Chokmah and Binah. Unto Kether is attributed Kerthiel which means "cut off from God," Ps. 37:34. "When the wicked are cutoff . . ." And the symbolic form is that of Black Evil Giants. Also to Kether belong the Thaumiel or Thamiel, the Bicephalous Ones; and their forms are those of Dual Giant Heads with bat-like wings. They have not bodies for they are those that seek continually to unite themselves unto the bodies of other beings and forces.

Unto Chokmah are referred to the Dukes of Edom; and the Zogiel (from Og of Bashan) or as it is sometimes written Ghogiel or Oghiel, and they attach themselves unto lying and material appearances, and their form is like that of Black-Evil Giants with loathsome serpents twined round them.

Unto Binah are referred the Satorial or Harasiel, the Concealers and Destroyers whose forms and appearances are as gigantic black veiled Heads with Horns, and hideous eyes seen through the veil, and they are followed by evil centaurs. These are also called Seriel, from Esau, because of their hairiness.

The Second Palace contains Chesed, unto which are attributed the Gagh Shekelah, the Disturbing Ones, and their symbolic forms are those of black cat-headed giants. They are also called Aziel, Charariel and Agniel.

The Third Palace containeth Geburah, whereunto are attributed Golahab, or Burners with Fire, otherwise called Zaphiel, and their forms are those of enormous black heads like a volcano in eruption.

The Fourth Palace containeth Tiphareth whereunto are attributed Zamiel, and they are great black giants, ever working against each other.

The Fifth Palace containeth Netzach. whereunto are attributed the Ghoreb Zereq, or Dispeasing ravens. Their form is that of hideous demon-headed Ravens issuing from a volcano, also called Getzphiel.

The Sixth Palace containeth Hod, whereunto are referred to the Samael or Deceivers (Jugglers), whose form is that of dull, demon headed dog like monsters.

---

[146] This translates as "where" and has a numerical value of 11 in Deut. 22:37.

The Seventh palace containeth Yesod and Malkuth. Unto Yesod are referred the Gamaliel, or Obscene bull-men, linked together. Thereunto are also referred Nachashiel, evil serpents, and Obriel. Thereunto belongeth the Blind Dragon-force.

Unto Malkuth is attributed Lilith, the Evil Woman and the appearance is that of a woman at first beautiful, but afterwards changing to a black monkey-like demon. The name of the serpent, Nachash, hath the same number as that of Messiah, who will root out the Qlippoth from the world.

THESE ARE THE EVIL CHIEFS

1. Kether — Satan and Moloch

2. Binah — Beelzebub

3. Chokmah — Lucifuge

4. Chesed — Ashtaroth

5. Geburah — Asmodeus

6. Tiphareth — Belphagor

7. Netzach — Baal

8. Hod — Adramalech

9. Yesod — Lilith

10. Malkuth — Nahemah

According to the opinion of some; but these names can hardly be referred to any one Sephirah, seeing their power extendeth over many and numberless orders.

Behemoth and Leviathan are two evil forms, of which the first is the synthesis of the Qlippoth already described under the head of Behemiron in the Qlippoth of the Months of the Year.

The Leviathan are, as it were, numberless Dragon forms united together so that each of his scales is like a separate Evil Serpent.[147]

---

[147] This ends the transcription of the Mathers lecture on the Qlippoth.

CHAPTER TEN

The Seven Heavens[148]

We are told in the *Zohar*[149] that the Hebrew name for the Heavens, Shaimaim, is composed of the words for Fire (ash) and Water (maim) in the spiritual sense. These were placed in the manner of a curtain and turned into the letter Vau which illuminated them. The Seven Heavens of Assiah[150] are, in descending order:[151]

> 7. ARABOTH — This means "cloud" or a mixture of them. In metaphysical terms it shows the potential to renew life and give blessing through rain. This is associated with Chesed-Mercy. Since Chesed is the first of the Sephiroth after the Supernals we are told in the Talmud[152] that Araboth is the peaceful abode where souls (freshly reincarnated) arrive (through Daath

---

[148] In the diagram the earth is the central circle, while on the left is the Garden of Eden and on the right the Gehenna.

[149] Part 4, folio 164b.

[150] See "The Seven Palaces in early Jewish Mysticism" by Dr. Deirdre Green in the *Hermetic Journal*, No. 31, which views the Heavens or Palaces from a different viewpoint than I have given here and is a very exhaustive scholarly work with a massive reference index.

[151] With traditional Hebrew literature there are many descriptions of the Visions of Paradise and they quite often contradict each other. I have used the descriptions of the Heavens as given in the Talmud as the basis and also been influenced by the translations of early pre-Christian works by Jellnick, Gaster, Friedmann and the Lesser Hecaloth texts.

[152] Hagigah 12b.

and across the Abyss) and is the place where the Ministering Angels oversee, for this is the heaven that encompasses all other heavens. It is the heaven of the Messiah.

6. MAKHON — This roughly translates as "place" and is mentioned in the Talmud as being the place where fatal doses of rain, snow, or dew (that can destroy vegetation) are kept. It is the heaven of discrimination for the stores kept here will be unleashed on the ungodly and it closely resembles the influence of Geburah which it is allied to. This is very much the sphere of the Law and retribution and is said to be the abode of Moses, Isaac and Jacob. When punishment is inflicted from this heaven, the Prophets who guard this heaven try to protect the righteous. It is basically a position of the Talmud differing from that of the *Zohar*[153] on its functions.[154] Since the Heavens are a reflection of the energies of the Sephiroth it would appear that Talmudic consideration seems more appropriate.

5. MAHON — meaning "dwelling" and is related to Tiphareth. The Talmud says that this heaven is the home of the Ministering angels who sing the praise of YHVH during the day and rest during the night so that the songs of the day will be with man during sleep as well. When Moses viewed this heaven he saw angelic combinations of both Fire and Ice working together in harmony. These were the Erelim,[155] who are also called the Ishim.[156] This harmony, of course, relates to the Middle Pillar of the Tree of Life where the polar opposites merge.

4. ZEBUL — meaning "habitation,"[157] relates to the Sephirah of Netzach. According to the Talmud, it relates to the Celestial Temple of Jerusalem where high sacrifices are made. When Moses saw this heaven his vision was of a Temple with columns of red and green fire and halls of sparkling gems. The angelic hosts of this level govern all those stars and planets in the heavens.

3. SHEHAKIM — meaning "clouds of glory" is analogous to the Sephirah of Hod. Using a modern conception of the Talmudic explanation of this heaven it shows us that this is the level where the grace and glory of God are given to those who deserve it and is literally the "manna from heaven."

---

[153] Part 1, folio 45a.

[154] This function differs from that given in the Golden Dawn rituals which Mathers took from Rosenroth.

[155] Some versions refer to the Kerubim being associated here.

[156] Prov. 8:4.

[157] Kings 8:13.

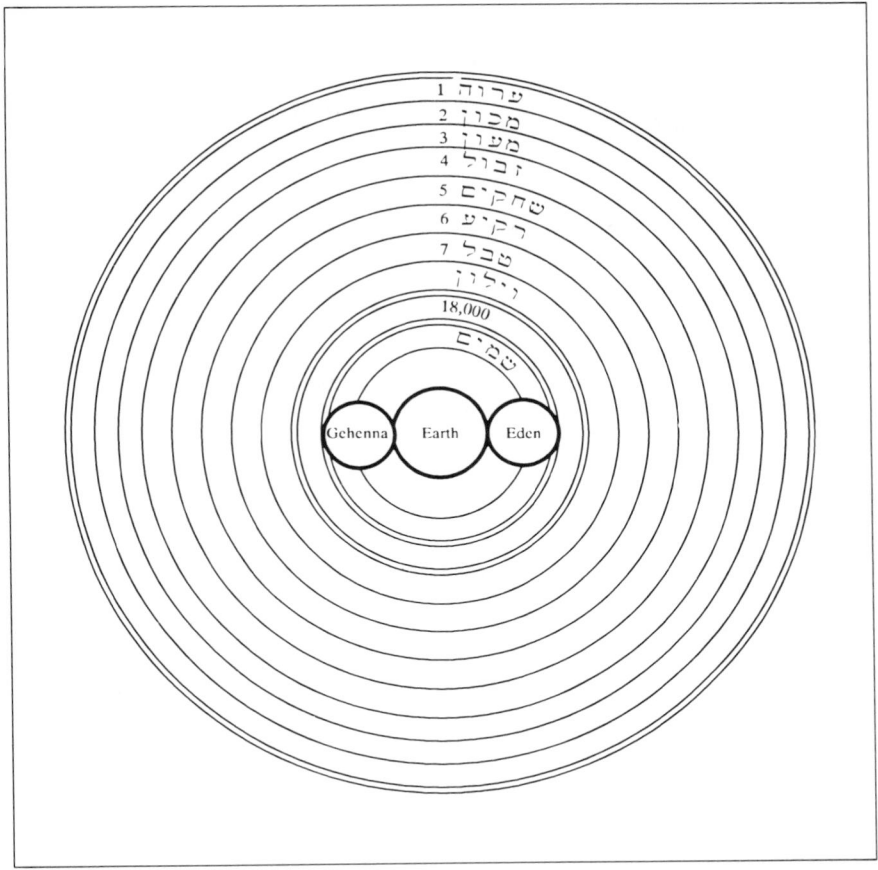

The Seven Heavens of Assiah

2. RAKIYAH — meaning "expanse of sky" or "firmament" where the support of the heavens is given through the knowledge imparted to the prophets who pass this information on to the Children of Israel. This level is analogous to the Sephirah of Yesod. The Angelic governors of this level teach souls to live in harmony with others through the process of purification. It is said that the brightness they emit relates to the level of purification they have received with the aim of reuniting with the Shekinah above them.

1. VILON — meaning "veil" or "curtain" and the Talmudic explanation of this level is that it resembles a veil and that it

is lowered during darkness and raised during the morning.[158] Vilon relates to the Sephirah of Malkuth. The vision of Moses at this level shows that he found Vilon a level of windows, with each window showing a particular joy and another a particular sorrow, polar opposite of the preceding window.[159]

SEVEN HEAVENS OF YETZIRAH[160]

Palaces	Holy Name	Sephiroth[161]
1.	AB, GI, ThTz	Kether, Chokmah, Binah
2.	QROShTN	Gedulah
3.	NGDIKSH	Geburah
4.	BTRTzTHG	Tiphareth
5.	ChQBTNO	Nezach
6.	IGLPZQ	Hod
7.	ShQVTzITH	Yesod, Malkuth

SEVEN HEAVENS OF BRIAH[162]

Palaces	Holy Name	Sephiroth	Meaning
1.	AL	Kether	Holy of Holies
		Chokmah	Holy of Holies
		Binah	Holy of Holies
2.	MATZPATZ[162]	Chesed	Love
3.	YEHEVID	Geburah	Merit
4.	YHVH	Tiphareth	Benevolence
5.	ELOHIM	Netzach	Substance of Heaven
6.	HOD & MATZPAT	Hod	Serenity
7.	YAH, ADONAI[164]	Yesod, Malkuth	Crystal Whiteness

---

[158] Issiah 40:42.

[159] An example of this would be the window of Joy and the window of Tears.

[160] According to Rosenroth, these names are derived from the first 42 letters of Genesis (up to the B in the word Bohu) which are then transmuted. Waite considers they are taken from the consonants of the name YHVH (as does Godwin in his *Cabalistic Encyclopedia*) expanded while Ginsburg says they are taken from the ten Divine names mentioned in the Bible and cites the *Zohar*, Part 3, folio 11a as a source.

[161] In the original Rosenroth translation there were quotes from Isaiah (6:2,3) but the Golden Dawn adapted this aspect to the Palaces of Briah. These associations were shown in the 3~8 Grade of Practicus.

[162] These associations were shown in the Portal Grade Ritual.

[163] This is the temurah of YHVH.

[164] A synthesis of both these names is in the word Taklith—perfection.

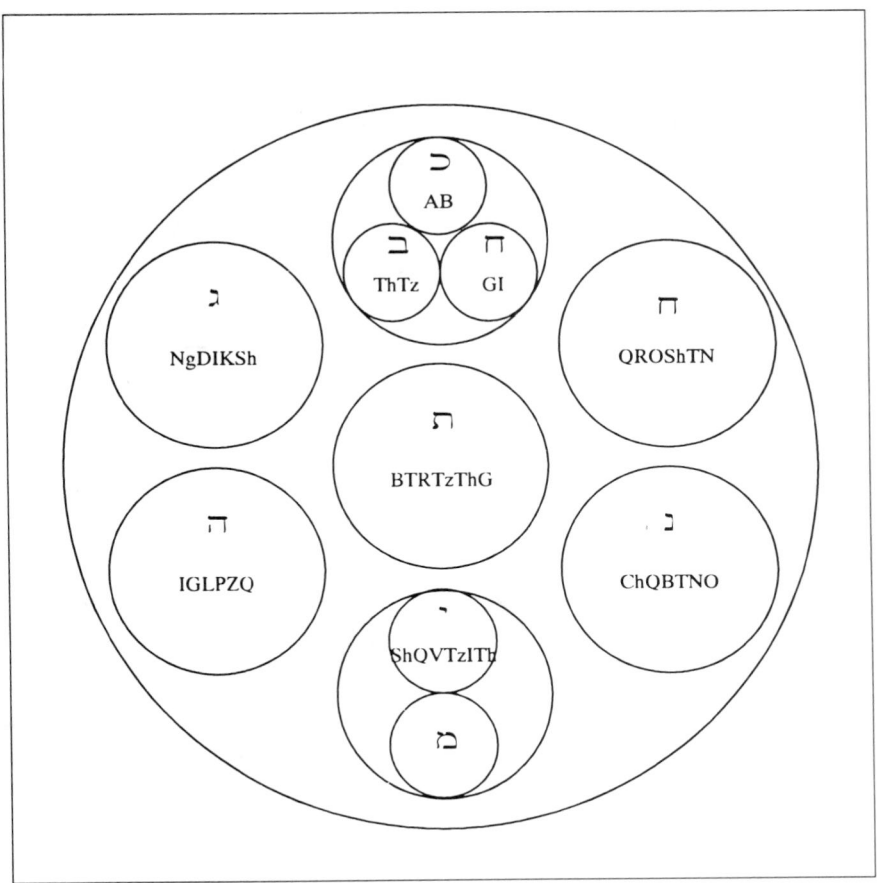

The Seven Heavens of Yetzirah

THE SERAPHIM

The name Seraphim is derived from the word "Saraph" meaning "burn." Their function is to burn the false doctrine and convert man back to the righteous. It is said that their functions also include passing on information (drawn from the Neschamah at night, during sleep) to the Creator, in Atziluth, for the Seraphim are in the Holy of Holies or the Highest

---

99 See Wilhelm Reich, *Selected Writings* (Farrar, Straus and Giroux, New York, 1951).

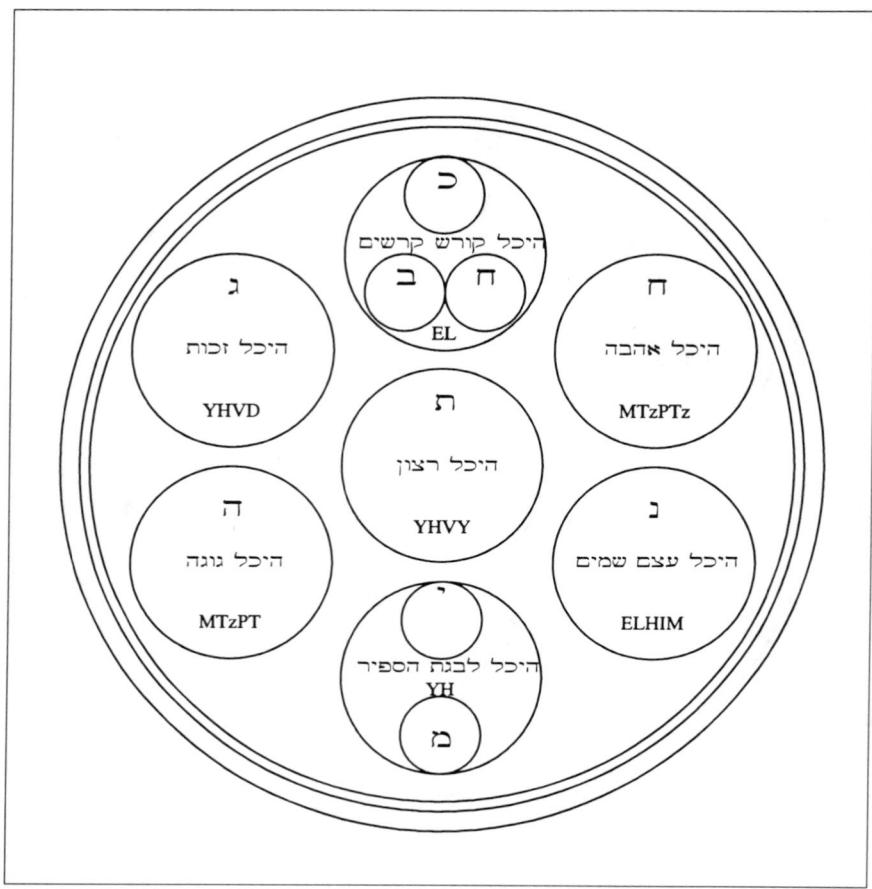

The Seven Heavens of Briah

heaven of Briah. They are four in number and correspond to the Four
Winds; they have six wings each, with each one corresponding to one day
of creation.

The Golden Dawn says of them:

> The Seraphim in the Vision of Issiah are described as hav-
> ing 6 wings: "With twain he covered his face, and with twain
> he covered his feet, with twain he did fly." That is, his synthe-
> sis is to be found in the Hexagram and in the idea of the 7,
> more especially dominating the planetary region. But the

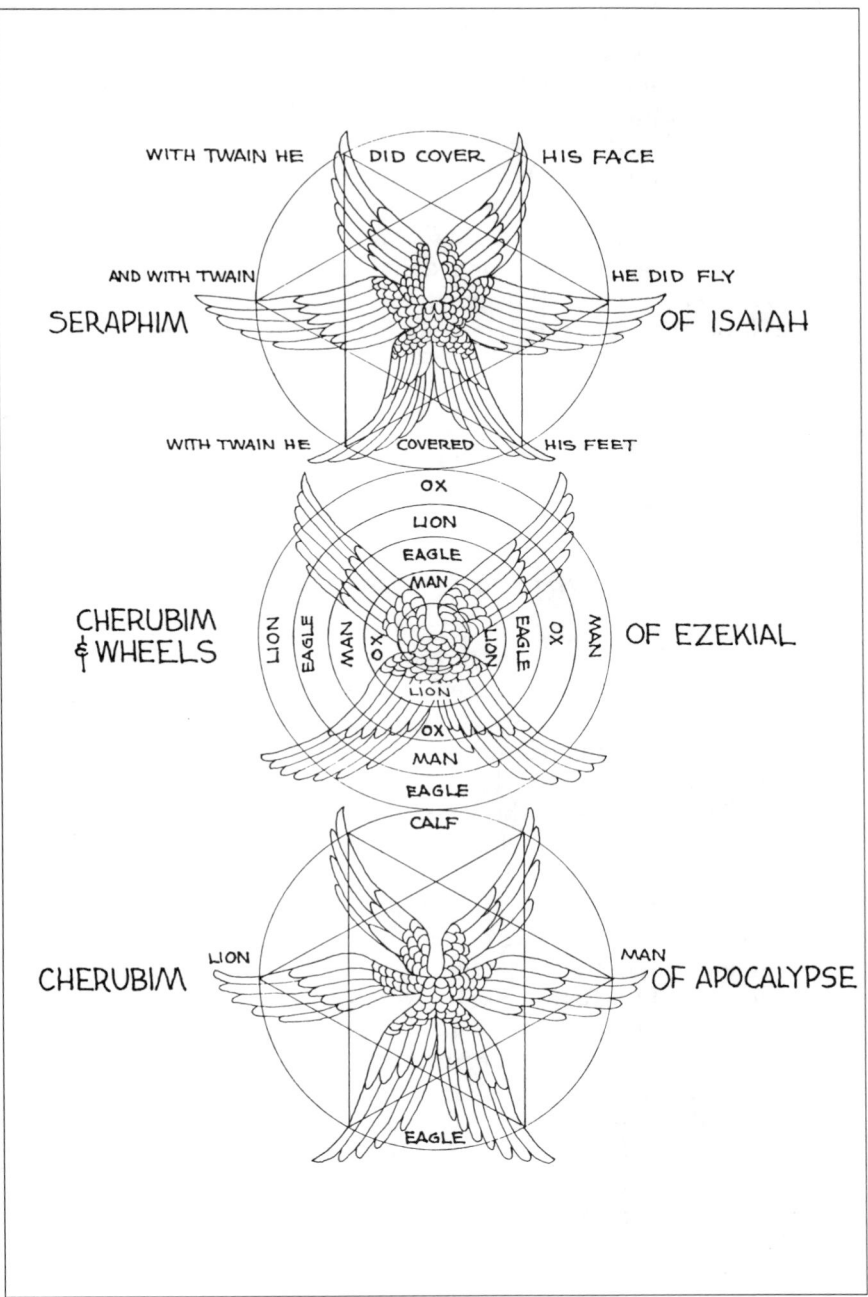

The Seraphim

Kerubim of Ezekiel each have four faces—those of the Lion, the Eagle, the man and the Bull—counterchanged with each other by revolution, whence the symbolic form of the wheels beside them wherein was the Spirit: and with two of the wings they their bodies, and were stretched upwards one to another. So the synthesis of the Kerubim is found in the revolving Cross, in the Pentagram, and the idea of one spirit dominating the Four Elements. But the Kerubim of St. John's vision in the Apocalypse are uncompounded, having single heads: but they have six wings, and thus unite with the powers of the seven and the four. And their cry is similar to that of the Seraphim of Isaiah: "Holy, Holy, Holy."

What the Golden Dawn was trying to do is reconcile the various visions of the Seraphim as one unit with the Kerubs being the lesser unit or lower part of the Seraphim proper.

SERPENT OF BRASS[165]

This is the Serpent Nehustan, which Moses made when the Children of Israel were bitten by the serpents of Fire in the Wilderness. It is the Serpent of the paths of the Tree. And he set it on a pole, that is, twined round the Middle Pillar of the Sephiroth. And the word used in the passage in Numbers 21, for "Fiery Serpents" is the same as the name of the Angels of Geburah, the same spelling, the same pointing Seraphim. Round the Middle Pillar of the Sephiroth, because that is the Reconciler between the Fires of Geburah or Severity and the Waters of Chesed or Mercy: and hence it is said in the New Testament that it is a type of Christ, the Reconciler. And the Serpent is of Brass, the metal of Venus, whose Sphere is called Nogah or External Splendour . . . And therefore it is said in the Zohar that, alone of the Shells is the Serpent Nogah found in Holiness, and he is called the Balance of Justice. Why then is he called the External of the False Splendour? Because he indeed uniteth the paths, but comprehendeth not the Sephiroth. nevertheless, he is also the Celestial Serpent of Wisdom. But the Serpent of Temptation is the Serpent of the Tree of Knowledge of Good and Evil, and not the Tree of Life.

---

[165] This is shown in the 4=7 ritual of Philosophus.

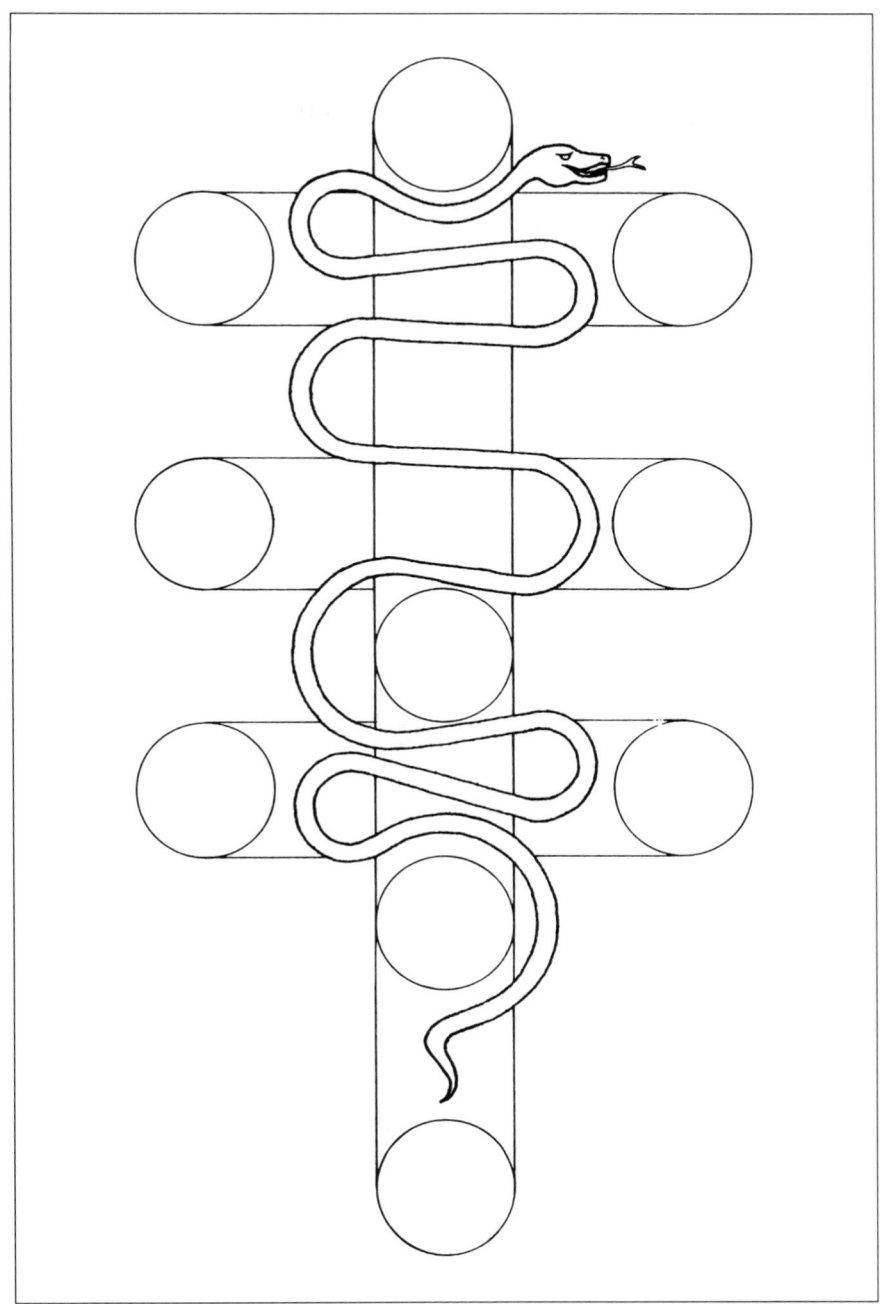

The Serpent of Brass

CHAPTER ELEVEN

Alchemy and the Kabbalah[166]

The subject of alchemy and its application to the Kabbalah and the teachings of the Golden Dawn has for many years been shrouded in mystery. Virtually no revelation has been made by former members of the Order who studied it. For all intents and purposes alchemy is the science of transmutation, whether it be animal, vegetable, or mineral. Israel Regardie was one of the first[167] to state the principles of alchemy in purely psychological terms and his book, *The Philosophers Stone*, which he published in 1938, actually predating the work on similar lines by Carl Jung published in his *Psychology and Alchemy*,[168] and *Mysterium Coniunctionis*. Regardie, as mentioned earlier, was an initiate of the Bristol Temple of the Stella Matutina, a successor of the Golden Dawn. Following his

---

[166] I have not included a breakdown of the modern Qabalah of Frater Albertus, *Qabalah of the Seven Rays*, which he based on the teachings of Lewis Spence and the Color Scales of the Golden Dawn and adapted them to alchemy. After studying Frater Albertus's *Qabalah* and related unpublished documents on the subject over the years, I find little in common with the traditional Kabbalah. In many respects Frater Albertus went his own way in developing the Qabalistic pulsation system he utilized for his Alchemical Paracelsus Organization.

[167] A member of the Golden Dawn, under the Mathers lineage, Langford Garstin, published a book *Secret Fire* in 1932 which leans towards to the psychological side of alchemy, but only in a very vague manner.

[168] Jung based this work on two lectures he delivered in 1935/36 for the *Eranos-Jahrbuch*, which Regardie had never seen.

time in the Order, he made the comment a number of times in print that he had seen no reference to practical alchemy in the Order.[169]

I am going to devote considerable space to this aspect of Kabbalistic work because of its importance within the Golden Dawn scheme, although, in fact, most Kabbalistic writers seem to gloss over or avoid it completely.

Within the Golden Dawn's Outer Order there are three areas where the initiate is introduced to Kabbalah as applied to alchemy. One is in the Second Knowledge Lecture where the metals are attributed to the planets as shown below.

The Names and Alchemical Symbols of the Three Principles of Nature are:

Sulphur	Salt	Mercury

The metals attributed to the planets are:

Saturn	Lead	Binah[170]
Jupiter	Tin	Chesed
Mars	Iron	Geburah
Sun	Gold	Tiphareth
Venus	Copper or Brass	Netzach
Mercury	Quicksilver	Hod
Moon	Silver	Yesod

This is the alchemical/Kabbalistic association the initiate has to comprehend and learn to apply along with two other associations taken from the book *Aesch Mezareph*.

---

[169] Ellic Howe's *Alchemist of the Golden Dawn* was really a bitter disappointment in terms of revealing the Golden Dawn's alchemical work, for it contains nothing but a series of letters to and from W. A. Ayton, alchemical matters being mentioned only briefly. Francis King in his *Ritual Magic in England* also includess a chapter on alchemy and the Golden Dawn.

[170] This final column of Sephirotic association was included in some temples and left out in others.

AESCH MEZAREPH[171] — PURIFYING FIRE

The *Aesch Mezareph*, or Purifying Fire, is in reality the only Zoharic text that refers directly to alchemy and the Kabbalah. Jewish Alchemy had been referred to by notable authors such as Thomas Vaughan (Eugenius Philalethes) yet the *Aesch Mezareph* was the first to put it into some sort of prospectus. In the *Zohar* proper there are some references to alchemical concepts,[172] but these are fragmented. In the Preface to the *Aesch Mezareph*, Westcott says:

> The Aesch Mezareph or Ash Metzareph, is only known to persons of Western Culture from the Latin translation found in a fragmentary condition in the work entitled *Kabala Denudata* by Knorr von Rosenroth, published at Salzbach in 1677–84. These volumes have a subtitle "Transcendental, Metaphysical and Theological Doctrines of the Hebrews," and they enshrine a Latin translation, with part of the Hebrew text and commentaries of the great Sohar or *Zohar*, "Book of Splendour." The Aesch Mezareph is still extant as a separate treatise in what is called the Hebrew language, but which is more properly Aramaic Chaldee: it was a companion volume to the *Chaldean Book of Numbers* so often referred to by H. P. Blavatsky.

There is no doubt that the *Aesch Mezareph* comes from the first volume of Rosenroth's work, which is in the form of a *Lexicon*,[173] and that it was fragmented and put into a single book form by *The Lover of Philalethes* in English in 1714. It has been suggested by numerous authors that this text is not a course in practical alchemy, but more of a discourse in rhetoric. Over the years I have had an opportunity of discussing this work from a practical viewpoint with a number of alchemists and am told that

---

[171] For a study on the practical side of alchemy as applied to this text see *Hermetic Journal*, vol.14, "The Alchemical Tree of Life," by Rafal T. Prinkle.

[172] Part 2, folio 249a–250b. Part 3, folio 23b–24b. Part 4, folio 171a–171b (this includes aspects of what could be considered herbal alchemy).

[173] Rosenroth stated that this portion of the Kabbalah Denudata had five sources:

1. *Garden of Pomegranates*.
2. *Gate of Light* by Rabbi Joseph Gikatilla ben Abraham.
3. *Kabala Recentior* by Rabbai Jizchak Loria.
4. Index plurimarium materiarum Cabalisticarum in ipso Libro Sohar propitarum.
5. Compendium Libri Cabalistico-Chymici, Aesch Metzareph dicti, de Lapide Philosphico.

The Tree of Metals (first version).

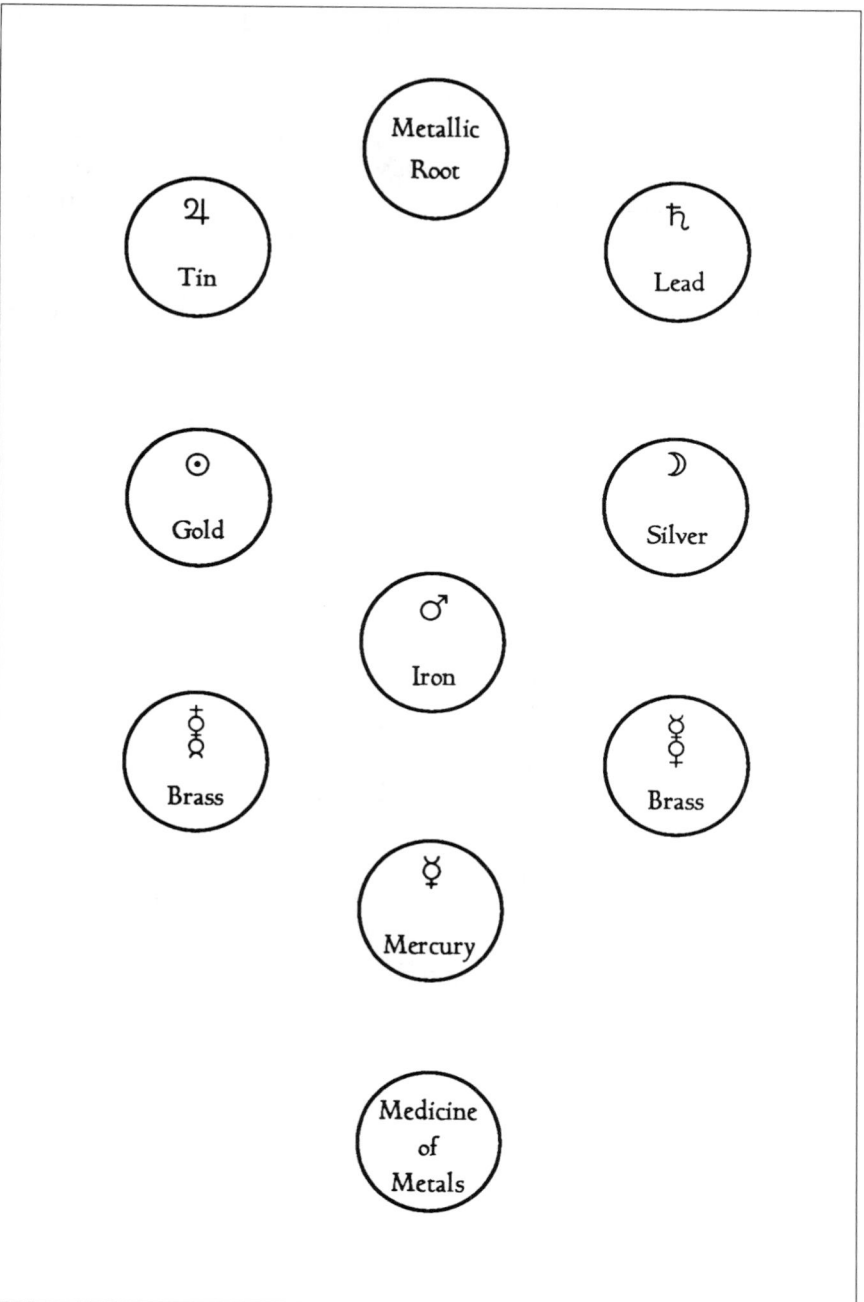

The Tree of Metals (second version).

if the text is read from start to finish then it is indeed hopeless, but if the text is read in parts then there are some experiments that can work on a practical level, but even these are only parts of experiments and not completed.

The dual associations of the metals with the Sephiroth are confusing and relate to various stages of the experiment. I must confess that I think that to introduce the student to these diagrams during ritual was a bad error of judgment by Mathers, and he would have done better to simply provide the standard associations of the Knowledge Lectures where associations are given to the Sephiroth.[174]

A rectification of this would be as follows:

Kether	Mercury
Chokmah	Sulphur
Binah	Salt
Daath	Lead
Chesed	Tin
Geburah	Iron
Tiphareth	Gold
Netzach	Copper
Hod	Quicksilver
Yesod	Silver
Malkuth	Metallic Root

There is no doubt that to take parts of a lexicon and try to make a book out of it can create difficulties, and this is apparent with the *Aesch Mezareph*. Yet it should be treated as a type of lexicon only, and nothing more, although each of its relevant parts does have some very important gleanings to give providing they are seen as parts and not the whole.

---

[174] I have placed Saturn to Daath for the sake of form but also because it is used there in the associations to the Hexagram Ritual of the Golden Dawn.

THE SEPHER YETZIRAH
AND ALCHEMY

Although the formation of the *Sepher Yetzirah* was discussed early in the book, we will now review parts of the text with an alchemical viewpoint in mind. While various authors have discussed how alchemy and the Kabbalah are related or not related, I have never seen any mention of the association of alchemy with one of the oldest of all the Kabbalistic books, when to my mind it is the most obvious. The previous section on the *Aesch Mezareph* has dealt with alchemy from the Sephirotic viewpoint, and now it is time to look at alchemy as seen from the PATHS—the Sephiroth are excluded.

The concept we are going to look at is very simplistic and involves alchemical steps or stages in a three-, seven- and twelvefold system.

Three-Stage System of Alchemy

The *Sepher Yetzirah* says:

> These Three Mothers did He produce and design, and combined them; and He sealed them as the three mothers in the Universe, in the year and in Man—both male and female. He caused the letter Aleph to reign in Air and crowned it, and combining it with the others He sealed it, as Air in the World, as the temperate (climate) of the Year, and as the chest (the lungs for breathing Air) in Man: the male with Aleph, Mem and Shin, the female with Shin, Mem and Aleph. He caused the letter Mem to reign in Water, crowned it, and combining it with the others formed the earth in the world, cold in the year, and the belly in man, male and female, the former with Mem, Aleph, Shin, the latter with Mem Shin, Aleph. He caused Shin to reign in Fire, and crowned it, and combining it with the others, sealed with it the heavens and the universe, heat in the year and the head in man, male and female.

Now at this point there is no indication which came first, just that there were three letters, each with its respective territory. These three letters then send their rays to the seven and the twelve letters. The Three letters correspond to the Three basic steps in alchemy which cover the process as a whole. These are the process of *Separation*, *Purification*, and *Cohobation*.

1. Aleph is the process of **Separation** of the Sulphur, Salt, and Mercury (regardless of the Kingdom concerned), the Three Vital Essences of the process.

2. Shin is analogous to the process of **Purification,** which takes the three components' parts and purifies them to a very high degree.

3. Mem is linked to the process of **Cohobation,** which is a series of successive distillations which unify the Three Principles of Sulphur, Salt, and Mercury and bring their vibration rate to the level required.

If these three stages are applied to a practical application, such as the making of a herbal alchemical tincture, they can be applied very generally, in the following manner.

1. Rectified or distilled alcohol is poured in a glass jar partly full of fresh herbs. This is the first stage of the Separation process (called Maceration) as the alcohol causes the oil to separate from the main body of the plant and float to the top. After a period of time the alcohol, that contains the Sulphur (oil), is then drained off into a distillation apparatus; then distillation takes place, thus separating the alcohol (Mercury) from the oil (Sulphur).

2. Purification occurs when the plant which had the alcohol drained from it is calcined to a white powder (salt) over a direct heat source. This is also where the Sulphur is evaporated to a hard substance and then calcined as above.

3. Cohobation is when the Mercury, Sulphur, and Salt are combined in a laboratory apparatus (such as a soxhlet) for further use, or simply placed together, which then forms the end result of the experiment, in this instance a tincture which is ready to be used for medicinal purposes.

---

[137] The Golden Dawn also adapted the Tarot Trump "Blasted Tower" to this theme.
[138] Part 1, folio 54–55a.

Seven-Stage System of Alchemy

These relate to the Double Letters and are in fact a further refinement of the above three-stage generalization, arranged in this order: Letter — Stage — Planet

1. Peh — Calcination — Mars
   Calcination is the process of reducing the size of the material worked with (Prima Materia—first matter) by fire, through four stages which can be seen by the color of the matter at each stage: The Blackening, Whitening, Yellowing, and Reddening. The first stage, the Blackening, is obtained by direct burning, while the other three stages are through the process of a consistent heat. Through this process pulverization occurs and impurities are removed which makes the matter ready for the next step.

2. Kaph — Sublimation — Jupiter
   Sublimation takes place when the matter is placed in a container (usually made of glass with a long neck above it) over a heated element. The vapor or essence is then extracted from the matter and remains in the top of the neck for a short time, then descends back down the tube to the matter (which is at the bottom of the flask) from which it was derived. This step actually covers the steps of separation and exaltation in alchemy. Part of the essence is taken from the matter, strengthened, then returned to it, changing the matter in its composition.

3. Daleth — Solution — Venus
   Solution is the aspect when the matter is dissolved in the liquid as a result of the previous step of sublimation.

4. Gimel — Putrefication — Moon
   Putrefication, to a certain extent, is still part of the dissolution process, where great care must be taken that the matter being dissolved must be stopped at a certain point in the experiment when complete separation has occurred, for at this critical level an entirely new substance has been formed or transmuted.

5. Beth — Distillation — Mercury
   Distillation covers other steps as well and relates to the separation of the spirit, through the vapor from the matter through a distillation train, with a receptacle at the end to catch the liquid. It is the separation of the volatile from the non-

volatile. It differs from the previous step of sublimation because the vapor is not returned to the matter which, in effect, has also changed in composition.

6. Tau — Coagulation[175] — Saturn
Coagulation is when all parts of the experiment are reunited and are brought back back to as solid state.

7. Resh — Tincture\Lapidication — Sun
This is the end result of the experiment where the matter can be increased in quantity.

The Twelve-Stage System.

These relate to the Twelve Simple Letters and are a further division of the seven stage system, arranged in this order: Letter — Stage — Sign

1. Heh — Calcination — Aries
The Calcination process differs only in the degree it is taken from the previous explanation of it. In this instance it is sim-ply a more refined process.

2. Vau — Fixation — Taurus
Fixation is the stabilization of a volatile matter or substance, generally done through Calcination.

3. Zain — Separation — Gemini
Separation is a phase that separates the pure from the impure, and also the component parts of the matter.

4. Cheth — Circulation — Cancer
Circulation is the process where heat circulates the liquid from the matter in a continuous uplifting movement. This contin-ues through varying states of the experiment (i.e., Dissolution, Coagulation, Digestion, Sublimation, Distillation, and Coho-bation). It is a method where the liquid is strengthened in vitality by being brought from the liquid to the gaseous state, then returned to the liquid once again.

5. Teth — Exaltation\Solution — Leo
This means to raise the vitality of the matter on the etheric or spiritual level.

---

[175] By Segregation and Comprehension.

6. Yod — Dissolution \ Subtilizing — Virgo
Dissolution is actually a part of the Putrefication process where the solid is reduced to a liquid but stops at the first phase of operation.

7. Lamed — Cohobation — Libra
Cohobation is a series of Distillations where a volatile substance is poured back over the matter. This process is repeated a number of times.

8. Nun — Digestion \ Ferment — Scorpio
Digestion is a process which through a mild heat the matter or substance gives up its vital essences. This process is also called Maceration. It is a process where the gross elements become much lighter as the essence is removed and to a certain extent Separation occurs.

9. Samech — Sublimation — Sagittarius
Sublimation takes place when the vapor is extracted from the matter and is driven upward into the upper part of the container. Like the previous step, it makes the spiritual part of the matter more ethereal in content.

10. Ayin — Coagulation \ Cibation — Capricorn
(Refer to the previous explanation.)

11. Tzaddi — Congelation — Aquarius
Congelation is a liquification of the materials used in the experiment to the consistency of water and letting them gradually produce a solid state.

12. Qoph — Conjunction \ Impregnate — Pisces
The Conjunction is the bringing together of the separated parts of the experiment into one homogenous commodity. It is the final step in which all component parts of the matter have been separated, strengthened, then placed back together, which results in a totally transmuted substance that is much stronger than when the experiment first started.

The steps of Multiplication and Projection are done after the work is completed and therefore not applicable to the above table.

A number of the associations here are not standard textbook quotes but are the results of a number of years of practical alchemical exploration. The entire process described here is one that works on a practical level. The *Sepher Yetzirah* is also allied to the mental process as well, for that is how the book was designed, yet when a theory holds a certain truth it can be applied almost on any level—whether it be mental, spiritual, or practical, and is the foundation for the concept of the Macrocosm and the Microcosm.

THE FIFTY GATES OF UNDERSTANDING

This section, which has been briefly mentioned earlier in the text, may be a surprise to find in the alchemical section. Within the past there have been some very weird and wonderful explanations of this document but, as I understand it, it is purely alchemical and is the skeletonic framework of and key to breaking down the alchemical manuscript "Homer's Golden Chain."[176] The text of this paper is related to the Sephirah of Binah—Understanding.

First Order: Elementary
1. Chaos, Hyle, The first matter
2. Formless, void, lifeless
3. The Abyss
4. Origin of the Elements
5. Earth (no seed germs)
6. Water
7. Air
8. Fire
9. Differentiation of qualities
10. Mixture and combination

Second Order: Decad of Evolution
11. Minerals differentiate
12. Vegetable principles appear
13. Seeds germinate in moisture

---

[176] Homers Golden Chain," was a manuscript that was given considerable attention at the 5=6 level of the Golden Dawn and was based on a translation by Pattinson, a prominent Golden Dawn and S.R.I.A member who was also an alchemist. This manuscript was never deemed official but was frequently referred to. In *Sword of Wisdom*, Ithel Colquhoun referred to the Kirchweger translation as the one being used in the Golden Dawn but this is in error; it was the Bacstrom version.

14. Herbs and Trees
15. Fructification in vegetable life
16. Origin of low forms of animal life
17. Insects and reptiles appear
18. Fishes, vertebrate life in the waters
19. Birds, vertebrate life in the air
20. Quadrupeds, vertebrate earth animals

Third Order: Decad of Humanity
21. Appearance of Man
22. Material human body
23. Human Soul conferred
24. Mystery of Adam and Eve
25. Complete Man as Microcosm
26. Gift of five human faces acting exteriorly
27. Gift of five powers of the Soul
28. Adam Kadmon, the Heavenly Man
29. Angelic beings
30. Man in the image of God

Fourth Order: World of Spheres
31. Moon
32. Mercury
33. Venus
34. Sol
35. Mars
36. Jupiter
37. Saturn
38. Firmament
39. Primum Mobile
40. Empyrean heaven

Fifth Order: The Angelic World
41. Ishim — Sons of Fire
42. Auphanim — Cherubim
43. Aralim — Thrones
44. Chashmalim — Dominions

45. Seraphim — Virtues
46. Malakim — Powers
47. Elohim — Principalitie
48. Beni Elohim — Angels
49. Cherubim — Archangels

Sixth Order: The Archetvpe

50. God. Ain Soph. He whom no mortal eye hath seen, and Who has been known to Jesus the Messiah alone.

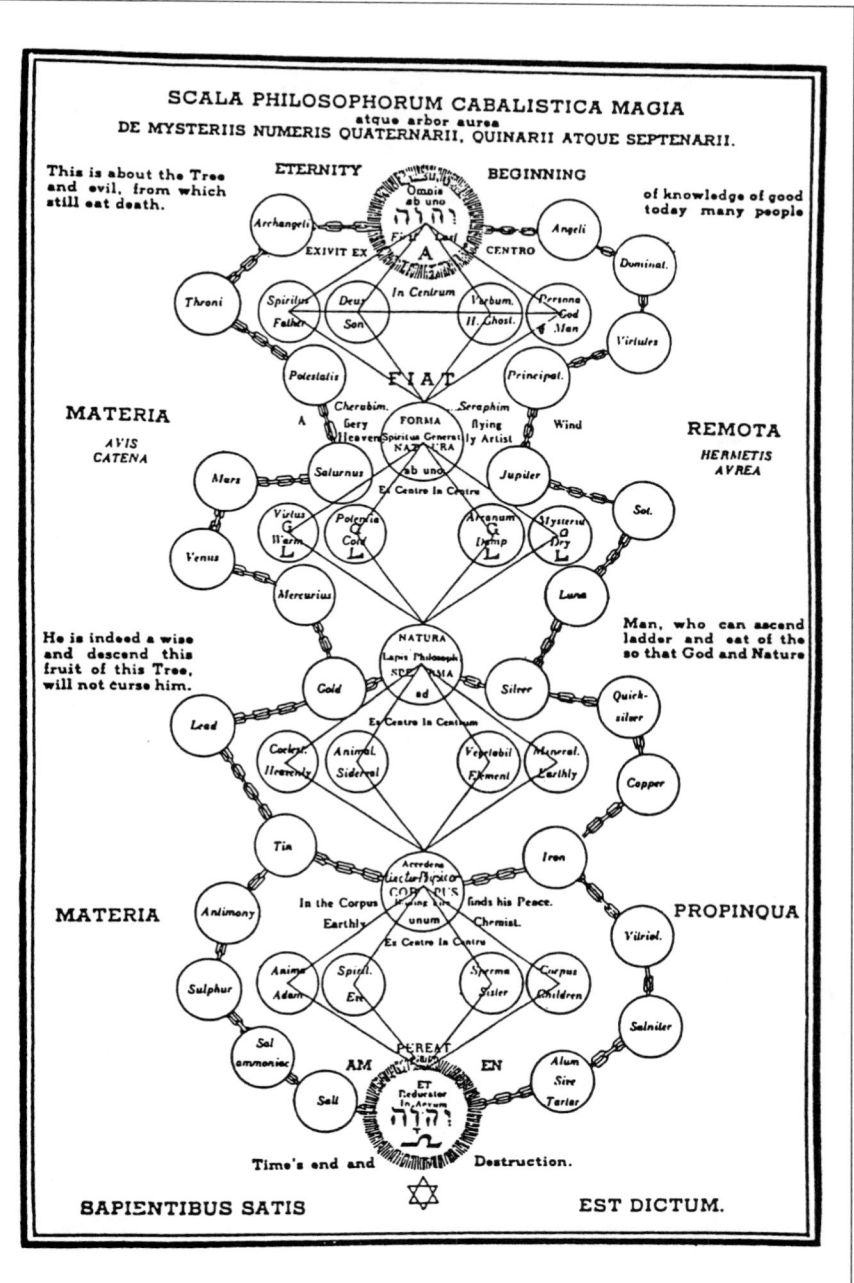

Homer's Golden Chain and the 50 Gates of Understanding.

CHAPTER TWELVE

The Twelve Tribes and Astrology

This lecture by Mathers has two versions. The only difference between them is the Enochian names being placed at the front of each Tribe in one version.

The Twelve Tribes[177] are thus attributed to the Twelve Zodiacal Signs and permutations of the Great and Holy Name of Tetragrammaton and the Angelic counterparts:

Sign	Letters of the Name	Tribe	Angel
Aries	Yod Heh Vau Heh	Gad	Melchidael
Taurus	Yod Heh Heh Vau	Ephraim	Asmodel
Gemini	Yod Vau Heh Heh	Manasseh	Ambriel
Cancer	Heh Vau Heh Yod	Issachar	Muriel
Leo	Heh Vau Yod Heh	Judah	Verchiel
Virgo	Heh Heh Vau Yod	Naphthali	Hamaliel
Libra	Vau Heh Yod Heh	Asshur	Zuriel
Scorpio	Vau Heh Yod Heh	Dan	Barchiel
Sagittarius	Vau Yod Heh Heh	Benjamin	Advachiel
Capricorn	Heh Yod Heh Vau	Zebulun	Hanael
Aquarius	Heh Yod Vau Heh	Reuben	Cambriel
Pisces	Heh Heh Yod Vau	Simeon	Amnitzel

---

[177] For an indepth study of theses tribes see "The Testament of the Twelve Patriarchs" in the *Forgotten Books of Eden*. Also Bullinger's *Witness to the Stars*.

Of these especially the Bull, the Lion, the Scorpion (but in good symbolism the Eagle) and the Man are to be noted as forming the Kerubic figures of Ezekiel and John. To these signs are allotted the tribes of Ephraim, Judah, Dan and Reuben, who, as we shall presently see, encamped towards the Cardinal Points around the Tabernacle of the Congregation, and as the leaders of the others. The signs of the Twins, the Fishes, and in a certain sense as a compounded figure,[178] the Centaur armed with a bow, are called bi-corporate or double-bodied signs. To these refer Manasseh, Simeon, and Benjamin. Manasseh was divided into two half-tribes with separate possessions (being the only tribe thus divided), and thus answers to the equal divisions of the sign of the Twins, Castor and Pollux, the Great Twin Brethren. Simeon and Levi are classed together, like the two Fishes in the Sign, but Levi is withdrawn later, to form as it were the binding and connecting link of the Tribes, as the priestly caste. Benjamin is the younger brother of Joseph, for Rachael had only these *two* sons, and is the only one of the Sons of Jacob who at his birth was called by two names, for Rachael called him "Ben oni," but his father Benjamin, and in the Sign of ♐ the two natures of Man and Horse are bound together in one symbol.

We shall find much light upon the connection between the Signs and the Tribes shown by the blessings of Jacob, and of Moses, from the former of which the Armorial bearings of the Twelve Tribes are derived.

Let us note also that as in the Tribes Levi was withdrawn, and the two Tribes of Ephraim and Manasseh substituted for the simple one of Joseph, so in the New Testament, Judas is withdrawn from the number of the twelve Apostles and his place filled by another, Matthias, who is chosen by lot to fill his place.

The following is the order by birth, of the children of Jacob:

Leah bore Reuben; Simeon; Levi, afterwards withdrawn, and Judah.
Bilhah (Rachel's maid) bore Dan and Naphtali.
Zilpah (Leah's maid) bore Gad and Asher.
Leah again bore Issachar, Zebulon and Dinah (a daughter).
Rachael bore Joseph, whose sons were Manasseh and Ephriam, but died at the birth of Benjamin, whom she wished to call Ben-oni.

---

[178] This is the Assyrian Fish God Oannes, who was half man and fish.

In the Wilderness the Tabernacle was pitched in the midst, and immediately surrounding it are the tents of Levi. At the distance towards the four cardinal points are the Standards of the Twelve Tribes erected there. *On the East,* Judah—the Kerubic Sign of the Lion, with Issachar and Zebulon (Leo, Cancer, Capricorn). *On the South,* Reuben— the Kerubic Sign of Man, Aquarius, with Simeon and Gad (Aquarius, Pisces and Aries). *On the West,* Ephraim—the Kerubic sign of the Bull, with Manasseh and Benjamin (Taurus, Gemini and Sagittarius). *On the North,* Dan, the Kerubic Sign of the Eagle, with Asher and Naphtali (Scorpio, Libra and Virgo). Save the Kerubic emblems the arrangement seems at first very confused, but when we notice the Maternal Ancestors of the Tribes, this confusion disperses, and we notice that at the East are three tribes descended from Leah, viz. Judah, Issachar, and Zebulon. Opposite to them, towards the West, three tribes descended from Rachel, viz. Ephraim, Manasseh and Benjamin. At the South are two descended from Leah, and one descended from Zilpah, viz. Reuben, Simeon and Gad, and at the North, two descended from Bilhah and one descended from Zilpah; viz. Dan, Naphtali and Asher. Here two Tribes descended from Zilpah, Gad, and Asher, are the only ones separated, and placed in opposition to each other, for these are the two signs of the Equinoxes.

The substitution of the two tribes of Ephraim and Manasseh for the single one of Joseph is given in Genesis 48, where Jacob blessed them prior to the general blessing of the Tribes, stating at the same time that Ephraim, though the younger, should take precedence over Manasseh;

> And Jacob said unto Joseph . . . And now thy two sons, Ephraim and Manasseh which were born unto thee in the land of Egypt before I came unto thee in Egypt, are mine; as Reuben and Simeon they shall be mine. And thy issue which thou begettest after them shall be thine and shall be called after the name of their brethren in their inheritance. . . . Moreover I have given unto thee one portion above of thy brethren.[179]

---

[179] He becomes the ancestor of two tribes instead of one.

Let us now notice the blessings of Jacob and Moses, and compare them with the Signs of the Zodiac attributed to each Tribe. We shall take them in the Zodiacal order.

Of Gad (Aries), Jacob says, "Gad, a troop shall overcome him, but he shall overcome at the last." Moses says, "Blessed be he that enlargeth Gad: he dwelleth as a lion, and teareth the arm with the crown of the head, and he provideth the first part for himself because there, in a portion of the law-giver, was he sealed; and he came with the heads of the people, he executed the justice of the Lord, and his judgements with Israel." The armorial bearings of Gad are, white, a troop of cavalry. All this coincides well with the martial and dominant nature of Aries, the only one of the twelve signs in which the superior planets alone bear sway, for it is the House of Mars, exaltation of Sun and triplicity of Sun and Jupiter. The symbolism of the Lion is also proper to Aries on account of its solar, fiery and martial nature.

Of Ephraim and Manasseh (Taurus and Gemini), classed together under their father's name, Jacob says, "Joseph is a fruitful bough, even a fruitful bough by a well, whose branches run over the wall; the archers have surely grieved him and shot at him, and hated him: but his bow abode in strength, and the arms of his hands were made strong by the hands of the mighty God of Jacob; (from thence is the shepherd, the stone of Israel): Even by the God of thy father, who shall help thee, and by the Almighty who shall bless thee with blessings of Heaven above, blessings of the deep that lieth under, blessings of the breasts and of the womb: the blessings of thy father have prevailed above the blessings of my progenitors unto the utmost bound of the everlasting hills: they shall be on the head of Joseph, and on the crown of the head of him who was separate from his brethren." Moses says, "Blessed of the Lord be his land, for the precious things of heaven, for the dew, and for the deep that coucheth beneath, and for the precious fruits brought forth by the Sun, and for the precious things put forth by the moon, and for the chief things of the lasting hills. And for the precious things of the earth, and the fullness thereof, and for the good will of him that dwells in the bush: let the blessing come upon the head of Joseph, and upon the top of the head of him that was separate from his brethren. His glory is like the firstling of a bullock, and his horns are like the horns of unicorns: with them he shall push the people together to the ends of the earth, and they are the ten thousands of Manasseh."

The Armorial Bearings of Ephraim are: Green, an Ox. Those of Manesseh are flesh-colour, a Vine by a Wall. All this refers to the natures of Taurus and Gemini, the firstling of the bullock and the earthy nature of the sign, shown by the hills, to Taurus while the archers over Manasseh, as Sagittarius, the sign of the Archer, is in opposition to Gemini.

Of Issachar, Cancer, Jacob says—"Issachar is a strong ass couching down between two burdens: and he saw that rest was good, and the land that it was pleasant, and he bowed his shoulder to bear, and became a servant under tribute." Moses says—"Rejoice Issachar, in thy tents . . . and they shall suck of the abundance of the seas." The armorial bearings of Issachar are—Blue, and an ass crouching beneath its burden. This coincides with the peaceful nature of the quiet and watery sign of Cancer.

Of Judah, Leo, Jacob says, "Judah, thou art he whom thy brethren shall praise: thy hand shall be in the neck of thine enemies; thy father's children shall bow down before thee. Judah is a lion's whelp: from the prey, my son, thou art gone up; he stooped down, he couched as a lion, and as an old lion; who shall rouse him up? The sceptre shall not depart from Judah, nor a lawgiver from between his feet, until Shiloh come; and unto him shall the gathering of the people be. Binding his foal unto the vine, and his ass's colt unto the choice vine; he washed his garments in wine, and his clothes in the blood of grapes: his eyes shall be red with wine, and his teeth white with milk." Moses says, "This is the blessing of Judah, and he said, Hear, Lord, the voice of Judah, and bring him unto his people, let his hands be sufficient for him and be thou an help to him from his enemies." The armorial bearings of Judah are—Scarlet, a lion rampant. All this well agrees with the regal and leonine nature of the Sign. "Binding the ass's colt unto the choice vine" may allude to the ass of Issachar, Cancer, lying between Judah, Leo, and the vine of Manasseh, Gemini.

Of Naphtali, Scorpio, Jacob says, "Naphtali is a hind let loose, he giveth goodly words." Moses says, "O Naphtali satisfied with favour, and full with the blessings of the Lord, possess thou the West and the South." The armorial bearings of Naphtali are—Blue, a hind.

Of Asher, Libra, Jacob says, "Out of Asher his bread shall be fat, and he shall yield royal dainties." Moses says, "Let Asher be blessed with children, let him be acceptable to his brethren, and let him dip his foot in oil. Thy shoes shall be iron and brass, and as thy days, so shall thy strength be." The armorial bearings of Asher are Purple, a Cup. All this coincides with the nature of Venus and Libra, while the feet refer to the sign of Pisces, which rule the feet, and in which Venus is exalted. Iron and Brass are the metals of the friendly planets Mars and Venus.

Of Dan, Scorpio, Jacob says—"Dan shall judge his people as one of the tribes of Israel. Dan shall be a serpent by the way, an adder in the path, that biteth the horse's heels, so that his rider shall fall backward. I have waited for thy salvation, O Lord." Moses says, "Dan is a lion's whelp, he shall leap from Bashan." The armorial bearings of Dan are Green, an Eagle. These things fit with the martial and fierce nature of this sign, in which Mars principally bears sway. To the sign of Scorpio, the Egyptians attributed the Serpent, and also Typhon, the Slayer of Osiris, and on this account they call it the "Accursed Sign." In good symbolism it is generally represented by the Eagle. The horse's heels which the Serpent bites are found in the Centaur figure of Sagittarius which follows Scorpio in the Zodiac.

Of Benjamin, Sagittarius, Jacob says, "Benjamin shall ravin as a wolf: in the morning he shall devour the prey, and at night he shall divide the spoil." Moses says—"The beloved of the Lord shall dwell in safety by him; and the Lord shall cover him all the day long, and he shall dwell between his shoulders." The armorial bearings of Benjamin are—Green, a Wolf. These suit the character of Sagittarius, partly keen, partly of the nature of Jupiter, and partly brutal.

Of Zebulon, Capricorn, Jacob says—"Zebulon shall dwell at the haven of the sea, and he shall be for a haven of ships, and his border shall be unto Sidon.'" Moses says, "Rejoice Zebulon in thy going out, and Issachar in thy tents, they shall call the people unto the mountain, there they shall offer sacrifices of righteousness, for they shall suck of the abundance of the sea, of the treasures hid in the sands." This suits well the tropical, earthy and water signs of Capricorn and Cancer. The armorial bearings of Zebulon are—Purple, a Ship.

Of Reuben, Aquarius, Jacob says—"Reuben, thou art my firstborn, my might, and the beginning of my strength, the excellency of dignity and the excellency of power. Unstable as water, thou shalt not excel, because thou wentest up to thy father's bed, then defiledst thou it; he went up to my couch."

Moses says—"Let Reuben live and not die, and let not his men be few." The armorial bearings of Reuben are—Red, a man. "Unstable as water" is still shown in the undulating hiero-glyphic which marks this aerial and brilliant, but often super-ficial sign of the Water-Bearer.

Of Simeon and Levi, Pisces, Jacob says—"Simeon and Levi are brethren; instruments of cruelty are in their habitations. O my soul, come not thou into their secret, unto their assembly, mine honour, be not thou united: for in their anger they slew a man, and in their selfwill they digged down a wall. Cursed be their anger, for it was fierce; and their wrath, for it was cruel: I will divide them in Jacob, and scatter them in Israel." This alludes to their smiting Shalem, the city of Hamor and Shechem, and slaying the latter because they had carried off Dinah, the daughter of Leah. Moses says of them—"Let thy Thummim and thy Urim be with thy Holy One, whom thou didst prove at Massah, and with whom thou didst strive at the waters of Meribah; who said unto his father and his mother, I have not seen him; neither does he acknowledge his brethren, nor knew his children; for they have observed thy word, and kept thy covenant. They shall teach Jacob thy judgments and Israel thy law: and they shall put incense before thee, and whole burnt sacrifice upon thine altar. Bless, Lord, his sub-stance, and accept the works of his hands; smite through the loins of them that rise against him, and of them that hate him, that they rise not again." The armorial bearings of Simeon are Yellow, a Sword.

These are the blessings of the twelve tribes of Israel, whose names were engraven upon the twelve stones of the High Priest's breastplate, upon which, according to some traditions, certain flashes of light appeared playing over certain of the let-ters, and thus returning the answer of the Deity to the consul-ter of the Oracle by Urim.

By comparing these blessings with the nature of the Signs attributed to the particular tribes, we have been thus enabled to trace more or less clearly the connection between them, and also the derivation of the armorial bearings ascribed to them in Royal Arch Freemasonry.[180]

---

[180] This ends the Mathers transcription.

CHAPTER THIRTEEN

Literal Kabbalah

The following is taken from Wynn Westcott's *Introduction to the Study of the Kabalah*, which was widely used in the Golden Dawn as a type of unofficial knowledge lecture. Though out of print today, it still has as much value as when it was first published. The literal Qabalah is referred to in several places, and therefore a knowledge of its leading principles is necessary. It is divided into three parts: GMTRIA, Gematria; NVTRIQVN, Notariqon; and ThMVRH, Temura. I originally found this paper among study lectures for the 4=7 grade at Whare Ra.

> GEMATRIA was a mode of interpretation by which a name or word having a certain numerical value was deemed to have a relation with some other words having the same number; thus certain numbers became representative of several ideas, and were considered to be interpretative one of the other. For example, Messiah spelled MShICh, numbered 358 and so does the phrase IBA ShILH, Shiloh shall come; and so this passage in Genesis 49 v.10, was considered be a prophecy of the Messiah: note that Nachash NChSh, the Serpent of Moses, is also 358. The letter Shin, Sh, 300, became an emblem of divinity by corresponding with Ruach Elohim, RUCh ALHIM, the Spirit of the Living God.

NOTARICON, or abbreviation, is of two forms, one word is formed from the initial and final letters of one or more words, or the letters of one name are taken as the initials or finals of the words of a sentence. For example, in Deut. 30 v. 12, Moses asks "Who shall go up for us to Heaven?" The initial letters of the original words MI IOLH LNV HShMILH, form the word MILH, mylah, which means circumcision, and the final letters are IHVH, the name Jehovah: hence it was suggested that circumcision was a feature of the way to God in heaven.

Amen, AMN, is from the initials of Adonai melekh namen. "The Lord and the faithful king"; and the famous Rabbinic word of power used for talismans, AGLA, is formed of the initials of the words "Ateh gibur leolam Adonai." "The lord ever powerful," or "Tu potens in soeculum Domine."

TEMURA is a more complex procedure, and has led to an immense variety of curious modes of divination: the letters of a word are transposed according to certain rules with many limitations: or again, the letters as arranged by a definite scheme, often shown in a diagram. For example, a common form was to write one-half of the alphabet over the other in reverse order, and so that the first letter A was placed by the last T, and B by Shin, and so on. On this plan the word Shesnak of Jeremiah 12 v. 26, is said to mean babel: this permutation was known as ATBSh. On this principle we find twenty-one other possible forms named in order ALbat, Abgat: the complete set was called "The combination of Tziruph." Other forms were rational, right, averse and irregular, obtained from a square of 22 spaces in each direction, that is of 404 secondary squares, and then putting a letter in each square in order up and down, and then reading across or diagonally, etc. Of this type is the so-called "Kabbalah of the Nine Chambers" of the Mark Masons.

300	30	3	200	20	2	100	10	1
000	00	0	000	00	0	000	00	0
Sh	L	G	R	K	B	Q	I	A
600	60	6	500	50	5	400	40	4
000	00	0	000	00	0	000	00	0
M(f)	S	V	K(f)	N	H	Th	M	D
900	90	9	800	80	8	700	70	7
000	00	0	000	00	0	000	00	0
Tz(f)	Tz	T	P(f)	P	Ch	N(f)	O	Z

A further development of the numerical arts was shown by the modés of Contraction and ·Extension; thus Jehovah, IHVH 26, was extended to IVD-HA-VV-HA and so l0, 5, 6, 5 or 26 became 20, 6, 12, 6, or 44. By extension Zain, z. 7, became 1, 2, 3, 4, 5, 6 and 7 or 28; or 28 was regarded as 2 and 8 or 10. The Tetragrammaton, Jehovah 26 was also at times regarded as 2 and 6 or 8: so El Shaddai, God Almighty. Al ShDI, 1, 30, 300, 4, l0, was 345 then 12 then 3, a trinity. A· quaint conceit was that of the change of spelling of the names of Abraham and Sara: at first Abram ABRM and Sari ShRI, became ABRHM and ShRH: they were 100 and 90 years old and were sterile: now H, Heh, was deemed of a fertile type, and so the letter H was added to ABRAM, and the Yod I, converted into an H of the name SARAI.

A MODERN APPROACH TO THE KABBALAH

Without doubt today the modern leaning toward the Kabbalah is through psychology and adopting what I prefer to call the "Inner Space Syndrome." Not that it is wrong to look at the Kabbalah from the viewpoint of different levels of consciousness or states of awareness, but, generally speaking, those that prefer this way tend to ignore the original approach of the religious devotee who tries to know his God through this method. An ideal situation would be to take the traditional approach of Rabbi Kaplan and marry it with that of Zev ben Halevi, if this could be done.

As a hermeticist, if there is such a word, I prefer to use both aspects when and where I need them, and this generally is where the Western Kabbalist seems to be heading. As we have seen in this volume, the Golden Dawn goes yet a step further by using the Kabbalah in magical ritual, which some of the old Jewish sects possibly did but in a much different manner. There is an old saying that "there is nothing new under the sun." Writers such as Edward Hoffman[181] have well and truly pointed this fact out to us, for many of the old mystical ways resemble Indian Tantric techniques and modern magical practices adopted by modern occultists, such as Kenneth Grant and his Typhonian OTO.

---

[181] See *Way of Splendor*.

All of these are, of course, tailored to fit the requirements of the particular individual or sect. The Kabbalah is an extremely versatile concept to familiarize oneself with, providing the dogma of the school we study under is considered as a guideline only, and the Higher Self is given free rein to explore other dimensions using a Kabbalistic framework.

Though I have tried to present the Golden Dawn viewpoint (which is of course as subjective as its practitioners), this too is changing, with modern studies of the Kabbalah being introduced today. Writers such as Regardie and Halevi have both added extra dimensions to the Kabbalah that cannot be ignored. The Golden Dawn will continue to grow and expand on its teachings, as the Kabbalistic viewpoint of 100 years ago is not necessarily what is taken today or even 100 years from now.

It is rather surprising to note how many of those who study the Golden Dawn tradition feel that the viewpoint of the Order goes only as far as the Rituals, the Knowledge Lectures, and the Flying Rolls,[182] then stops. At Whare Ra Temple in New Zealand there were literally stacks of lectures on the Kabbalah that were given out in Temple over a 60-year period; many of them have never been published. A number of these, mainly being Zoharic quotes, have been included in this book, but unfortunately there were a number destroyed. Many of these same documents were also given out in Golden Dawn lectures as early as the early 1890s by various Golden Dawn temples, while a number were added later.

While visiting Los Angeles in 1988, I was pleasantly surprised to find yet further dimensions of the Kabbalah given in a series of lectures by the Chief of the Los Angeles Golden Dawn Temple, Laura Jennings-Yorke, who presented the day-to-day aspects of the Kabbalah in a refreshingly clear and concise manner and in a style of her own which, no doubt, was well suited to the American temperament. It is new ground like this that brings the teachings of the Kabbalah to the masses in a more readily acceptable form than either the Traditionalist or the Psychological viewpoint. Both the teachings of Dion Fortune and Paul Foster Case, though written in the first half of this century, also bear out this fact.

Kabbalistic doctrine, no matter which school one studies, is a continually evolving process that should be kept abreast of 20th- and 21st-century developments and must not be left solely to 13th-century

---

[182] See *Astral Projection, Ritual Magic and Alchemy*, edited by Francis King.

rhetoric; though, by the same token, it should not be solely ignored either. The Kabbalah is a living Tree with its own growth organisms and which in every generation bears its own style of fruit, whether forbidden or otherwise, so that all can gain insight from its teachings.

APPENDIX

Seals of the Schemhamphoresch

These seals[183] were given out to some members of the Golden Dawn at 5=6 Grade or Inner Order level. They were used at Whare Ra Temple in New Zealand and had no associated documentation with them as to their origin. Some years ago I was sent a copy of a set of seals in the handwriting of Mathers, which were almost identical to the ones here save the circular border. The Mathers paper had the notation "By the Great Magician Blaise Viginaire – A.R. 2494."

There were three ways to use these seals. The first was to use them on talismans for additional potency. The second was for evocation work where the angel of the seal is summoned to perform a desired task. The third method was to scry the sigils for astral work in experiencing these potencies to see their full potential. My old mentor from Whare Ra, Jack Taylor, informed me that there was a small paper on these seals, written by Mathers, but he had only seen the original copy back in the 1930s. The three methods of study of them that I have advocated above were the basis of that paper, and Taylor simply made some condensed notes on it during a lecture at Whare Ra.

---

183   Also see the Goetia, one of the parts of the Lesser Key of Solomon (which is included in many publications to-date, including Waite and Crowley) for what can be called the mirror image of these angels along with associated seals. The Grimoire of Armadel and the The Key of Solomon The King, both edited by Mathers, also throw additional light on how these seals can be studied.

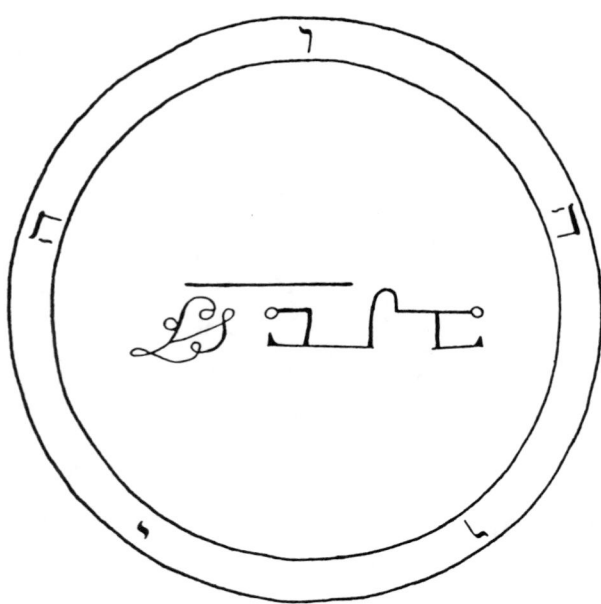

1. VAHUAIH

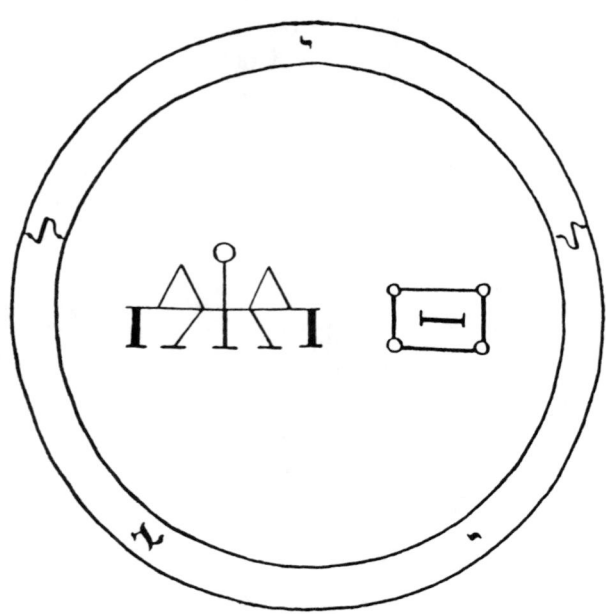

2. YELAVIEL

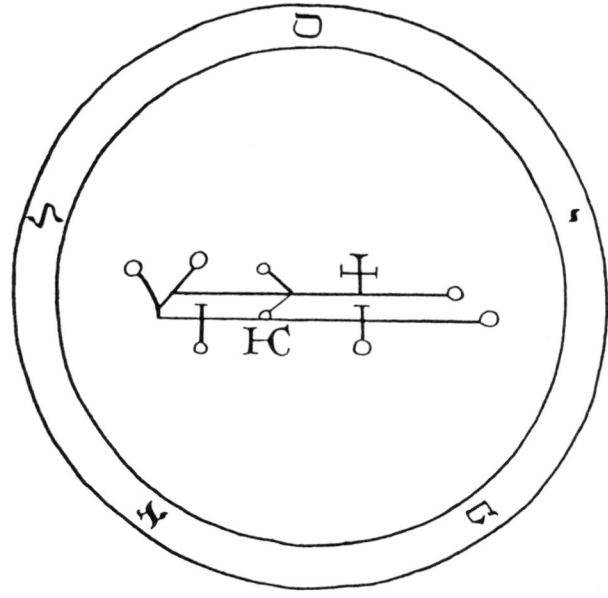

3. SATIEL

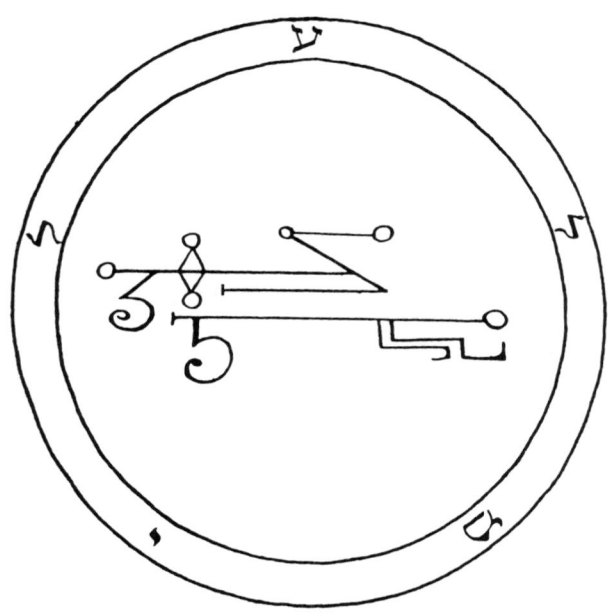

4. NGHELAMIAH

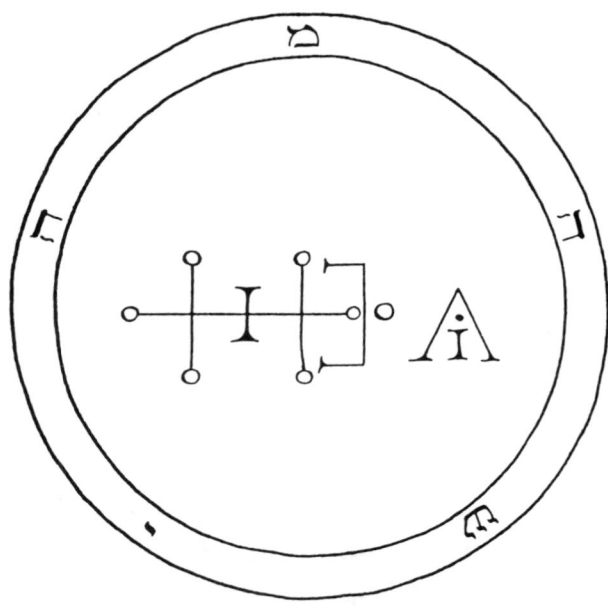

5. MAHASIAH

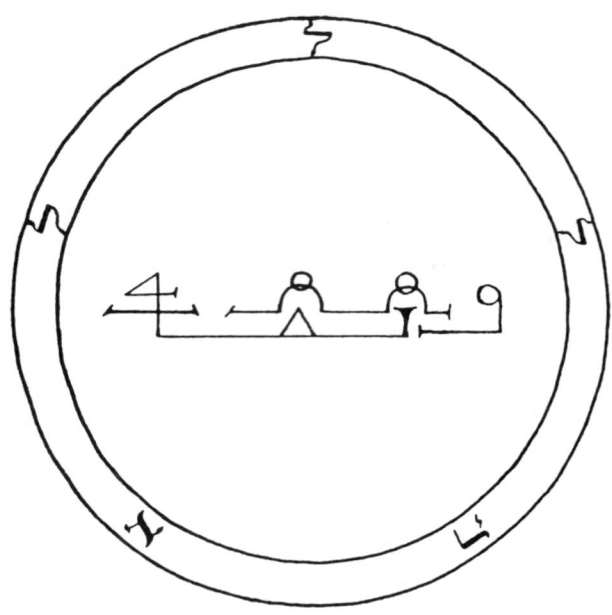

6. LELAHEL

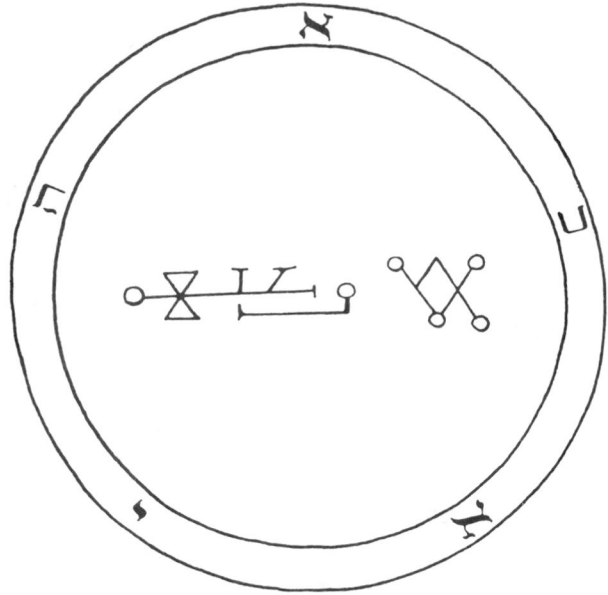

7. AKAIAH

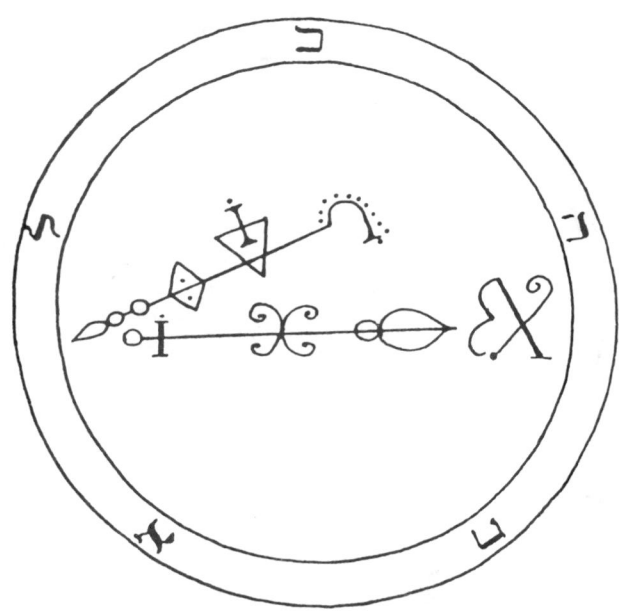

8. KEHETHEL

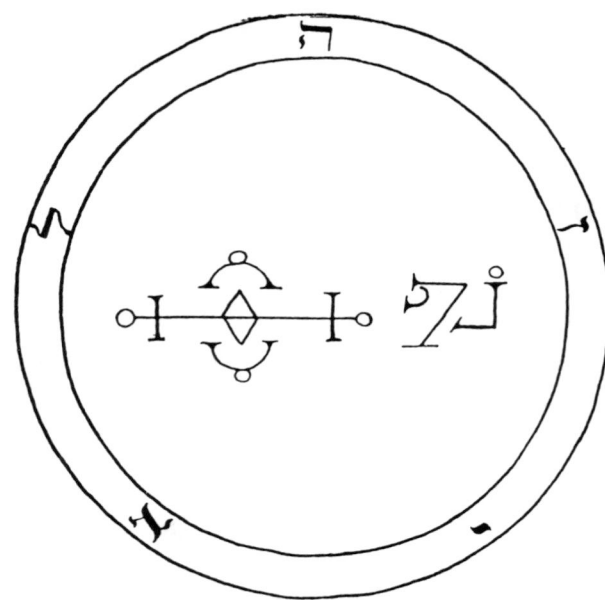

9. HAZEYAEL

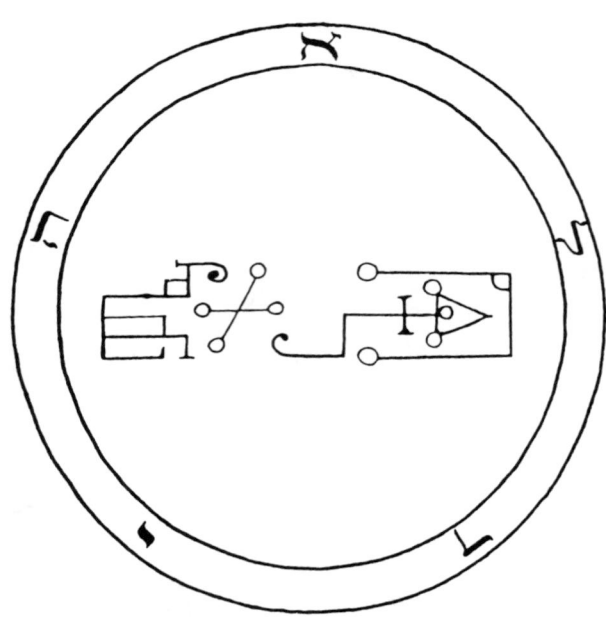

10. ELDIAH

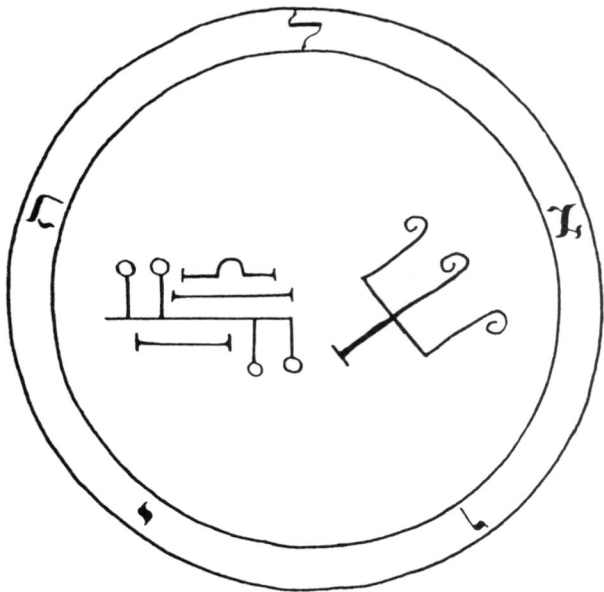

11. LEVIAH

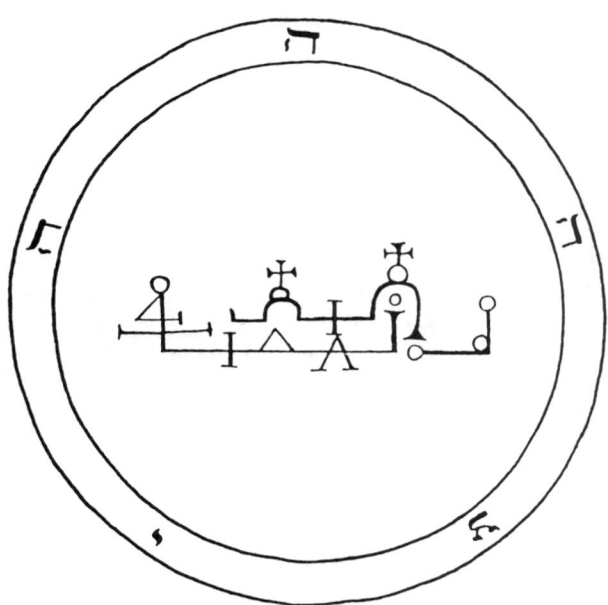

12. HIHAIAH

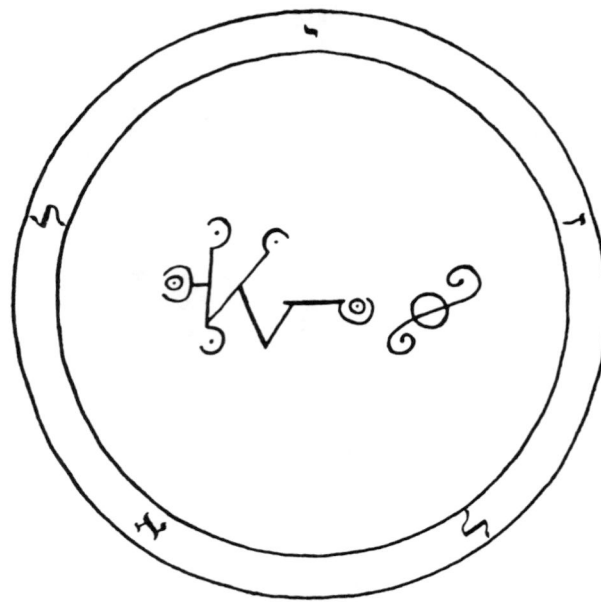

13. IEZALEL

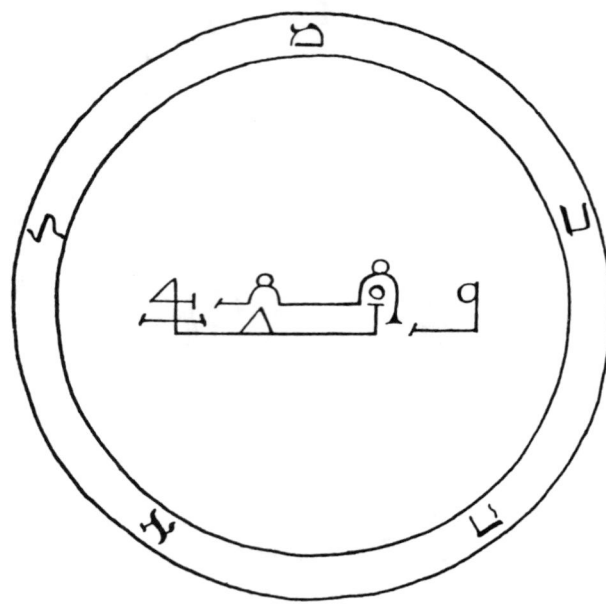

14. MEBANAEL

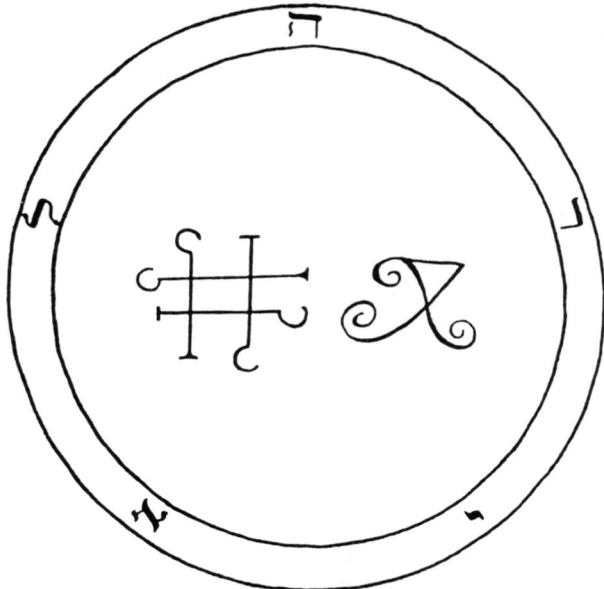

15. HARAYEL

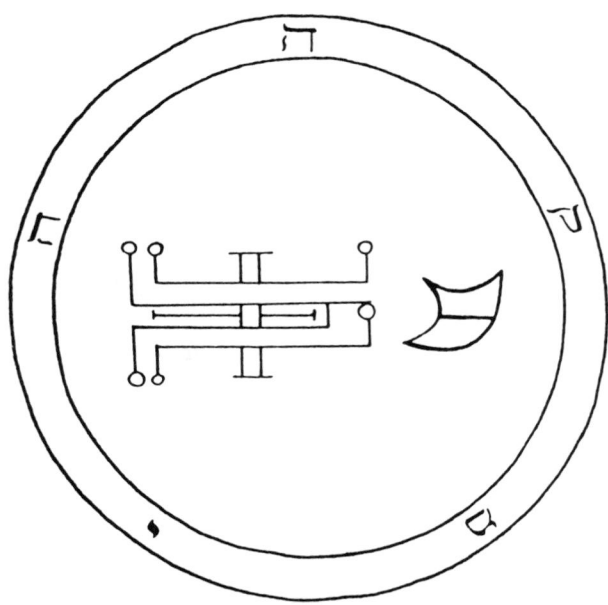

16. HOQAMIAH

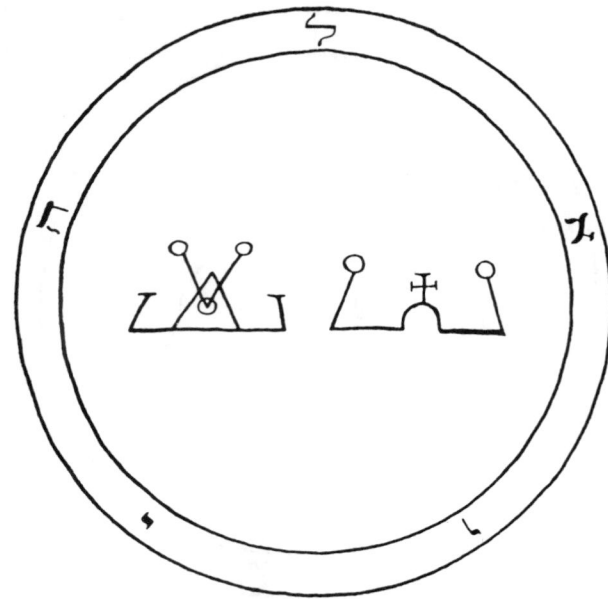

17. LAVIAH

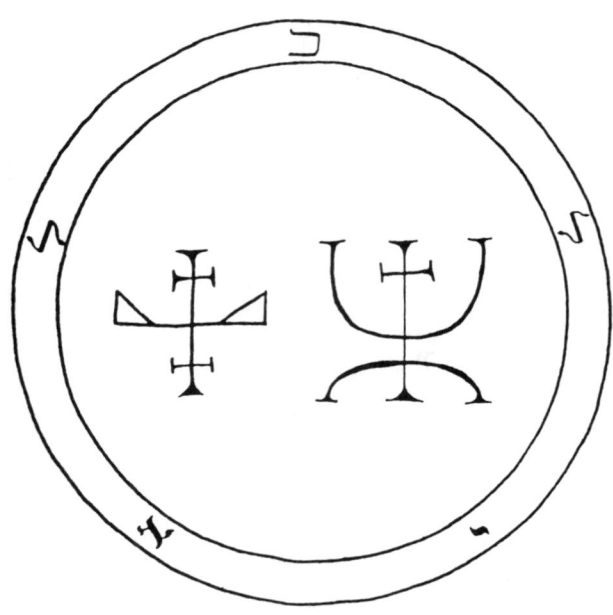

18. KELIEL

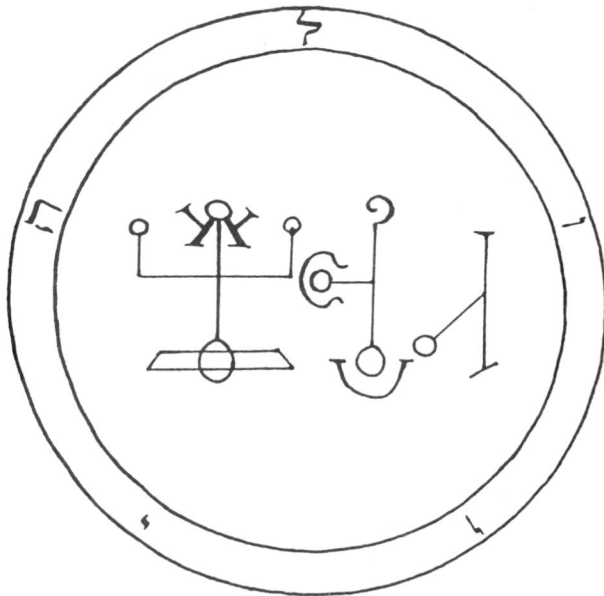

19. LIVOIH

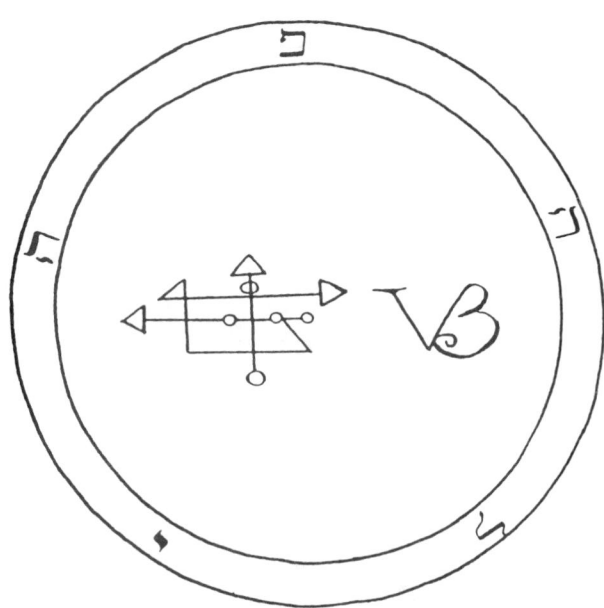

20. PEHELIAH

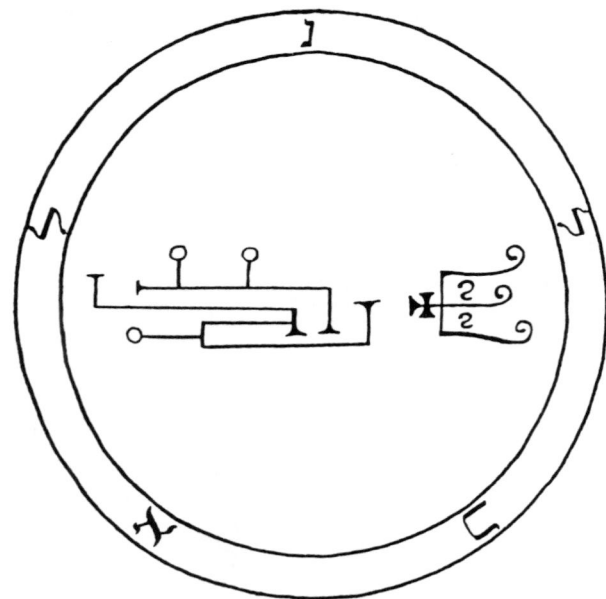

21. NELAKHEL

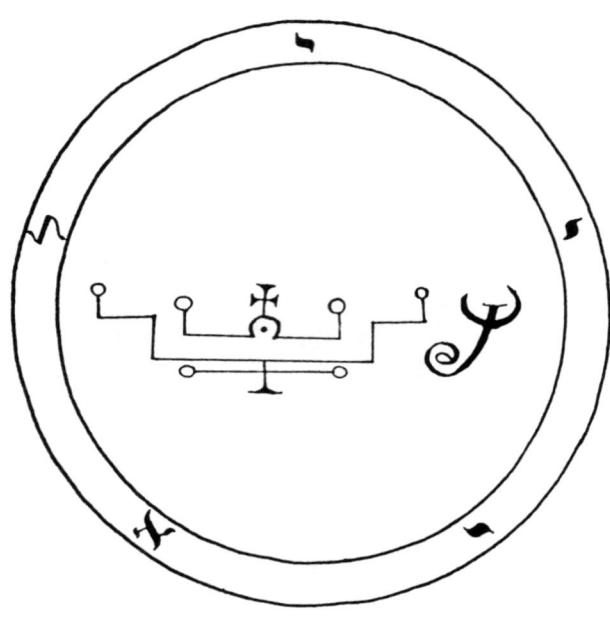

22. YEIAEL

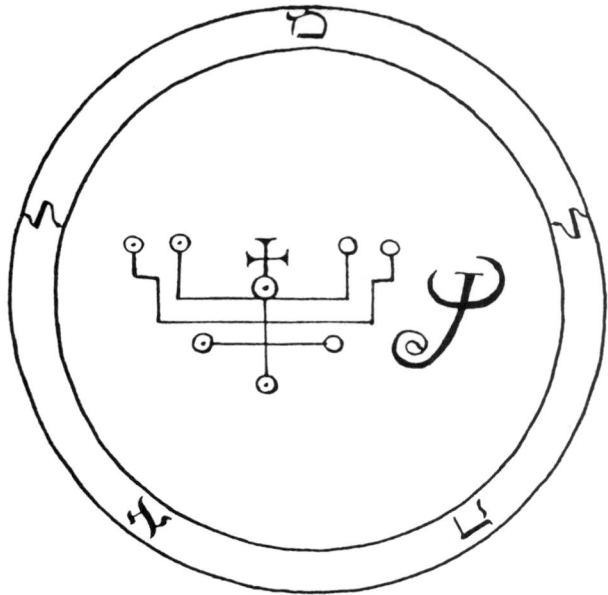

23. MALAHEL

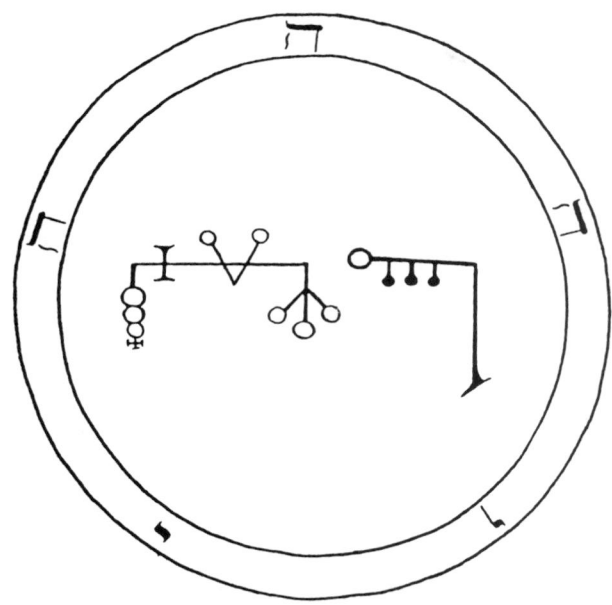

24. HAHAUIAH

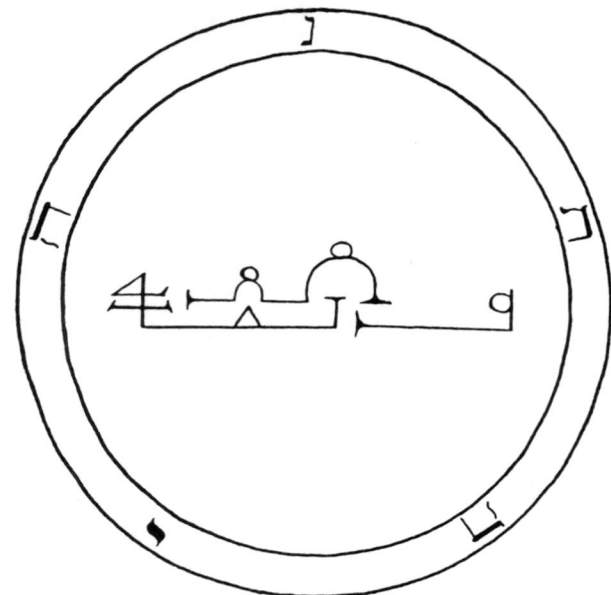

25. NETHHIAH

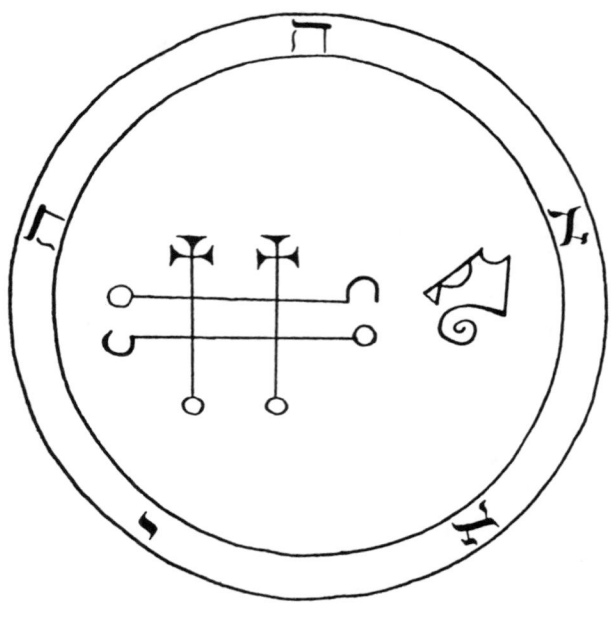

26. HEEIAH

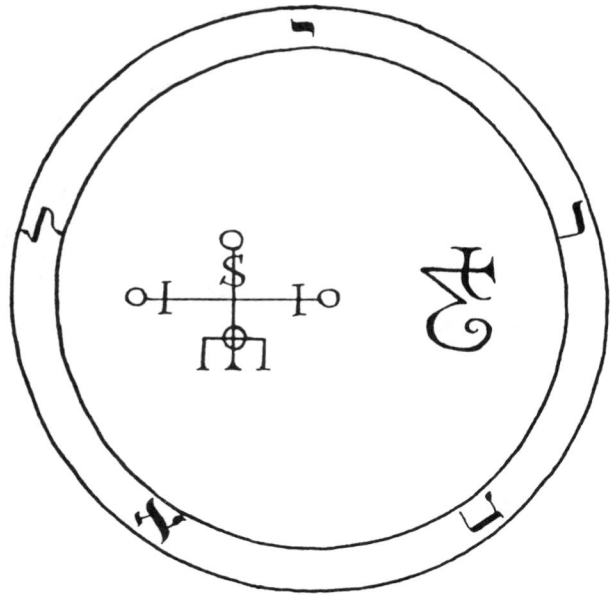

27. IRTHEL

28. SEHAIAH

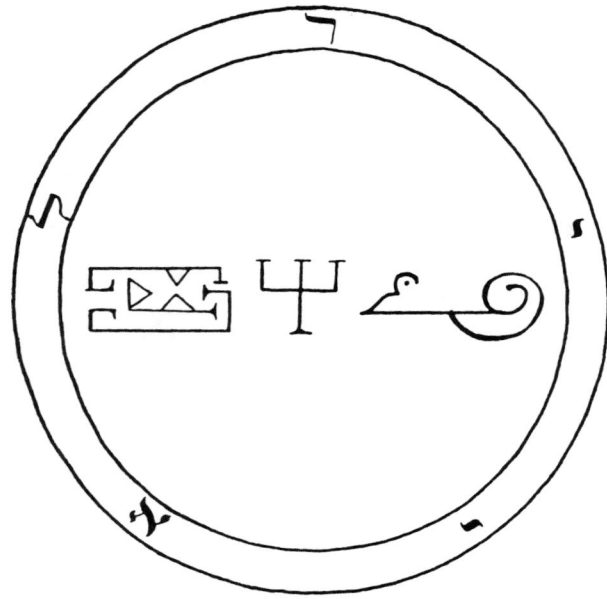

29. RAYAYEL

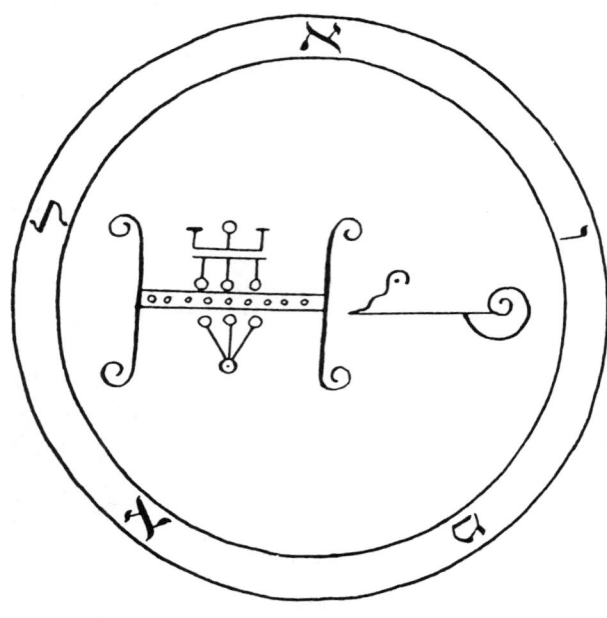

30. EVAMEL

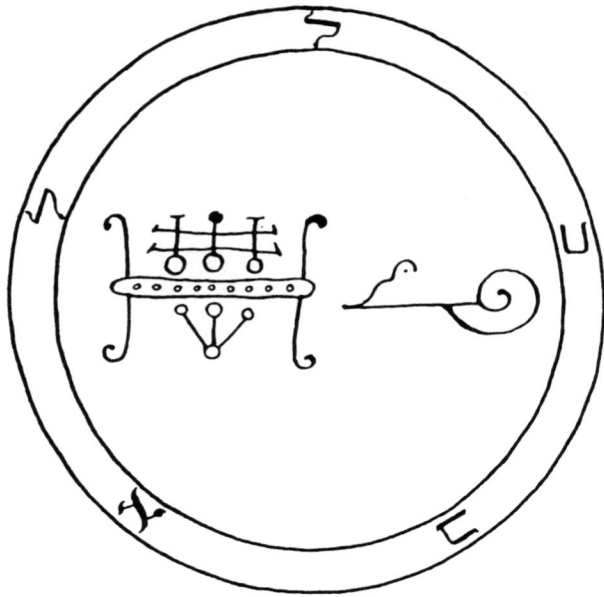

31. LEKABEL

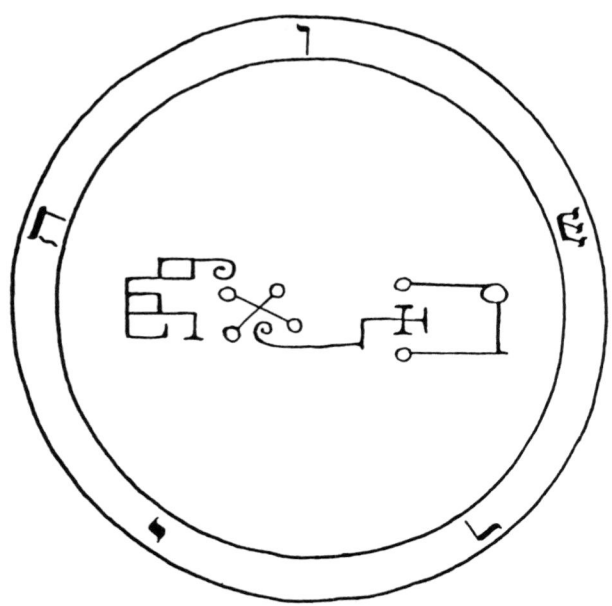

32. VESHERIAH

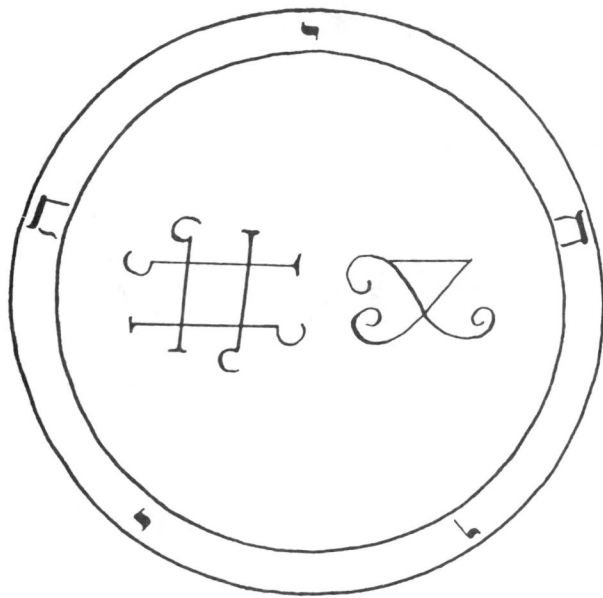

33. YECHVIAH

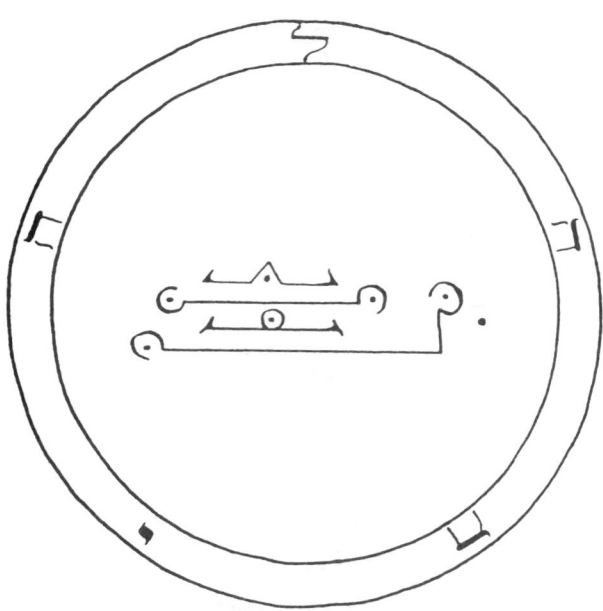

34. LEHAHAIH

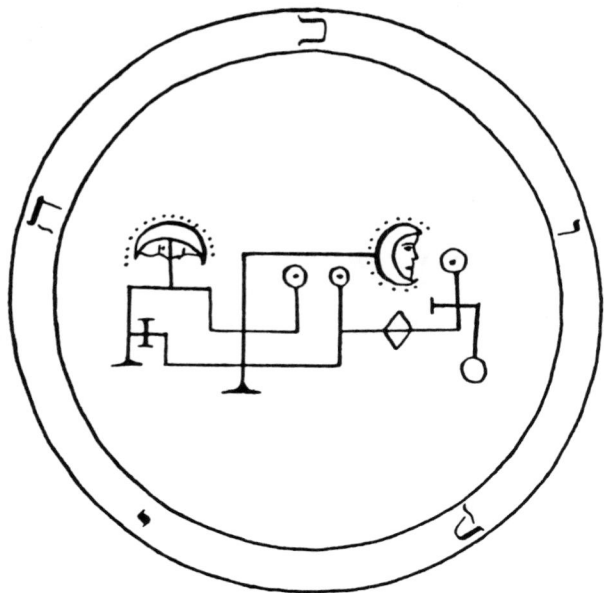

35. KEVEQAIAH

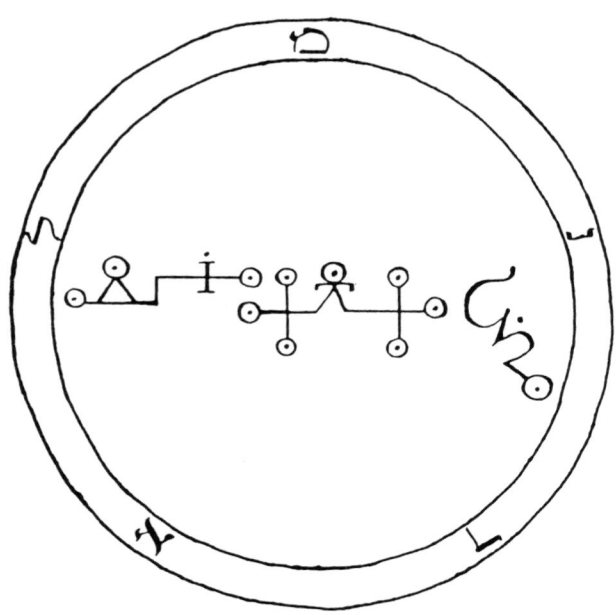

36. MENDIEL

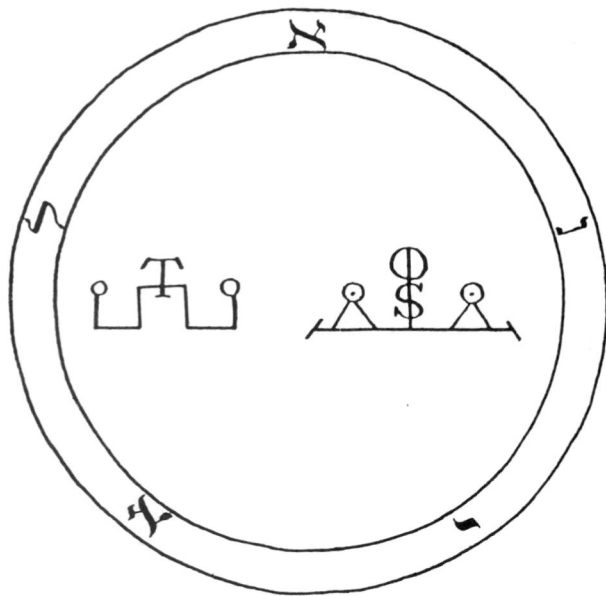

37. ANAIEL

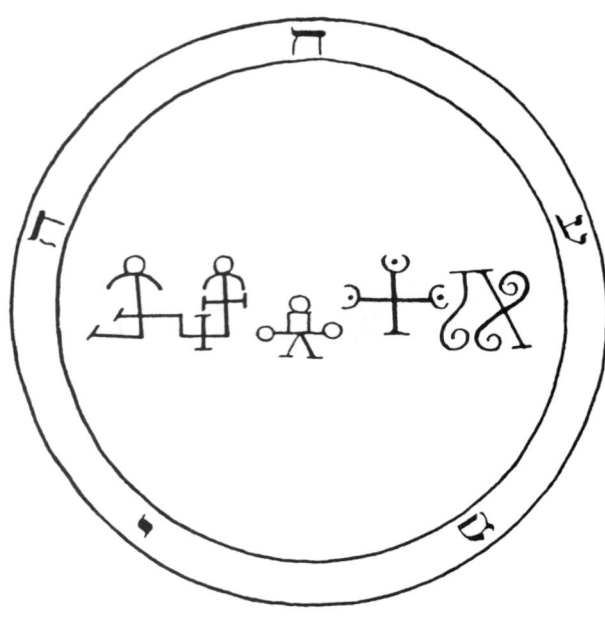

38. CHAAMIAH

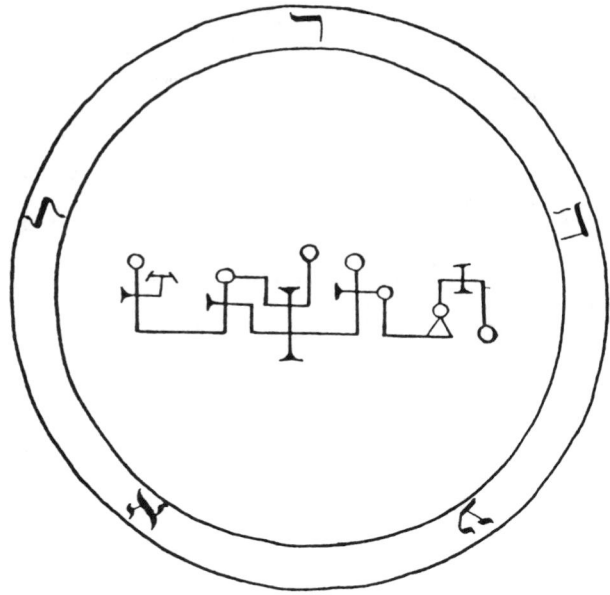

39. REHEAEL

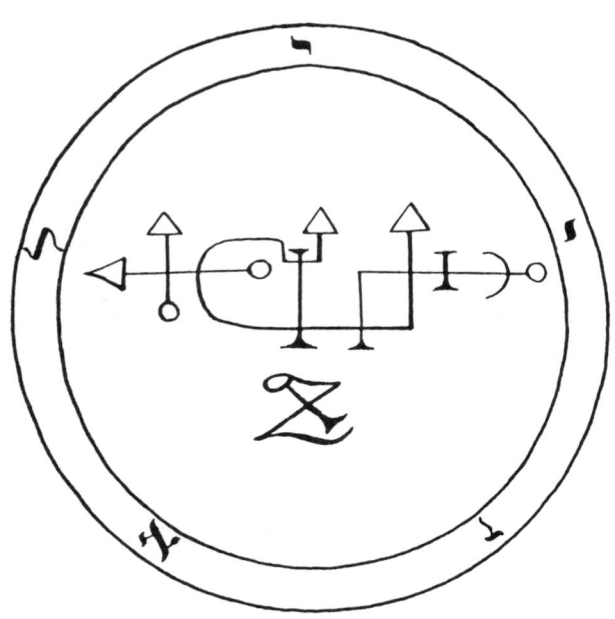

40. YEIZAEL

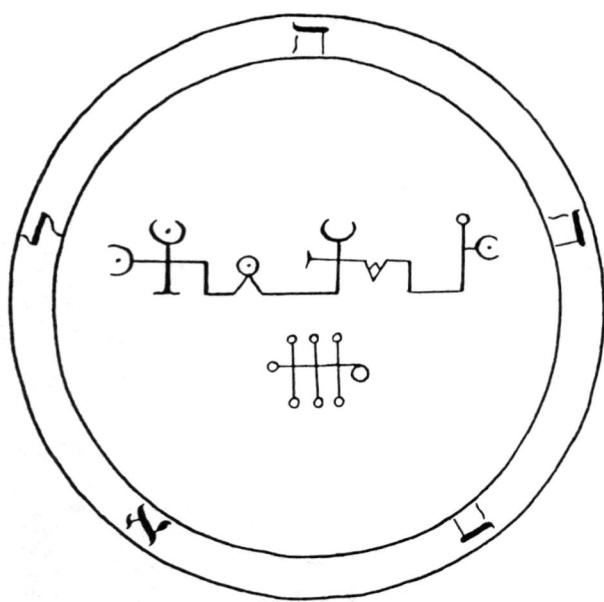

41. HEHIHEL

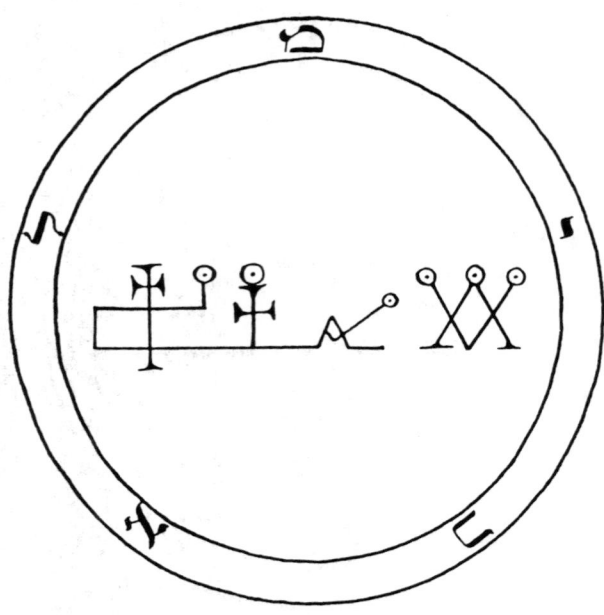

42. MIKHAEL

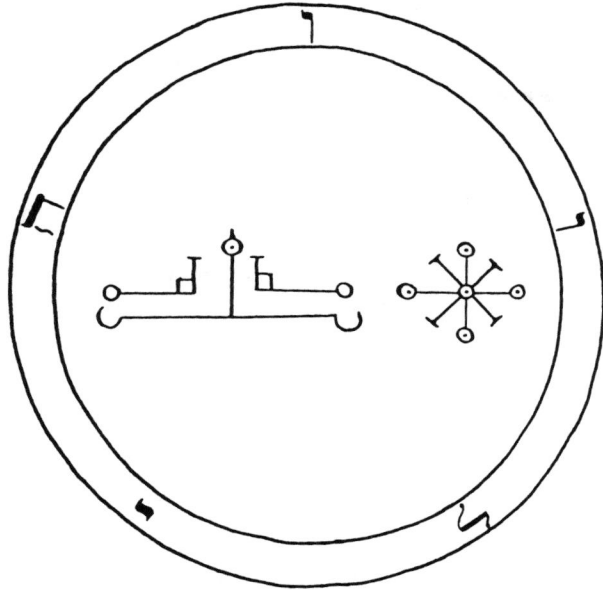

43. VAVALIAH

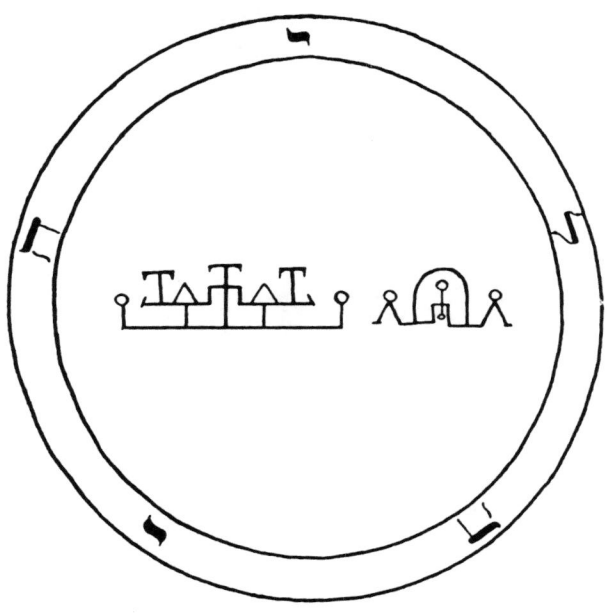

44. IHAIAH

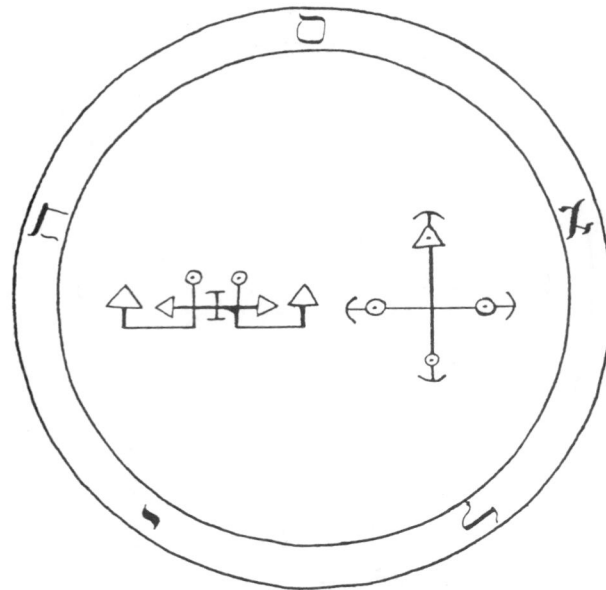

45. SAELAIH

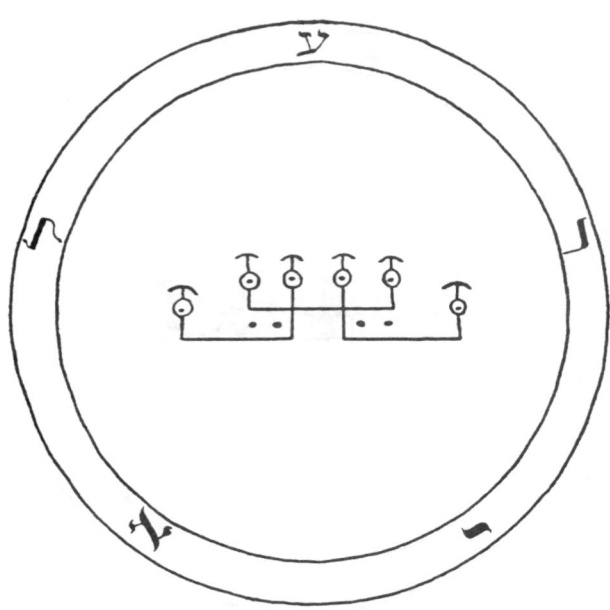

46. NGHARAIEL

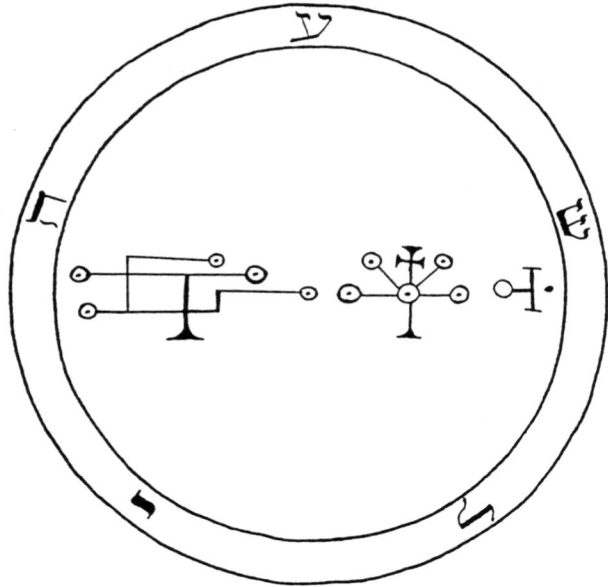

47. ASLAIAH

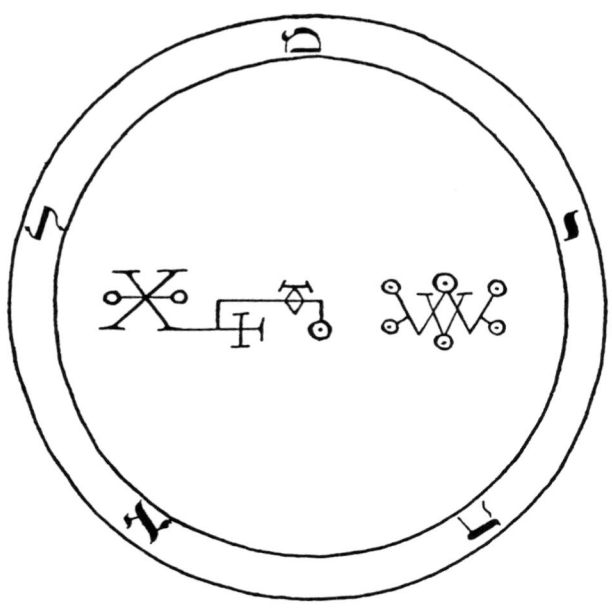

48. MIHEL

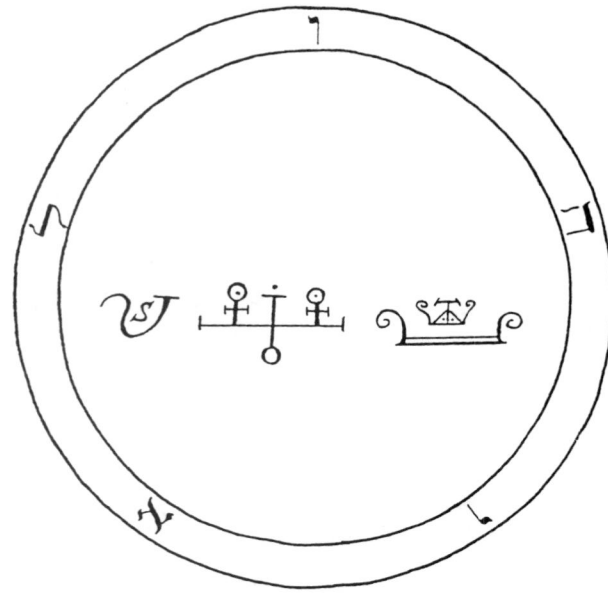

49. UHAUEL

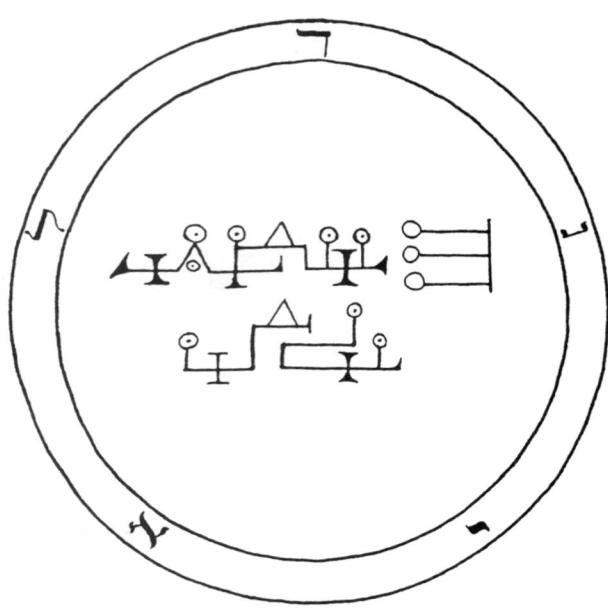

50. DENEYAEL

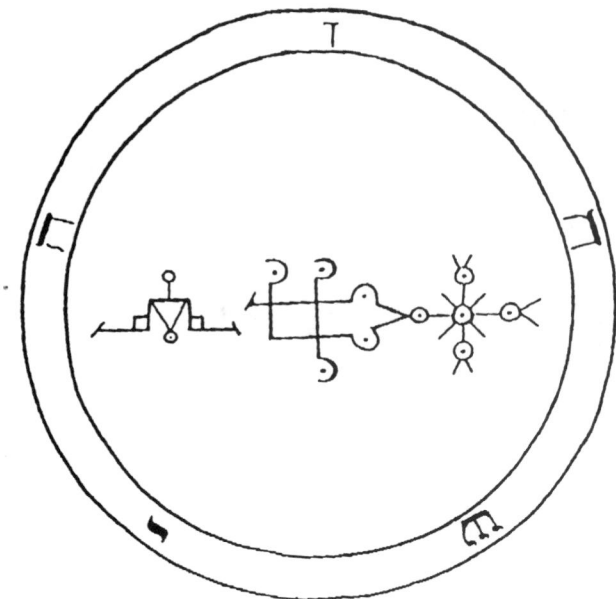

51. HECHASHEIAH

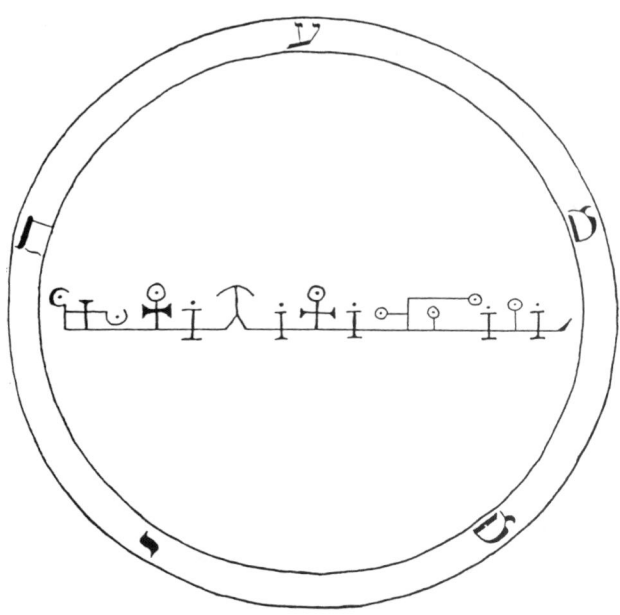

52. AMAMIAH

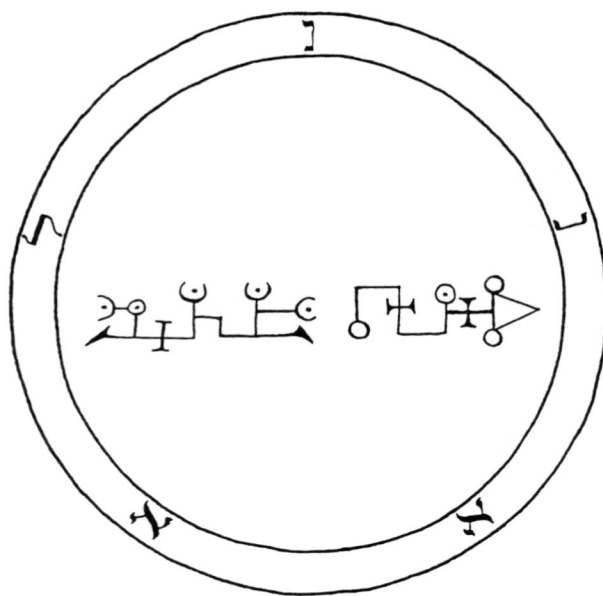

53. NANAEL

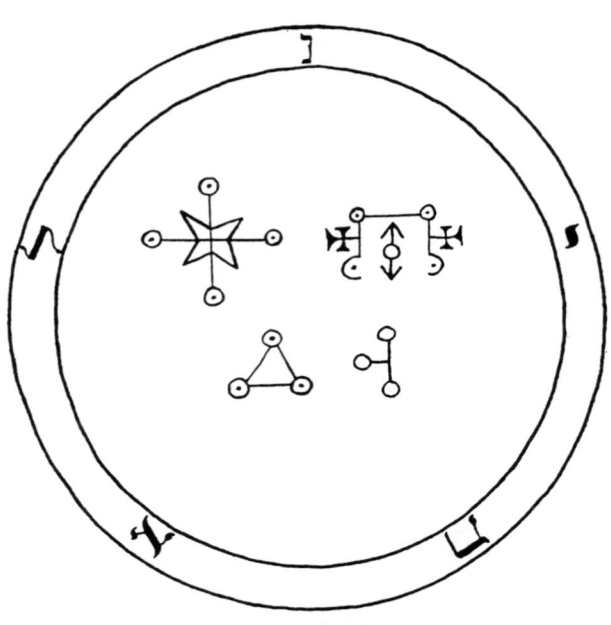

54. NITHAEL

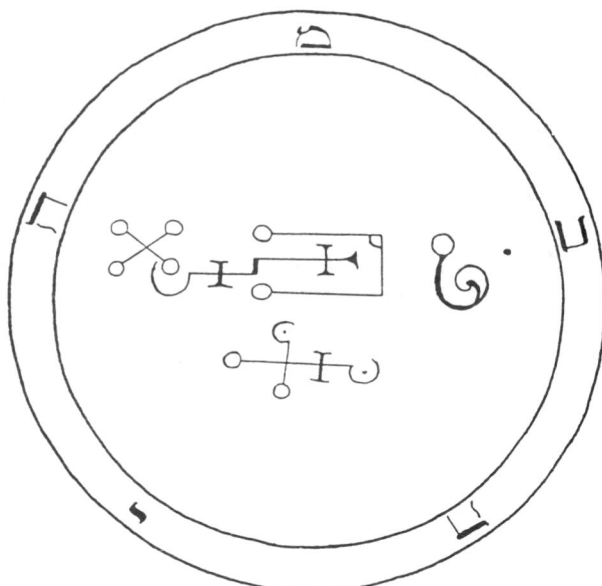

55. MIBAHAIH

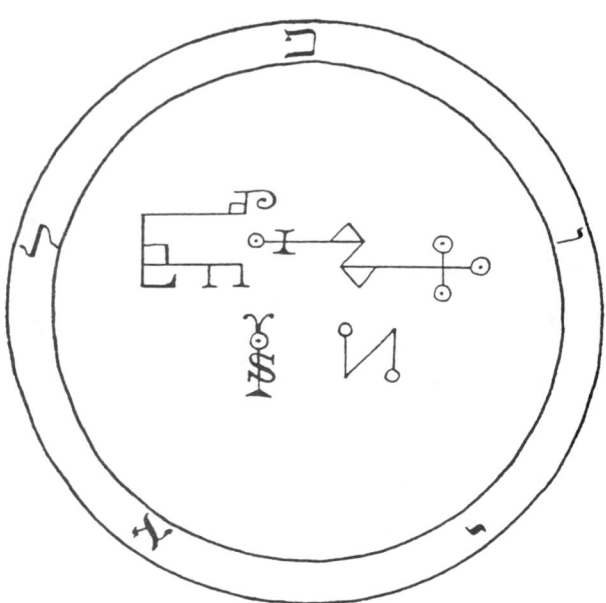

56. PUIAEL

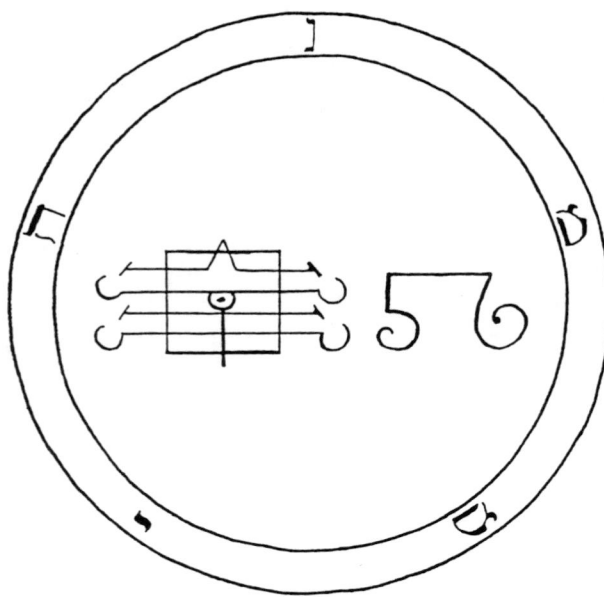

57. NEMAMIAH

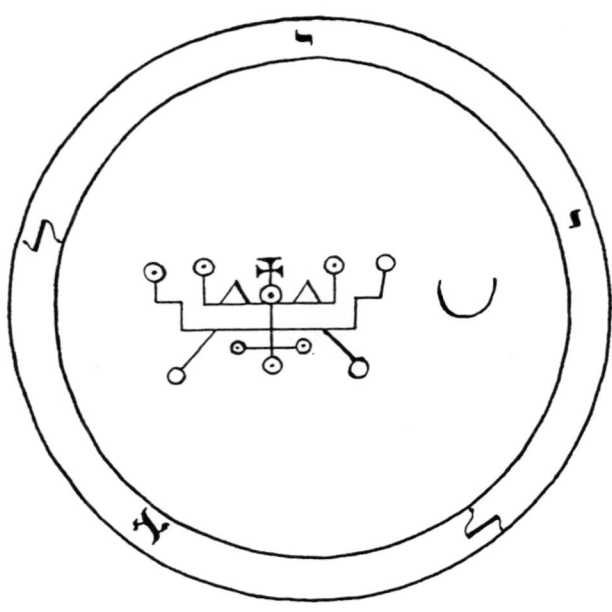

58. YEILEEL

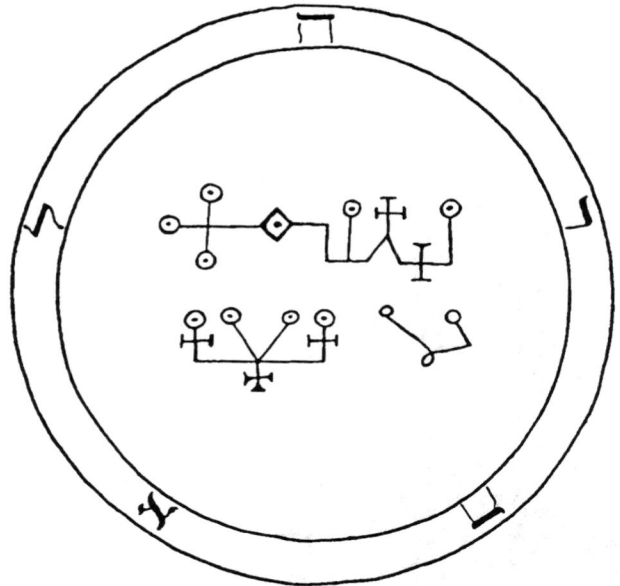

59. HERACHAEL

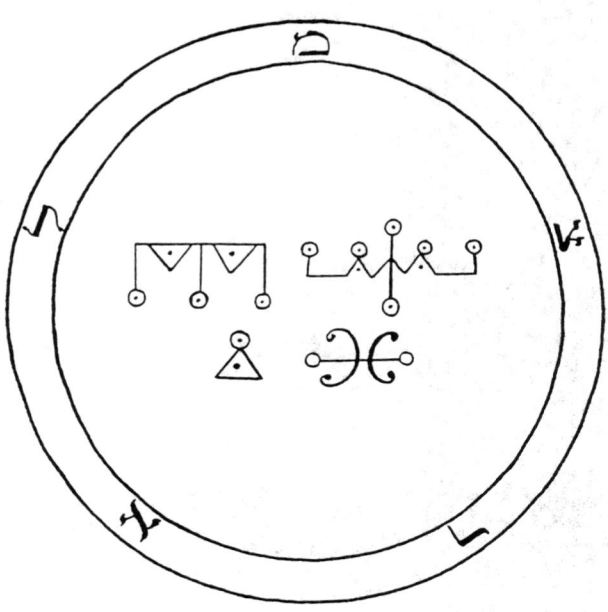

60. METZRAEL

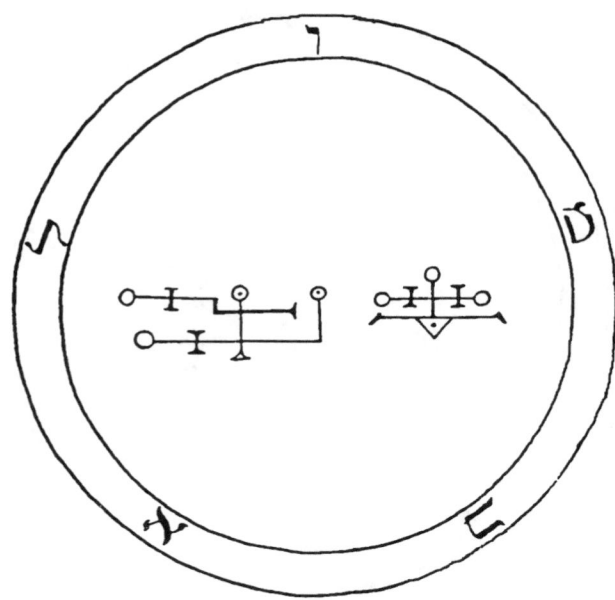

61. VAMIBAEL

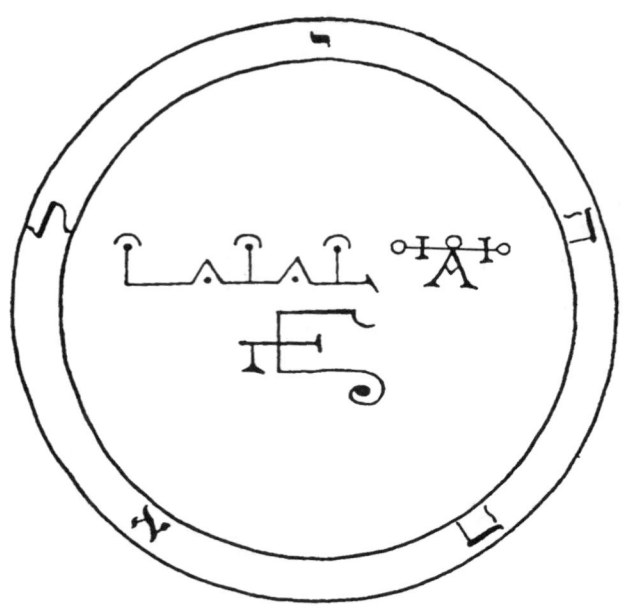

62. IAHAHEL

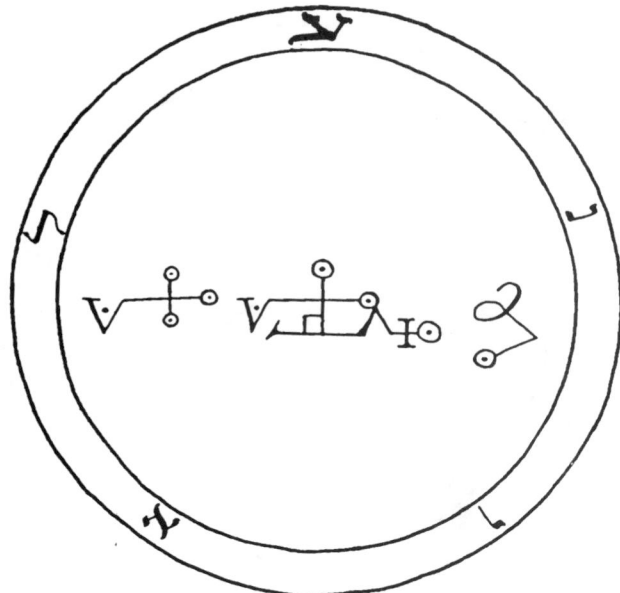

63. NGHANEAUEL

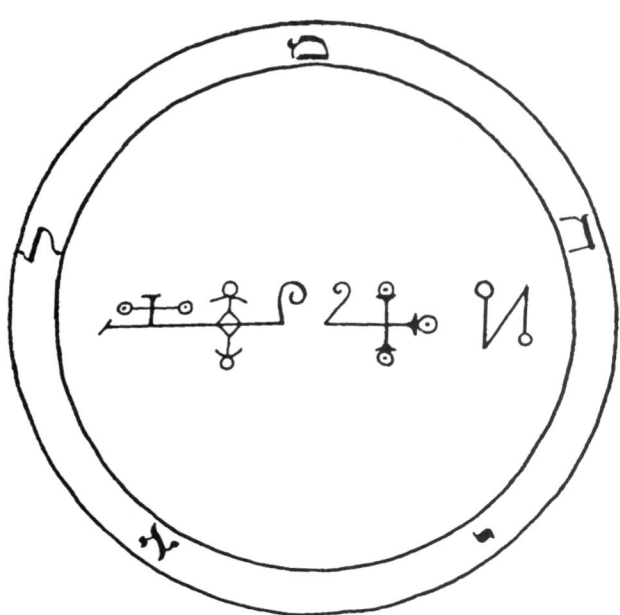

64. MOCHAIEL

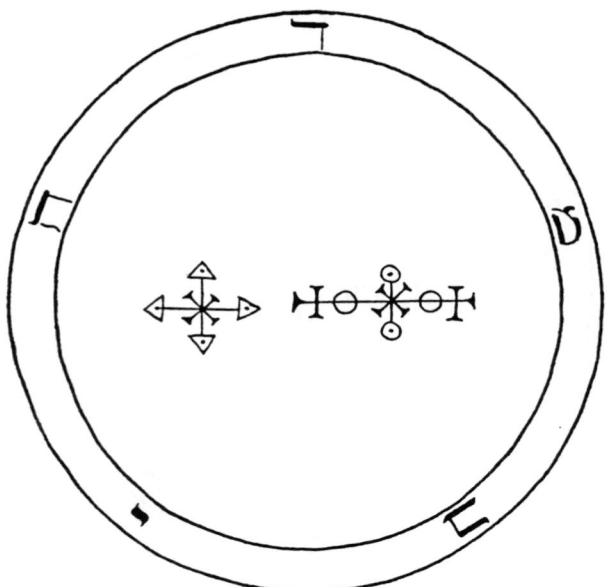

65. DAMABAIAH

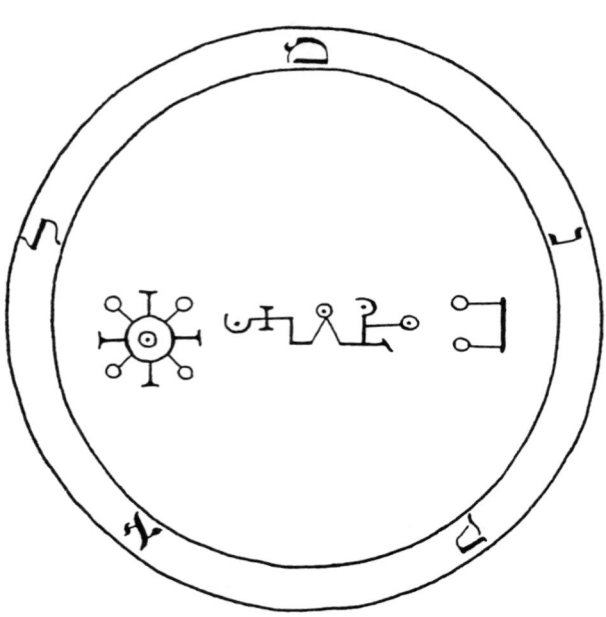

66. MENQEL

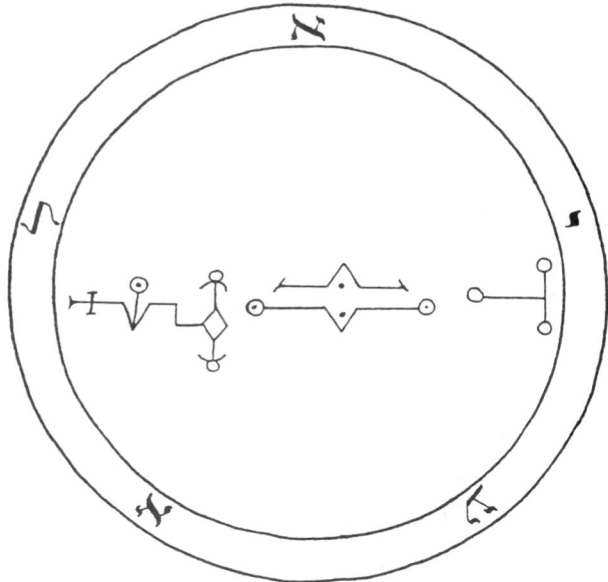

67. AIAEL

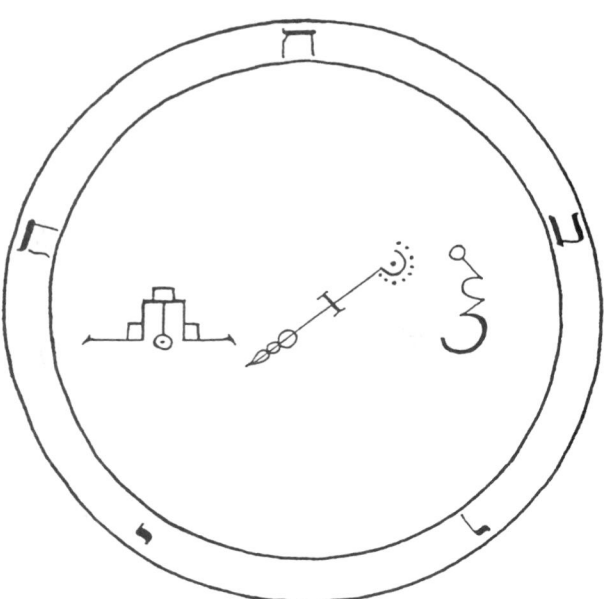

68. CHABEOIAH

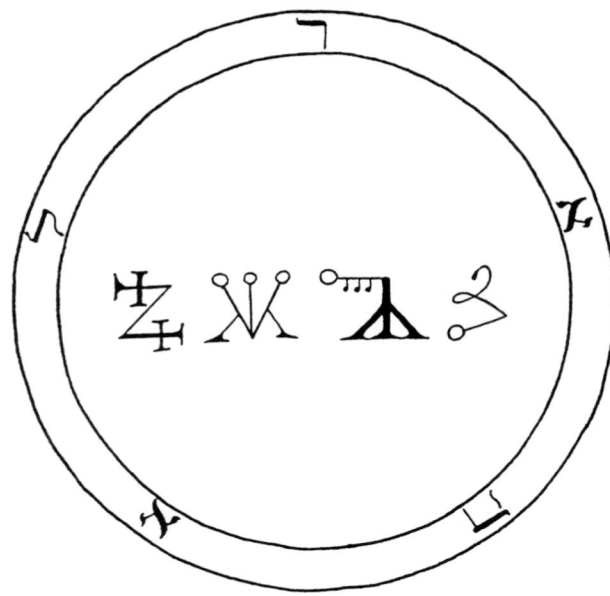

69. ROHAEL

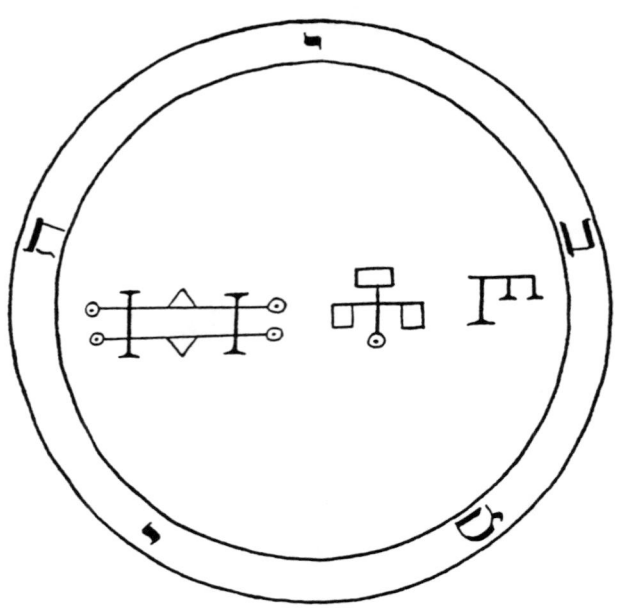

70. YEBAMAIAH

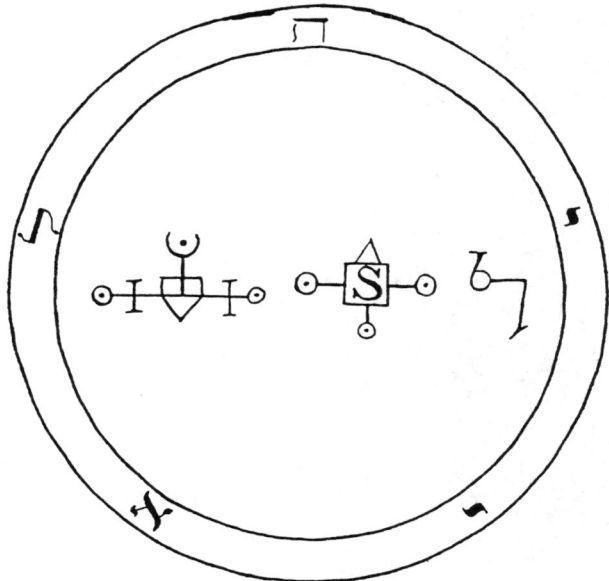

71. HAYAIEL

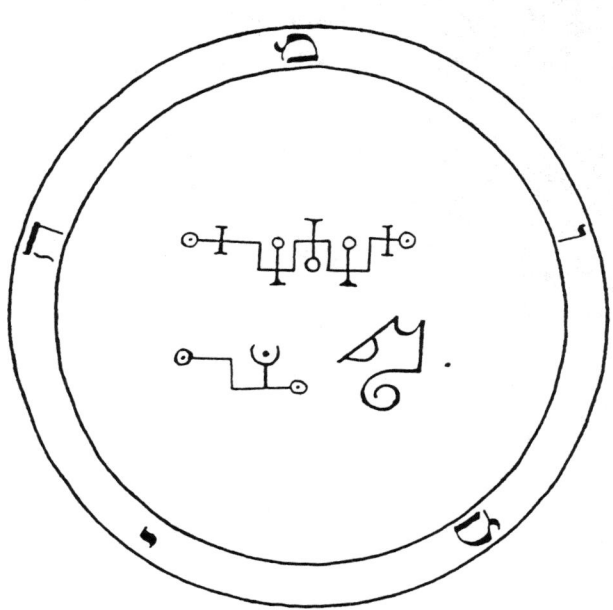

72. MEVAMIAH

STAY IN TOUCH

On the following pages you will find some of the books now available on related subjects. Your book dealer stocks most of these and will stock new titles in the Llewellyn series as they become available. We urge your patronage.

To obtain our full catalog, to keep informed about new titles as they are released and to benefit from informative articles and helpful news, you are invited to write for our bimonthly news magazine/catalog, *Llewellyn's New Worlds of Mind and Spirit*. A sample copy is free, and it will continue coming to you at no cost as long as you are an active mail customer. Or you may subscribe for just $10.00 in the U.S.A. and Canada ($20.00 overseas, first class mail). Many bookstores also have *New Worlds* available to their customers. Ask for it.

Llewellyn's New Worlds of Mind and Spirit
P.O. Box 64383-873, St. Paul, MN 55164-0383, U.S.A.

* * *

TO ORDER BOOKS AND TAPES

If your book dealer does not have the books described, you may order them directly from the publisher by sending full price in U.S. funds, plus $3.00 for postage and handling for orders *under* $10.00; $4.00 for orders *over* $10.00. There are no postage and handling charges for orders over $50.00. Postage and handling rates are subject to change. We ship UPS whenever possible. Delivery guaranteed. Provide your street address as UPS does not deliver to P.O. Boxes. UPS to Canada requires a $50.00 minimum order. Allow 4-6 weeks for delivery. Orders outside the U.S.A. and Canada: Airmail—add retail price of book; add $5.00 for each non-book item (tapes, etc.); add $1.00 per item for surface mail.

FOR GROUP STUDY AND PURCHASE

Because there is a great deal of interest in group discussion and study of the subject matter of this book, we offer a special quantity price to group leaders or agents. Our Special Quantity Price for a minimum order of five copies of *The Kabbalah of the Golden Dawn* is $38.85 cash-with-order. This price includes postage and handling within the United States. Minnesota residents must add 6.5% sales tax. For additional quantities, please order in multiples of five. For Canadian and foreign orders, add postage and handling charges as above. Credit card (VISA, MasterCard, American Express) orders are accepted. Charge card orders only ($15.00 minimum order) may be phoned in free within the U.S.A. or Canada by dialing 1-800-THE-MOON. For customer service, call 1-612-291-1970. Mail orders to:

LLEWELLYN PUBLICATIONS
P.O. Box 64383-873, St. Paul, MN 55164-0383, U.S.A.

Prices subject to change without notice.